THE

ANTI-SLAVERY CRUSADE

IN AMERICA

AM I NOT A MAN AND A BROTHER?

THE SLAVE POWER

Theodore Parker

ARNO PRESS
&
THE NEW YORK TIMES
NEW YORK   1969

Reprint edition 1969 by Arno Press, Inc.

*

Library of Congress Catalog Card No. 74–82209

*

Reprinted from a copy in
The New York State Library

*

Manufactured in the United States of America

THE SLAVE POWER

The Slave Power

BY

THEODORE PARKER

EDITED WITH NOTES

BY

JAMES K. HOSMER

IN·LUCE· VERITATIS

BOSTON

AMERICAN UNITARIAN ASSOCIATION

25 BEACON STREET

EDITOR'S PREFACE.

The present volume, containing anti-slavery papers written by Theodore Parker between the years 1841 and 1852, does not present all that he wrote upon this topic during the period. In many essays and sermons he refers to slavery in passages sometimes brief and sometimes extended. In particular the discourse on the death of Daniel Webster in 1852 abounds in references to this theme. For such papers the reader is referred to other volumes of this series. In the papers presented here, however, Parker's battle against slavery may be studied in its entire development. While the sermon of 1841 is unimpassioned, as from a heart not deeply stirred, the address of 1852 is almost frenzied in its heat, an utterance in which fire could not burn more fiercely. In the documents between may be traced the gradual deepening of earnestness.

Fifty years ago the present editor, as a youth, often heard the voice of Theodore Parker and was among the thousands over whom his spell was powerful. Coming again to him after an interval so long and so charged with events of vast moment, he is again deeply affected by the force and sincerity of the prophet. Where have we seen better courage, a greater singleness of purpose, a more active humanity, a fiercer invective — applied to the wrong-doer, a better equipment in the champion of a cause?

Nevertheless, looking after a half century at Parker's positions, there is much in them to find fault with. Though professing patriotism, he scoffs bitterly at the " Union-savers," and Mr. Chadwick cites him as declaring: " I have thought if any State wished to go she had a perfect right to do so."—(I. Theodore Parker, p. 260.)

However Parker may have expressed himself in private, there is little in his public utterances to show that he saw in African slavery an evil out of which good might come. But Booker T. Washington, accepted now everywhere as the best spokesman of the colored race, asserts:

" We must acknowledge that notwithstanding the cruelty and moral wrong of slavery, the ten million negroes inhabiting this country, who themselves or their ancestors went through the school of American slavery, are in a stronger and more hopeful condition, materially, intellectually, morally, and religiously, than is true of an equal number of black people in any other portion of the world." *

Parker's denunciation was directed especially at the men, among whom Daniel Webster was chief, who to save the Union were willing to postpone for a time the grapple with slavery. Yet in this company stood Abraham Lincoln, in Parker's time unrevealed as yet in his greatness, but whom his countrymen were soon to regard as the best and wisest American of his century. He was the arch " temporizer "; he announced with all definiteness that his purpose to save the Union was paramount; he was willing to execute the Fugitive Slave Law and not at all impelled by his conscience to interfere with slavery where it existed. Under him it came about as an incident, not at all as an end sought for, that slavery fell. Had Parker lived into the war-time, Lincoln scarcely less than Webster would perhaps have been the object of his scorn.

* *Up from Slavery*, p. 16.

The truth is that Parker, with all his fine scholarship blinked somewhat the facts as to human slavery.

His moral sense was impatient and the calamities consequent upon civil war and the disruption of the nation were in his mind not to be compared with suffering slavery to exist a moment longer. Webster no doubt had many frailties, but his love for the Union was consuming, and his conviction fixed that the welfare of men required its preservation,— a conviction which Americans to-day adhere to universally as a fundamental principle. Webster felt the evil of slavery, but thought that to save the Union, the struggle with it might be postponed. Says the latest historian who has considered his period: " The mission which he felt the circumstances of his era had committed to him was to defend the Union till the bonds had grown too strong to break. The anti-slavery crusade must fall to the men of a younger generation, whose work, had it come sooner, would have placed American nationality in deadlier peril than was brought by the Civil War." * George Frisbie Hoar, too, ascribed Webster's hesitation in the anti-slavery path upon which in earlier years he so distinctly entered, not to sordid ambition but to superior prescience, which in 1850 foresaw a catastrophe to which Parker and his friends were blind. The conservatives felt that reform must proceed gradually. Slavery had existed from the beginning of the human race. No evil that afflicts society is more inveterate; there is no evil to the enormity of which the moral sense of mankind awakened more slowly. In vast masses of Americans, even in the North, the conscience was still silent when slavery was held up as a national sin.

* Garrison, *American Nation,* vol. XVII., p. 327.

EDITOR'S PREFACE

To Webster and the other conservative spirits who stood with him, the Compromise of 1850, of which the Fugitive Slave Law was the feature most repugnant, seemed, with good reason, necessary to avert civil war. Had civil war come at that time, it can scarcely be doubted that the destruction of the country would have resulted. The North in 1850 was far less able to make a good fight than ten years later. Its resources were much smaller, the foreign immigration which reinforced so effectively the anti-slavery strength was in its halfway stage; the work of railroads was only beginning, transit was comparatively slow and difficult; the great Northwest, dependent for its trade upon watercourses, was bound far more closely to the South than in the following decade. Even in 1861, under vastly improved conditions, the North had the narrowest possible escape from defeat. The " temporizing " policy at which Parker cast so much scorn, probably saved the national life.*

I have said that if Theodore Parker had lived he would perhaps have assailed Lincoln with no less bitterness than he assailed Webster. In 1848 both men sat in Congress, one in the Senate the other in the House, old line Whigs not far apart. Though Lincoln favored and Webster rejected the Wilmot Proviso, that made no important chasm between them. Both men favored the exclusion of slavery from the territories, but while Lincoln thought an enactment might be necessary, Webster believed that natural conditions made slavery in the new territory impossible. Why " re-enact the will of God "? Again in 1860, though Webster was gone, the statesmen who carried on his

* James Ford Rhodes, *History of the United States from the Compromise of 1850,* vol. I., 193.

tradition did not find an entire ally in their old associate Abraham Lincoln. He was willing to accept the nomination to the Presidency of a " sectional party," whereas they desired " to know no North and no South." But these were comparatively trifling differences. In the main Lincoln's ideas were those of his old Whig associates. Like them he thought slavery wrong and desired its restriction within limits, but nothing was farther from his purpose than to attack it within those limits. To save the Union he was quite ready to execute the Fugitive Slave Law. He clearly repudiated the idea that the war was for emancipation; he strove simply and solely to save the Union. " My paramount purpose in this struggle is to save the Union, and is not either to save or destroy slavery. If I could save the Union without freeing any slaves I would do it, and if I could save it by freeing all the slaves I would do it. What I do about slavery and the colored race I do because I believe it helps to save the Union, and what I forbear I forbear because I do not believe it will help to save the Union." * When the Emancipation Proclamation came its announced purpose was to cripple the Union-threatening enemy, any design of benefiting the negro thereby was secondary in Lincoln's thought.

Theodore Parker mocked at " Union-saving " with great bitterness. The threats of the South he contemned, as " the barking of a dog that will not bite." The Union to him was not a paramount consideration. As it stood, it was a thing intolerable; it had better be done away with if slavery must persist in it. So thought generally the more zealous abolitionists. So did not think the masses of their countrymen. A

* *Lincoln's Works,* (ed. of 1894), vol. II., p. 227.

champion came forth from the camp which they ridiculed and denounced, who pursued a policy of patience and tact suffering long himself and teaching the multitudes, both white and black, also to suffer long, until at last, discerning the right moment, he struck at once and with power. The Union was saved and throughout its entire extent the shackles fell from the bondmen.

Unmistakably slavery was a terrible wrong. To deprive men of freedom, unless that freedom is used to the detriment of society as in the case of criminals, or stands in the way of proper training as in the case of children, must always and everywhere be injustice. When in the past the strong have imposed bonds upon the weak it has almost invariably been for selfish ends, and it was never more selfish than when the American slave-holders imposed bonds upon the African. A vast wrong was committed, and as the universe is constituted, it must necessarily be followed by its penalty. Upon whom in the order of Providence ought the penalty to fall? Certainly not upon the innocent victim, but upon the guilty enslaver. Accordingly we see in antiquity the rotting out of the master-races, however strong and brilliant, while the barbarians they held in subjection, though for a time tortured and distressed, emerged at length from the harsh schooling to become in turn conquerors with the world at their feet. Has American experience gone counter to that of former times? Those among us whose immediate fathers were slaves, speaking through the voice of the man of their race best qualified to represent them, declare that they have been lifted through bondage above the savagery in which their race has been for ages involved. If it be asked, on the other hand, where among white civil-

ized races ignorance is most rife, homicide most preva-
lent, law in general least respected, it must be sadly
answered that all this is found in that part of our
country where until lately slavery prevailed. That is
the sharp penalty which the descendants of an arbitrary master-class must pay for the evil which their
fathers so long maintained and strove so strenuously
to make permanent.

Though it was not the leadership of Parker and his
friends which brought us out of our strait it would be
quite wrong to declare that they did no good in their
time. One of the group is said to have gloried in the
name fanatic, confessing that his positions were extreme
even in his own eyes, maintaining that in a great movement some should be extravagant, perhaps even frantic,
as a counterpoise to the recalcitrants. No such avowal
as this could have come from Theodore Parker. He
was not conscious that he was extreme. He thought
himself centered upon justice, in the only place it was
possible for a true man to stand. He was fervid, per-
fervid, in his abolitionism, and it was that per-fervid-
ness which, when the fire had smouldered long, at length
evoked the conflagration. In spite of the cost of our
Civil War,— more than a million lives and the loss to
the North alone of perhaps five billions of treasure,* as
the world feels to-day, it is well that it came when it
did. It had to come, and though the memory of all its
agonies is a most solemn shadow within our consciousness, few will say to-day that the result was not worth
all it cost. We are thankful then to those who fought
it through from whatever camp they came,— to the
conservative spirits who forebore until after long wait-

* *American Nation,* vol. XXI., *Outcome of the Civil War,* p.
304.

EDITOR'S PREFACE

ing the right moment came to act; and also to the impatient consciences that leaped before, dragging into the arena those who were holding back too long.

JAMES K. HOSMER.

CONTENTS

I

A SERMON OF SLAVERY

Know ye not that to whom ye yield yourselves servants to obey, his servants ye are whom ye obey; whether of sin unto death, or of obedience unto righteousness?— Rom. vi. 16.

In our version of the New Testament the word *servant* often stands for a word in the original, which means *slave*. Such is the case in this passage just read, and the sense of the whole verse is this: — " If a man yields unconditional service to sin, he is the *slave* of sin, and gets death for his reward." Here, however, by a curious figure of speech, not uncommon in this apostle, he uses the word *slave* in a good sense — *slave* of obedience unto righteousness. I now ask your attention to a short sermon of slavery.

A popular definition has sometimes been given of common bodily slavery, that it is the holding of property in man. In a kindred language it is called body-property. In this case, a man's body becomes the possession, property, chattel, tool, or thing of another person, and not of the man who lives in it. This foreign person, of course, makes use of it to serve his own ends, without regard to the true welfare, or even the wishes, of the man who lives in that body, and to whom it rightfully belongs. Here the relation is necessarily that of force on one side and suffering on the other, though the force is often modified and the suffering sometimes disguised or kept out of sight.

Now man was made to be free, to govern himself, to be his own master, to have no cause stand between him and God, which shall curtail his birthright of freedom. He is never in his proper element until he attains this condition of freedom; of self-government. Of course, while we are children, not having reached the age of discretion, we must be under the authority of our parents and guardians, teachers, and friends. This is a natural relation. There is no slavery in it; no degradation. The parents, exercising rightful authority over their children, do not represent human caprice, but divine wisdom and love. They assume the direction of the child's actions, not to do themselves a service, but to benefit him. The father restrains his child, that the child may have more freedom, not less. Here the relation is not of force and suffering, but of love on both sides; of ability, which loves to help, and necessity, which loves to be directed. The child that is nurtured by its parent gains more than the parent does. So is it the duty of the wise, the good, the holy, to teach, direct, restrain the foolish, the wicked, the ungodly. If a man is wiser, better, and holier than I am, it is my duty, my privilege, my exaltation to obey him. For him to direct me in wisdom and love, not for his sake but for my own, is for me to be free. He may gain nothing by this, but I gain much.

As slavery was defined to be holding property in man, so freedom may be defined as a state in which the man does, of his own consent, the best things he is capable of doing at that stage of his growth. Now there are two sorts of obstacles which prevent, or may prevent, men from attaining to this enviable condition of freedom.

These are: —

I. Obstacles external to ourselves, which restrict our freedom; and

II. Obstacles internal to ourselves, which restrict our freedom.

A few words may be said on the condition to which men are brought by each of these classes of objects.

I. Of the slavery which arises from a cause external to ourselves. By the blessing of Providence, seconding the efforts, prayers, tears of some good men, there is no bodily, personal slavery sanctioned by the law amongst us in New England. But at the South we all know that some millions of our fellow-citizens are held in bondage; that men, women, and children are bought and sold in the shambles of the national Capital; are owned as cattle; reared as cattle; beaten as cattle. We all know that our fathers fought through the War of Independence with these maxims in their mouths and blazoned on their banners: that all men are born free and equal, and that the God of eternal justice will at last avenge the cause of the oppressed, however strong the oppressor may be; yet it is just as well known that the sons of those very fathers now trade in human flesh, separating parent and child, and husband and wife, for the sake of a little gain; that the sons of those fathers eat bread not in the sweat of their own brow, but in that of the slave's face; that they are sustained, educated, rendered rich, and haughty, and luxurious by the labor they extort from men whom they have stolen, or purchased from the stealer, or inherited from the purchaser. It is known to you all, that there are some millions of these forlorn children of Adam, men whom the Declaration of Independence declares " born free and equal " with their master before God and the law; men whom the Bible names " of the same blood " with the prophets and apostles; men " for whom Christ died," and who are " statues of God in ebony "— that they are held in this condition and made to feel the full burden of a corrupt society, and doomed from their birth to degradation and infamy, their very name a mock-word; their life a retreat, not a progress,— for the general and natural effect of slavery is to lessen the qualities of a man in the slave as he increases in stature or in years,— their children, their wives, their own bones and sinews at the mercy of a master! That these things are so, is known to all of us; well known from our childhood.[1]

Every man who has ever thought at all on any subject, and has at the same time a particle of manhood in him, knows that this state of slavery would be to him worse than a thousand deaths; that set death in one scale, and hopeless slavery for himself and children in the other, he would not hesitate in his choice, but would say, " Give me death, though the life be ground out of me with the most exquisite tortures of lingering agony that malice can invent or tyranny inflict." To the African thus made the victim of American cupidity and crime, the state of slavery, it will be said, may not appear so degrading as to you and me, for he has never before been civilized, and though the untaught instinct of man bid him love freedom, yet Christianity has not revealed to him the truth, that all men are brothers before God, born with equal rights. But this fact is no excuse or extenuation of our crime. Who would justify a knave in plundering a little girl out of a fortune that she inherited, on the ground that she was a little girl " of tender years," and had never enjoyed or even beheld her birthright? The fact that the injured party was ignorant and weak, would only enhance and aggravate the offense, adding new baseness and the suspicion of cowardice to guilt. If the African be so low that the condition

of slavery is tolerable in his eyes, and he can dance in
his chains — happy in the absence of the whip — it is
all the more a sin, in the cultivated and the strong,
in the Christian (!) to tyrannize over the feeble and
defenseless. Men at the South with the Bible in one
hand—with the Declaration of Independence in the
other hand — with the words of Jesus, " Love your
neighbor as yourself," pealing upon them from all
quarters, attempt to justify slavery; not to excuse,
to cloak, or conceal the thing, but to vindicate and
defend it. This attempt, when made by reflecting
men in their cool moments, discovers a greater degree
of blackness of heart than the kidnapping of men
itself. It is premeditated wickedness grown conscious
of itself. The plain truth of the matter is this: —
men who wish for wealth and luxury, but hate the
toil and sweat, which are their natural price, brought
the African to America; they make his chains; they
live by his tears; they dance to the piping of his
groans; they fatten on his sweat and are pampered
by his blood. If these men spoke as plainly as they
must needs think, they would say openly; " Our sin
captured these men on the African sands; our sin
fettered them in slavery; and, please God, our sin
shall keep them in slavery till the world ends." This
has been thought long enough, it is high time it was
said also, that we may know what we are about and
where we stand.[2]

Men at the North sometimes attempt to gloss the
matter over, and hush it up by saying the least possible on the subject. They tell us that some masters
are " excellent Christians." No doubt it is so, estimating these masters by the common run of Christians,—
you find such on the deck of pirate ships; in the dens

of robbers. But suppose some slaveholders are as good Christians as Fenelon or St. Peter; still a sin is sin, though a Christian commit it. Our fathers did not think " taxation without representation " any the less an evil because imposed by " his most Christian Majesty," a king of Christians.

Then, too, it is said, " The slaves are very happy, and it is a great pity to disturb them," that " the whole mass are better fed and clothed, and are troubled with fewer cares, than working men at the North." Suppose this true also, what then? Do you estimate your welfare in pounds of beef; in yards of cloth; in exemption from the cares of a man! If so all appeal to you is vain, your own soul has become servile. The Saviour of the world was worse fed and clothed, no doubt, than many a Georgian slave, and had not where to lay his head, wearied with many cares; but has your Christianity taught you that was an evil, and the slave's hutch at night, and pottage by day, and exemption from a man's cares by night and day, are a good, a good to be weighed against freedom! Then are you unworthy the soil you stand on; you contaminate the air of New England, which free men died to transmit to their children free!

Still further it is said, " The sufferings of slaves are often exaggerated." This may be true. No doubt there have been exaggerations of particular cases. Every slave-owner is not a demon, not a base man. No doubt there are what are called good Christians, men that would be ornaments to a Christian church, among slaveholders. But though there have been exaggerations in details, yet the awful sum of misery, unspeakable wretchedness, which hangs over two millions of slaves is such that eye hath not seen it; nor

ear heard it; nor heart conceived of it. It were so
if all their masters were Christians in character, in
action, still retaining slaves. How much deeper and
wilder must swell that wide weltering sea of human
agony, when the masters are what we know so many
are, hard-hearted and rapacious, insolent and brutal!

This attempt to gloss the matter over and veil the
fact, comes from two classes of men.

1. Some make the attempt from a real design to
promote peace. They see no way to abate this mischief; they see " the folly and extravagance " of such
as propose " dangerous measures," and therefore they
would have us say nothing about it. The writhing
patient is very sick; the leech more venturesome than
skilful; and the friends, fearful to try the remedy,
unwilling to summon wiser advice, declared the sick man
is well as ever if you will only let him alone! These
men mourn that any one should hold another in bondage; they think our fathers were illustrious heroes,
for fighting dreadful wars with the parent country
rather than pay a little tax against their will, but that
this evil of slavery can never be healed; therefore, in
the benevolence of their heart, they refuse to believe all
the stories of suffering that reach their ears. The imagination of a kind man recoils at the thought of so
much wretchedness; still more, if convinced that it cannot be abated. Now these men are governed by the
best of motives, but it does not follow that their opinions are so just as their motives are good.

2. But there are others, who are willing to countenance the sin and continue it, well knowing that it is
a sin. They would not have it abated. They tell you
of the stupidity of the African; that he is made for
nothing but a slave; is allied to the baboon and the

ape, and is as much in his place when fettered, ignorant and savage, in a rice field, to toil under a taskmaster's whip, as a New Englander, free and educated, is in his place, when felling forests, planning railroads, or "conducting" a steam-engine. Hard treatment and poor fare, say they, are the black man's due. Besides, they add, there is a natural antipathy between the black race and the white, which only the love of money, or the love of power, on the part of the white is capable of overcoming; that the blacks are an inferior race, and therefore the white Saxons are justified in making them slaves. They think the strong have a right to the services of the weak, forgetting that the rule of reason, the rule of Christianity, is just the other way; "We that are strong ought to bear the infirmities of the weak." They would have us follow the old rule, that "they should get who have the power, and they should keep who can." Of this class nothing further need be said save this: that they are very numerous, and quote the New Testament in support of slavery, thus contriving to pass for Christians, and have made such a stir in the land that it is scarce safe to open one's mouth and strip the veil from off this sin.

If some one should come and tell us that a new race of men had been discovered living at the bottom of the sea, who had a government which declared that all men were "born free," and a religion which laid down these excellent maxims: that all men were brothers; that God was no respecter of persons; and that man's chief earthly duty was to love and serve his fellow-mortals, keeping the law God Himself had made for man; we should say, what an admirable government! what a beautiful religion! what a free, religious, and blessed people they must be! "Happy is the people that is in such a case. Yea, happy is that people whose God is the Lord." But if we were told that a part of that nation had seized certain men weaker than themselves, whom their government had declared "free," whom their religion called "brothers" to the best of men; that they held these men in bondage, making them do all their masters' work, and receive no recompense, but a wretched life which they were to transmit to their children; and that in the mean time the other part of the nation looked on, and said nothing against this shameful wrong; they encouraged the crime and lent their wisdom, their wealth, and their valor to support and perpetuate this infamous institution; what should we say? Certainly that these men were liars! Liars before their government! Liars before their God! Such is the fact. This people does not live at the bottom of the sea, but on the firm land, and boasts the name of republic and Christian commonwealth!

The opinion of good and religious men here amongst us seems to be that slavery is a good sin and ought to be abolished as soon as possible; that the talent and piety of the nation cannot be better employed than in devising the speediest and most effectual way of exterminating the evil. Such of them as see a way to abolish the wrong cry aloud and publish the tidings; others who see no way state that fact also, not failing to express their dread of all violent measures. Such is the conviction of good and religious men at the North. But there is another opinion a little different, which is held by a different class of men at the North; — they think that slavery is a great sin, and ought to be kept up so long as

men can make money by it. But if the suppression
of slavery could be effected — not as our fathers won
their freedom, by blood and war — so gently as not
to ruffle a sleeping baby's eyelid, yet if it diminished
the crop of rice, or cotton, or tobacco, or corn, a single
quintal a year, it would be a great mistake to free,
cultivate, Christianize, and bless these millions of men!
No one, I take it, will doubt this is a quite common
opinion here in New England. The cause of this opinion will presently be touched upon. To show what
baseness was implied in holding such opinions, would
be simply a waste of time.

We all know there is at the North a small body of
men, called by various names, and treated with various
marks of disrespect, who are zealously striving to
procure the liberation of slaves, in a peaceable and
quiet way. They are willing to make any sacrifice
for this end. They start from the maxim that slavery
is sin, and that sin is to be abandoned at once, and for
ever, come what will come of it. These men, it is said,
are sometimes extravagant in their speech; they do not
treat the " patriarchal institution " with becoming reverence; they call slaveholders hard names, and appeal
to all who have a heart in their bosoms, and to some
who find none there, to join them and end the patriarchal institution by wise and Christian measures. What
wonder is it that these men sometimes grow warm in
their arguments! What wonder that their heart burns
when they think of so many women exposed to con-
tamination and nameless abuse; of so many children
reared like beasts, and sold as oxen; of so many men
owning no property in their hands, or their feet, their
hearts, or their lives! The wonder is all the other side,
that they do not go to further extremities, sinful as

it might be, and like St. John in his youth, pray for fire to come down from heaven and burn up the sinners, or like Paul, when he had not the excuse of youthful blood, ask God to curse them. Yet they do none of these things; never think of an appeal to the strong arm, but the Christian heart. When a man in this land of ours begins to feel this desperate iniquity and sees the deadness of those around him; the silly game played over his head by political parties and political leaders; the game yet sillier played by theological parties and theological leaders, while the land lies overgrown with " trespasses and sins," — he may be pardoned if he shrieks over human sufferings and human crime; if he cries out and spares not, but wishes he had a mouth in his hands, and a mouth in his feet, and was speech all over, that he might protest in every limb against this abomination which maketh the heart desolate. There is no doubt that these men are sometimes extravagant! There need be no wonder at that fact. The best of men have their infirmities, but if this extravagance be one of them, what shall we call the deadness of so many more amongst us? An infirmity? What shall we say of the sin itself? An infirmity also? Honest souls engaged in a good work, fired with a great idea, sometimes forget the settled decorum of speech, commonly observed in forum and pulpit, and call sin sin. If the New Testament tell truth, Paul did so, and it was thought he would " turn the world upside down," while he was only striving to set it right. John the Baptist and Jesus of Nazareth did the same thing, and though one left his head in a charger, and the other his body on a cross, yet the world thinks at this day they did God's great work with their sincerity of speech.

The men who move in this matter encounter opposition from two classes of men; from the moderate, who do not see the wisdom of their measures, and who fear that the slave if set free will be worse off than before, or who think that the welfare of the masters is not sufficiently cared for. These moderate men think "We had better not meddle with the matter at present," but by and by, at a convenient season, they will venture to look into it. Now these moderate men it is not likely would ever think of doing the work until it is all done, yet deserve the gratitude of the public, of the more enthusiastic abolitionists. A balance wheel is useful to a machine; though it renders more force necessary at first to start the machine, it gives it stability and power when once set a-moving. In certain stages of vegetation a chilly day is a most auspicious event.

Then too they encounter opposition from the selfish, who see, or think they see, that the white masters will lose some thousands of millions of dollars, if slavery be abolished! Who has forgotten the men that opposed the introduction of Christianity at Ephesus,— the craftsmen that made silver shrines for Diana!

I know some men say, "We have nothing to do with it. Slavery is the affair of the slaveholders and the slaves, not yours and mine. Let them abate it when they will." A most unchristian saying is this. Slavery! we have something to do with it. The sugar and rice we eat, the cotton we wear, are the work of the slave. His wrongs are imported to us in these things. We eat his flesh and drink his blood. I need not speak of our political connection with slavery. You all know what that is, and its effect on us here. But socially, individually, we are brought into contact with it every

day. If there is a crime in the land known to us, and
we do not protest against it to the extent of our ability,
we are partners of that crime. It is not many years
since it was said, temperate men had nothing to do
with the sin of drunkenness; though they paid for it
out of their purse! When they looked they found
they had much to do with it, and sought to end it.
I have no doubt, to go back to the Hebrew mythical
tale, that when God called Cain, "Where is Abel?"
he said, "I have nothing to do with it; that is Abel's
affair. Am I my brother's keeper?" If the law of
Moses made it the duty of a Hebrew to lift up the
beast of a public enemy which had stumbled in the
street, how much more does the law of God make it
a Christian's duty to tell his brother of his sin, and
help him out of it; how much more to rescue the oppressed,—" to bind up the broken-hearted; to proclaim
liberty to the captives, the opening of the prison to
them that are bound."

Such then is slavery at the South; such the action
of men at the North to attack or to defend it. But
look a moment at the cause of this sin, and of its defense. It comes from the desire to get gain, comfort,
or luxury; to have power over matter, without working
or paying the honest price of that gain, comfort, luxury, and power; it is the spirit which would knowingly
and of set purpose injure another for the sake of
gaining some benefit to yourself. Such a spirit would
hold slaves everywhere, if it were possible. Now when
the question is put to any fair man,— Is not this spirit
active at the North as well as the South? there is but
one answer. The man who would use his fellow-man
as a tool merely, and injure him by that use; who
would force another in any way to bend to his ca-

price; who would take advantage of his ignorance, his credulity, his superstition, or his poverty, to enrich and comfort himself; in a word, who would use his neighbor to his neighbor's hurt,— that man has the spirit of slaveholding, and were circumstances but different, he would chain his brethren with iron bonds. If you, for your own sake, would unjustly put any man in a position which degrades him in your eyes, in his own eyes, in the eyes of his fellow-men, you have the spirit of the slaveholder. There is much of this affair with us still. This is the reason that slavery finds so many supporters amongst us; that we deliver up the fugitives, and " betray him that wandereth," sheltering ourselves under the plea that we keep the law of the land, written by man on parchment half a century ago, while we violate the law of nature, written everlastingly by God on the walls of the world. It was through this spirit,— so genial to our Anglo-Saxon blood,— that our fathers slew the Indians, who would not work, and the Southern planter enslaves the African, who will work. Both acted from the same motives, at North and South; killing or enslaving. That spirit is still with us, and shows itself in many shapes that need not be touched on now. It is not owing so much to our superior goodness, perhaps, as to a fortunate accident, that we have no slaves here at this day. They are not profitable. The shrewd men of our land discerned the fact long ago, and settled the question. Doubtless we have still social institutions which eyes more Christian than ours shall one day look upon as evils only less than that of slavery itself. But it is gradually that we gain light; he that converts it to life as fast as it comes, does well.[3]

II. Let a word be said on the other kind of slavery;

that which comes from a cause internal to ourselves.
This is common at the North, and South, and East,
and West.   In this case the man is prevented from doing what is best for him, not by some other man who
has bound him, but by some passion or prejudice, superstition or sin.   Here the mischief is in his own heart.
If you look around you, you find many that bear the
mark of the beast; branded on the forehead and the
right hand; branded as slaves.   " He that committeth
sin is the slave of sin."   The avaricious man is a
slave.   He cannot think a thought but as his master
bids.   He cannot see a truth if a dollar intervene.   He
cannot relieve the poor, nor sympathize with the distressed, nor yield to the humane impulse of his natural
heart.   If he sees in the newspaper a sentence on the
wastefulness or the idleness of the poor, he remembers
it for ever; but a word in the Bible to encourage
charity,— he never finds that.

The passionate man is a slave; he lies at the mercy
of the accidents of a day.   If his affairs go well he is
calm and peaceful; but if some little mistake arise he
is filled with confusion, and the demon that rules him
draws the chain.   This master has many a slave under
his yoke.   He is more cruel than any planter in Cuba
or Trinidad.   He not only separates friend from
friend, parent from child, and husband from wife, but
what is worse yet, prevents their loving one another
while they are together.   This makes man a tyrant,
not a husband; woman a fiend, not an angel, as God
made her to be.   This renders marriage a necessary
evil, and housekeeping a perpetual curse, for it takes
the little trifles which happen everywhere, except between angels, and makes them very great matters; it
converts mistakes into faults, accidents into vices, er-

rors into crimes; and so rends asunder the peace of
families, and in a single twelvemonth disturbs more
marriages than all the slaveholders of Carolina in a
century.

So the peevish man is a slave. His ill humor watches
him like a demon. Ofttimes it casteth him into the fire,
and often into the water. In the morning he com-
plains that his caprice is not complied with; in the
evening that it is. He is never peaceful except when
angry; never quiet but in a storm. He is free to do
nothing good; so he acts badly, thinks badly, feels
badly,— three attributes of a devil. A yoke of iron
and fetters of brass were grievous to bear, no doubt;
the whip of a task-master makes wounds in the flesh;
but God save us from the tyranny of the peevish, both
what they inflict and what they suffer.

The intemperate man also is a slave; one most totally subjugated. His vice exposes him to the contempt and insult of base men, as well as to the pity of
the good. Not only this, but his master strips him of
his understanding; takes away his common sense, conscience, his reason, religion,— qualities that make a
man differ from a beast; on his garments, his face, his
wife and child, is written in great staring letters, so
that he may read that runs — This man also has sold
his birthright and become a slave. The jealous planter
forbids his slave to learn; but he cannot take from him
the understanding he has got. This refinement of torture it was left for intemperance to exercise, levelling
at once the distinctions between rude and polished.

Bodily slavery is one of the greatest wrongs that
man can inflict on man; an evil not to be measured by
the external and visible woe which it entails on the victim, but by the deep internal ruin which it is its direct

tendency to produce.   If I had the tongue of the arch-
angel I could not give utterance to the awfulness of
this evil.   There is no danger that this be exaggerated,
— no more than that the sun in a picture be painted
too bright.   A wise man would do anything within the
compass of righteousness, or suffer a hundred deaths,
if that were possible, rather than yield himself a slave,
to be the tool and chattel of a master who views him
as a dog.   A religious man will do all within the compass of religion to rescue others from a fate so hard.
What we can do for this, then, let us do with faith
in Him who brings good out of evil.   You and I cannot move multitudes of men, but we can each move
one, and so contribute our mite to remove the outward
obstacles that oppose the freedom of man.

I know men say that you and I ought not to move
in this matter; that we have nothing to do with it.
They urge in argument that the Constitution of the
United States is the supreme law of the land, and that
sanctions slavery.   But it is the supreme law made by
the voters, like the statutes denouncing capital punishment.   What voters have made can voters unmake.
There is no supreme law but that made by God; if our
laws contradict that, the sooner they end or the sooner
they are broken, why, the better.   It seems to be
thought a very great thing to run counter to a law of
man, written on parchment; a very little thing to run
counter to the law of Almighty God, Judge of the
quick and the dead.   Has He sanctioned slavery?
" Oh yes," say some, and cite Old Testament and New
Testament in proof thereof.   It has been said, " The
devil can quote Scripture for his purpose."   We need
not settle that question now, but it is certain that men
can quote it to support despotism when that is the

order of the day,— or freedom when that is the " law
of the land; " certain that men defend drunkenness and
war, or sobriety and peace, out of its pages. A man
finds what he looks for. Now some tell us that Paul
said, " Let every soul be subject unto the higher
powers," meaning the " law of the land,"—" for the
powers that be are ordained of God." Did Paul do
so? Not at all; he resisted the very religion established by the powers that were. But it will be said,
he did not war directly with slavery, yet lived in the
midst of slaveholders. Paul had work enough to do,
no doubt, without that of abolishing slavery; perhaps
he had not his eyes open to this great sin,— not seeing
it as a sin. This is certain, that he thought the world
was to end in his own lifetime, and therefore if he did
see the wickedness of the " institution," he may have
thought it not worth while to attempt to remove what
would so soon perish, at the " coming of the Lord."
But it is said still further, Jesus himself did not forbid
slavery in set speech. Did he forbid by name any one
of a hundred other vices that might be mentioned?
He did not forbid the excessive use of intoxicating
liquors in that way. Nay, we are told in the fourth
Gospel that he made three or four barrels of wine —
of superior quality too — for a single wedding in a
little country town, in Cana of Galilee! Does his silence or his alleged action afford any excuse for that
sin also? It is a very sad state of mind in which a
man can forget all the principles which Jesus laid
down, all the spirit of his doctrine and his life, and
then quibble about this,— that he did not forbid
slavery in words! Men that cite him in defense of
slavery seem to forget the " Sermon on the Mount; "
yes, all of his teachings, and would do well to read for

their special edification, what is said to their proto-
types in the twenty-third chapter of Matthew, and elsewhere.

Bodily slavery, though established by the powers
that be, is completely in the hands of the voters, for
they are the powers that be, is no more sanctioned by
the supreme law of the land than stealing or murder.
No enactment of man can make that right which was
wrong before. It can never be abstractly right in any
circumstances to do what is abstractly wrong.

But that other slavery, which comes from yourself,
that is wholly within your power. And which, think
you, is the worse, to be unwillingly the slave of a man
and chained and whipped, or to be the voluntary slave
of avarice, passion, peevishness, intemperance! It is
better that your body be forcibly constrained, bought
and sold, than that your soul, yourself, be held in
thraldom. The spirit of a slave may be pure as an
angel's; sometimes as lofty and as blessed too. The
comforts of religion, when the heart once welcomes
them, are as beautiful in a slave's cabin as in a king's
court. When death shakes off the slave's body, the
chain falls with it, and the man, disenthralled at last,
goes where the wicked cease from troubling, where the
weary are at rest, where the slave is free from his
master; yes, where faithful use of the smallest talent
and humblest opportunity has its reward, and unmer-
ited suffering finds its ample recompense. But the
voluntary slavery under sin — it has no bright side.
None in life; in death no more. You may flee from a
taskmaster, not from yourself.

Body-slavery is so bad that the sun might be pardoned if it turned back, refusing to shine on such a
sin; on a land contaminated with its stain. But soul-

slavery, what shall we say of that? Our fathers bought political freedom at a great price; they sailed the sea in storms; they dwelt here aliens on a hostile soil, the world's outcasts; in cold and hunger, in toil and want they dwelt here; they fought desperate wars in freedom's name! Yet they bought it cheap. You and I were base men, if we would not give much more than they paid, sooner than lose the inheritance.

But freedom for the soul to act right, think right, feel right, you cannot inherit; that you must win for yourself. Yet it is offered you at no great price. You may take it who will. It is the birthright of you and me and each of us; if we keep its conditions it is ours. Yet it is only to be had by the religious man — the man true to the nature God gave him. Without His spirit in your heart you have no freedom. Resist His law, revealed in nature, in the later scripture of the Bible, in your own soul; resist it by sin, you are a slave, you must be a slave. Obey that law, you are Christ's freeman; nature and God are on your side. How strange it would be that one man should be found on all the hills of New England, of soul so base, of spirit so dastardly, that of his own consent took on him the yoke of slavery; went into the service of sin; toiled with that leprous host, in hopeless unrecompensed misery, without God, without heaven, without hope. Strange, indeed, that in this little village there should be men who care not for the soul's freedom, but consent to live, no, to die daily, in the service of sin.

II

THE MEXICAN WAR

MR. CHAIRMAN,— We have come here to consult for the honor of our country. The honor and dignity of the United States are in danger. I love my country; I love her honor. It is dear to me almost as my own. I have seen stormy meetings in Faneuil Hall before now, and am not easily disturbed by a popular tumult. But never before did I see a body of armed soldiers attempting to overawe the majesty of the people, when met to deliberate on the people's affairs. Yet the meetings of the people of Boston have been disturbed by soldiers before now, by British bayonets; but never since the Boston Massacre on the 5th of March, 1770! Our fathers hated a standing army. This is a new one, but behold the effect! Here are soldiers with bayonets to overawe the majesty of the people! They went to our meeting last Monday night, the hireling soldiers of President Polk, to overawe and disturb the meetings of honest men. Here they are now, and in arms!

We are in a war; the signs of war are seen here in Boston. Men, needed to hew wood and honestly serve society, are marching about your streets; they are learning to kill men, men who never harmed us nor them; learning to kill their brothers. It is a mean and infamous war we are fighting. It is a great boy fighting a little one, and that little one feeble and sick. What makes it worse is, the little boy is in the right, and the big boy is in the wrong, and tells solemn lies

21

to make his side seem right. He wants, besides, to make the small boy pay the expenses of the quarrel.

The friends of the war say, " Mexico has invaded our territory! " When it is shown that it is we who have invaded hers, then it is said, " Ay, but she owes us money." Better say outright, " Mexico has land, and we want to steal it! "

This war is waged for a mean and infamous purpose, for the extension of slavery. It is not enough that there are fifteen slave States, and 3,000,000 men here who have no legal rights — not so much as the horse and the ox have in Boston; it is not enough that the slaveholders annexed Texas, and made slavery perpetual therein, extending even north of Mason and Dixon's line, covering a territory forty-five times as large as the State of Massachusetts. Oh, no; we must have yet more land to whip negroes in!

The war had a mean and infamous beginning. It began illegally, unconstitutionally. The Whigs say, " The President made the war." Mr. Webster says so! It went on meanly and infamously. Your Congress lied about it. Do not lay the blame on the Democrats; the Whigs lied just as badly. Your Congress has seldom been so single-mouthed before. Why, only sixteen voted against the war, or the lie. I say this war is mean and infamous, all the more because waged by a people calling itself democratic and Christian. I know but one war so bad in modern times, between civilized nations, and that was the war for the partition of Poland. Even for that there was more excuse.

We have come to Faneuil Hall to talk about the war; to work against the war. It is rather late, but " better late than never." We have let two opportunities for work pass unemployed. One came while the annexation of Texas was pending. Then was the time to push and be active. Then was the time for Massachusetts and all the North, to protest as one man against the extension of slavery. Everybody knew all about the matter, the Democrats and the Whigs. But how few worked against that gross mischief! One noble man lifted up his warning voice; [1] a man noble in his father — and there he stands in marble; noble in himself — and there he stands yet higher up; — and I hope time will show him yet nobler in his son — and there he stands, not in marble, but in man! He talked against it, worked against it, fought against it. But Massachusetts did little. Her tonguey men said little; her handy men did little. Too little could not be done or said. True, we came here to Faneuil Hall and passed resolutions; good resolutions they were, too. Daniel Webster wrote them, it is said. They did the same in the State House; but nothing came of them. They say "Hell is paved with resolutions;" these were of that sort of resolutions, which resolve nothing, because they are of words, not works!

Well, we passed the resolutions; you know who opposed them; who hung back and did nothing — nothing good I mean; quite enough not good. Then we thought all the danger was over; that the resolution settled the matter. But then was the time to confound at once the enemies of your country; to show an even front hostile to slavery.

But the chosen time passed over, and nothing was done. Do not lay the blame on the Democrats; a Whig Senate annexed Texas, and so annexed a war. We ought to have told our delegation in Congress, if Texas were annexed, to come home, and we would breathe upon it and sleep upon it, and then see what to do next. Had our resolutions, taken so warmly here in Faneuil Hall in 1845, been but as warmly worked out, we had now been as terrible to the slave power as the slave power, since extended, now is to us!

Why was it that we did nothing? That is a public secret. Perhaps I ought not to tell it to the people. (Cries of " Tell it.")

The annexation of Texas, a slave territory big as the kingdom of France, would not furl a sail on the ocean; would not stop a mill-wheel at Lowell! Men thought so.

That time passed by, and there came another. The Government had made war; the Congress voted the dollars, voted the men, voted a lie. Your representative men of Boston voted for all three — the lie, the dollars, and the men; all three, in obedience to the slave power! Let him excuse that to the conscience of his party; it is an easy matter. I do not believe he can excuse it to his own conscience. To the conscience of the world it admits of no excuse. Your President called for volunteers, 50,000 of them. Then came an opportunity such as offers not once in one hundred years, an opportunity to speak for freedom and the rights of mankind! Then was the time for Massachusetts to stand up in the spirit of '76, and say, " We won't send a man, from Cape Ann to Williamstown — not one Yankee man, for this wicked war." Then was the time for your Governor to say, " Not a volunteer for this wicked war." Then was the time for your merchants to say, " Not a ship, not a dollar, for this wicked war; " for your manufacturers to say, " We will not make you a cannon, nor a sword, nor a kernel of powder, nor a soldier's shirt, for this wicked war." Then was the time for all good men to

say, " This is a war for slavery, a mean and infamous
war; an aristocratic war, a war against the best interests of mankind. If God please, we will die a
thousand times, but never draw blade in this wicked
war." (Cries of " Throw him over," &c.) Throw
him over, what good would that do? What would
you do next, after you have thrown him over?
(" Drag you out of the hall! ") What good would
that do? It would not wipe off the infamy of this
war! would not make it less wicked!

That is what a democratic nation, a Christian people
ought to have said, ought to have done. But we did
not say so; the Bay State did not say so, nor your
Governor, nor your merchants, nor your manufacturers, nor your good men; the Governor accepted the
President's decree, issued his proclamation calling for
soldiers, recommended men to enlist, appealing to their
" patriotism " and " humanity."

Governor Briggs is a good man; and so far I honor
him. He is a temperance man, strong and consistent;
I honor him for that. He is a friend of education;
a friend of the people. I wish there were more such.
Like many other New England men, he started from
humble beginnings; but unlike many such successful
men of New England, he is not ashamed of the lowest
round he ever trod on. I honor him for all this. But
that was a time which tried men's souls, and his soul
could not stand the rack. I am sorry for him. He
did as the President told him.

What was the reason for all this? Massachusetts
did not like the war, even then; yet she gave her consent to it. Why so? There are two words which
can drive the blood out of the cheeks of cowardly men
in Massachusetts any time. They are " Federalism "

and "Hartford Convention"! The fear of those words palsied the conscience of Massachusetts, and so her Governor did as he was told. I feel no fear of either. The Federalists did not see all things; who ever did? They had not the ideas which were destined to rule this nation; they looked back when the age looked forward. But to their own ideas they were true; and if ever a nobler body of men held state•in any nation, I have yet to learn when or where. If we had had the shadow of Caleb Strong in the Governor's chair, not a volunteer for this war had gone out of Massachusetts.

I have not told quite all the reasons why Massachusetts did nothing. Men knew the war would cost money; that the dollars would in the end be raised, not by a direct tax, of which the poor man paid according to his little, and the rich man in proportion to his much; but by a tariff which presses light on property, and hard on the person — by a tax on the backs and mouths of the people. Some of the Whigs were glad last spring when the war came, for they hoped thereby to save the child of their old age, the tariff of '42. There are always some rich men, who say, "No matter what sort of a government we have, so long as we get our dividends;" always some poor men, who say, "No matter how much the nation suffers, if we fill our hungry purses thereby." Well, they lost their virtue, lost their tariff, and gained just nothing; what they deserved to gain.

Now a third opportunity has come; — no, it has not come; we have brought it. The President wants a war tax on tea and coffee. Is that democratic, to tax every man's breakfast and supper, for the sake of getting more territory to whip negroes in? (Numerous cries of "Yes.") Then what do you think despotism would be? He asks a loan of $28,000,000 for this war. He wants $3,000,000 to spend privately for this war. In eight months past, he has asked, I am told, for $74,000,000. Seventy-four millions of dollars to conquer slave territory! Is that democratic too? He wants to increase the standing army, to have ten regiments more! A pretty business that. Ten regiments to gag the people in Faneuil Hall. Do you think that is democratic? Some men have just asked Massachusetts for $20,000 for the volunteers! It is time for the people to rebuke all this wickedness.

I think there is a good deal to excuse the volunteers. I blame them, for some of them know what they are about. Yet I pity them more, for most of them, I am told, are low, ignorant men; some of them drunken and brutal. From the uproar they make here to-night, arms in their hands, I think what was told me is true! I say, I pity them. They are my brothers; not the less brothers because low and misguided. If they are so needy that they are forced to enlist by poverty, surely I pity them. If they are of good families, and know better, I pity them still more! I blame most the men that have duped the rank and file! I blame the captains and colonels, who will have least of the hardships, most of the pay, and all of the " glory." I blame the men that made the war; the men that make money out of it. I blame the great party men of the land. Did not Mr. Clay say he hoped he could slay a Mexican? (Cries, " No, he didn't.") Yes, he did; said it on Forefather's day! Did not Mr. Webster, in the streets of Philadelphia, bid the volunteers, misguided young men, go and uphold the stars of their country? (Voices,

" He did right!") No; he should have said
the stripes of his country, for every volunteer to this
wicked war is a stripe on the nation's back! Did not
he declare this war unconstitutional, and threaten to
impeach the President who made it, and then go and
invest a son in it? Has it not been said here, " Our
country, howsoever bounded," bounded by robbery or
bounded by right lines! Has it not been said, all
round, " Our country, right or wrong!"

I say, I blame not so much the volunteers as the famous men who deceived the nation! (Cries of " Throw
him over; kill him, kill him!" and a flourish of bayonets.) Throw him over! you will not throw him over.
Kill him! I shall walk home unarmed and unattended,
and not a man of you will hurt one hair of my head.

I say again, it is time for the people to take up this
matter. Your Congress will do nothing till you tell
them what and how. Your 29th Congress can do little
good. Its sands are nearly run, God be thanked! It
is the most infamous Congress we ever had. We began with the Congress that declared Independence, and
swore by the eternal justice of God. We have come
down to the 29th Congress, which declared war existed
by the act of Mexico — declared a lie; the Congress
that swore by the Baltimore Convention! We began
with George Washington, and have got down to James
K. Polk.

It is time for the people of Massachusetts to instruct their servants in Congress to oppose this war;
to refuse all supplies for it; to ask for the recall of the
army into our own land. It is time for us to tell them
that not an inch of slave territory shall ever be added
to the realm. Let us remonstrate; let us petition; let
us command. If any class of men have hitherto been

remiss, let them come forward now and give us their names — the merchants, the manufacturers, the Whigs and the Democrats. If men love their country better than their party or their purse, now let them show it.

Let us ask the General Court of Massachusetts to cancel every commission which the Governor has given to the officers of the volunteers. Let us ask them to disband the companies not yet mustered into actual service; and then, if you like that, ask them to call a convention of the people of Massachusetts, to see what we shall do in reference to the war; in reference to the annexation of more territory; in reference to the violation of the Constitution. (Loud groans from crowds of rude fellows in several parts of the hall.) That was a Tory groan; they never dared groan so in Faneuil Hall before; not even the British Tories, when they had no bayonets to back them up! I say, let us ask for these things!

Your President tells us it is treason to talk so! Treason is it? treason to discuss a war which the Government made, and which the people are made to pay for? If it be treason to speak against the war, what was it to make the war, to ask for 50,000 men and $74,000,000 for the war? Why, if the people cannot discuss the war they have got to fight and to pay for, who under heaven can? Whose business is it, if it is not yours and mine? If my country is in the wrong, and I know it, and hold my peace, then I am guilty of treason, moral treason. Why, a wrong — it is only the threshold of ruin. I would not have my country take the next step. Treason is it, to show that this war is wrong and wicked? Why, what if George III, any time from '75 to '83, had gone down to Parliament and told them it was treason to discuss the war then waging against these colonies! What do you think the Commons would have said? What would the Lords say? Why, that king, foolish as he was, would have been lucky, if he had not learned there was a joint in his neck, and, stiff as he bore him, that the people knew how to find it.

I do not believe in killing kings, or any other men; but I do say, in a time when the nation was not in danger, that no British king, for two hundred years past, would have dared call it treason to discuss the war — its cause, its progress, or its termination!

Now is the time to act! Twice we have let the occasion slip; beware of the third time! Let it be infamous for a New England man to enlist; for a New England merchant to loan his dollars, or to let his ships in aid of this wicked war; let it be infamous for a manufacturer to make a cannon, a sword, or a kernel of powder to kill our brothers with, while we all know that they are in the right, and we in the wrong.

I know my voice is a feeble one in Massachusetts. I have no mountainous position from whence to look down and overawe the multitude; I have no background of political reputation to echo my words. I am but a plain, humble man; but I have a background of truth to sustain me, and the justice of heaven arches over my head! For your sakes, I wish I had that oceanic eloquence whose tidal flow should bear on its bosom the drift-weed which politicians have piled together, and sap and sweep away the sand-hillocks of soldiery blown together by the idle wind; that oceanic eloquence which sweeps all before it, and leaves the shore hard, smooth, and clean! But feeble as I am, let me beg of you, fellow-citizens of Boston, men and brothers, to come forward and protest against this wicked war, and the end for which it is waged. I call on the Whigs, who love their country better than they love the tariff of '42; I call on the Democrats, who think justice is greater than the Baltimore Convention — I call on the Whigs and Democrats to come forward and join with me in opposing this wicked war! I call on the men of Boston, on the men of the old Bay State, to act worthy of their fathers, worthy of their country, worthy of themselves! Men and brothers, I call on you all to protest against this most infamous war, in the name of the State, in the name of the country, in the name of man — yes, in the name of God; leave not your children saddled with a war debt, to cripple the nation's commerce for years to come. Leave not your land cursed with slavery, extended and extending, palsying the nation's arm and corrupting the nation's heart. Leave not your memory infamous among the nations, because you feared men, feared the Government; because you loved money got by crime, land plundered in war, loved land unjustly bounded; because you debased your country by defending the wrong she dared to do; because you loved slavery, loved war, but loved not the eternal justice of all-judging God. If my counsel is weak and poor, follow one stronger and more manly. I am speaking to men; think of these things, and then act like men!

III

A LETTER ON SLAVERY

Fellow-Citizens of the United States:
It may seem strange and presumptuous that an obscure man, known even by name to but very few in the land, should write you a public letter on a theme so important as this of slavery. You may call it foolish and rash. Say that if you will; perhaps you are right. I have no name, no office, no rank amongst men, which entitle my thoughts to your consideration. I am but one of the undistinguished millions, who live unnoticed, and die remembered only by their family and friends; humble and obscure. If any of the famous men accustomed to sway the opinions of the political parties and the theological sects, had suitably treated this matter, showing you the facts and giving manly counsel, I should not have presumed to open my mouth. It is their silence which prompts me to speak. I am no aspirant for office or for fame; have nothing to gain by your favor; fear nothing from your frown. In writing this letter I obey no idle caprice, but speak from a sense of duty, in submission to the voice of conscience. I love my country, and my kind; it is patriotism and humanity which bid me speak. I ask you to read and consider, not to read without your prejudices, but with them, with them all; then to consider, to decide, to act, as you may or must. I address myself to no party, to no sect, but speak to you, as Americans and as men, addressing my thoughts to all the citizens of the slave States and the free.

I am to speak of a great evil, long established, wide spread, deeply rooted in the laws, the usages, and the ideas of the people. It affects directly the welfare of three millions of men, one sixth part of the nation: they are slaves. It affects directly half the States: they are slaveholders. It has a powerful influence on the other half, though more subtle and unseen. It affects the industry, laws, morals, and entire prosperity of the whole nation to a degree exceeding the belief of men not familiar with its history and its facts. The evil increases with a rapid growth; with advancing flood it gains new territory, swells with larger volume; its deadly spray and miasma gradually invade all our institutions. The whole nation is now legally pledged to its support; the public legislation for the last sixty years has made slavery a federal institution. Your revenue boats and your navy are bound to support it; your army acts for its defense. You have fought wars, spending money and shedding blood, to gain new soil wherein to plant the tree of slavery. You have established it in your districts and your territories. You have recently annexed to your realm a new territory as large as the kingdom of France, and extended slavery over that soil whence a semi-barbarous people had expelled it with ignominy. You are now fighting a war in behalf of slavery, a war carried on at great cost of money and of men. The national capital is a great slave market; in her shambles your brothers are daily offered for sale. Your flag floats over the most wicked commerce on earth — the traffic in men and women. Citizens of the United States breed youths and maidens for sale in the market, as the grazier oxen and swine.

VIII—3

The Bey of Tunis has abolished slavery as a disgrace to Africa and the Mahometan religion. Your Constitution of the United States supports this institution, and binds it upon the free States; the South fondly clings to it; the free men of the North bend suppliant necks to this yoke. With a few exceptions, your representatives and senators in Congress give it their countenance and their vote; their hand and their heart. Your great and famous men are pledged to this. or their silence practically purchased. Seven Presidents of your Christian Democracy have been holders of slaves; three only free from that taint. You will soon be called on to elect another slaveholder to sit in the presidential chair and rule over a republic containing twenty millions of men.

In all the Union there is no legal asylum for the fugitive slave; no soil emancipates his hurrying feet. The States which allow no slavery within their limits legally defend the slaveholder: catch and retain the man fleeing for his manhood and his life.

I cannot call upon the political leaders of the nation. You know what they look for, and how they would treat a letter exposing a national evil, and talking of truth and justice. I do not address you as members of the political parties; they have their great or petty matters to deal with, differing in regard to free trade or protection, but are united in one policy as it respects slavery. Demagogues of both parties will play their little game, and on your shoulders ride into fame, and ease, and wealth, and power and noise. The sects also have their special work and need not be addressed on the subject of slavery — of human wrong.

I speak to the people, not as sectarians, Protestant

or Catholic — not as Democrats or Whigs, but as Americans and as men. I solemnly believe if you all knew the facts of American slavery and its effects, as I know them, that you would end the evil before a twelvemonth had passed by. I take it for granted that you love justice and truth. I write to you, having confidence in your integrity and love of men, having confidence also in the democratic ideas on which a government should rest.

In what I write you will doubtless find mistakes — errors of fact or of reasoning. I do not ask to be screened from censure even for what no diligence could wholly escape, only that you will not reject nor refuse to consider the truth of fact and of reasoning which is presented to you. A few mistakes in figures or in reasoning will not affect the general argument of this letter. Read with what prejudice you may, but decide and act according to reason and conscience.

I. *Statistics and History of Slavery*

I will first call your attention to the statistics and history of slavery. In 1790 there were but 697,897 slaves in the Union; in 1840, 2,487,355. At the present day their number probably is not far from 3,000,000. In 1790, Mr. Gerry estimated their value at $10,000,000; in 1840 Mr. Clay fixed it at $1,200,-000,000. They are owned by a population of perhaps about 300,000 persons, and represented by about 100,000 voters.

At the time of the Declaration of Independence slavery existed in all the States; it gradually receded from the North. In the religious colonies of New England it was always unpopular and odious. It was there seen and felt to be utterly inconsistent with the ideas and spirit of their institutions, their churches, and their State itself.[1]   After the revolution therefore it speedily disappeared — here perishing by default, there abolished by statute. Thus it successively disappeared from Rhode Island, Massachusetts, New Hampshire, New York, Pennsylvania, and New Jersey. By the celebrated Ordinance of 1787, involuntary servitude, except as a punishment after legal conviction of crime, was for ever prohibited in the Northwest Territory. Thus the new States, formed in the western parallels, were, by the action of the Federal Government, at once cut off from that institution. Besides, they were mainly settled by men from the Eastern States, who had neither habits nor principles which favored slavery. Thus Ohio, Indiana, Illinois, Michigan, Wisconsin, and Iowa, have been without any legal slaves from the beginning.

In the South the character of the people was different; their manners, their social and political ideas, were unlike those of the North. The Southern States were mainly colonies of adventurers, rather than establishments of men who for conscience' sake fled to the wilderness. Less pains were taken with the education — intellectual, moral, and religious — of the people. Religion never held so prominent a place in the consciousness of the mass as in the sterner and more austere colonies of the North. In the Southern States — New Jersey, Delaware, Maryland, Virginia, the Carolinas, and Georgia,— slavery easily found a footing at an early day. It was not at all repulsive to the ideas, the institutions, and habits of Georgia and South Carolina. The other Southern States protested against it; — they never.

Consequences follow causes; it is not easy to avoid

the results of a first principle. The Northern States, in all their constitutions and social structure, consistently and continually tend to Democracy — the government of all, for all, and by all; — to equality before the State and its laws; to moral and political ideas of universal application. In the mean time the Southern States, in their constitutions and social structure, as consistently tend to oligarchy — the government over all, by a few, and for the sake of that few; — to privilege, favoritism, and class-legislation; to conventional limitations; to the rule of force, and inequality before the law. In such a state of things when slavery comes, it is welcome. In 1787, South Carolina and Georgia refused to accept the Federal Constitution unless the right of importing slaves was guaranteed to them for twenty years. The new States formed in the southern parallels — Kentucky, Tennessee, Alabama, Mississippi — retaining the ideas and habits of their parents, kept also the institution of slavery.

At the time of forming the Federal Constitution some of the Southern statesmen were hostile to slavery, and would gladly have got rid of it. Economical considerations prevailed in part, but political and moral objections to it extended yet more widely. The Ordinance of 1787, the work mainly of the same man who drafted the Declaration of Independence, passed with little opposition.[2] The proviso for surrendering fugitive slaves came from a Northern hand. Subsequently opposition to slavery, in the North and the South, became less. The culture of cotton, the wars in Europe creating a demand for the productions of American agriculture, had rendered slave labor more valuable. The day of our own oppression was more distant and forgotten. So in 1802, when Congress purchased from Georgia the western part of her territory, it was easy for the South to extend slavery over that virgin soil. In 1803, Louisiana was purchased from France; then, or in 1804, when it was organized into two territories, it would have been easy to apply the Ordinance of 1787, and prevent slavery from extending beyond the original thirteen States. But though some provisions restricting slavery were made, the ideas of that Ordinance were forgotten. Since that time five new States have been formed out of territory acquired since the revolution,— Louisiana, Missouri, Arkansas, Florida, Texas,— all slave States; the last two with constitutions aiming to make slavery perpetual. The last of these was added to the Union on the 22nd of December, 1845, two hundred and twenty-five years after the day when the Forefathers first set foot on Plymouth Rock; while the sons of the Pilgrims were eating and drinking and making merry, the deed of annexation was completed, and slavery extended over nearly 400,000 square miles of new territory, whence the semi-barbarous Mexicans had driven it out.

Slavery might easily have been abolished at the time of the Declaration of Independence. Indeed in 1744 the Continental Congress, in their celebrated " non-importation agreement," resolved never to import or purchase any slaves after the last of December in that year. In 1775, they declare in a " Report " that it is not possible " for men who exercise their reason to believe that the Divine Author of our existence intended a part of the human race to hold an absolute property in and unbounded power over others." Indeed the Declaration itself is a denial of the national right to allow the existence of slavery: "We hold these truths to be self-evident, that all men are created equal; that they are endowed by their Creator with certain unalienable rights; that among these are [the right to] life, liberty, and the pursuit of happiness; — that to secure these rights governments are instituted among men deriving their just powers from the consent of the governed."

But the original draft of this paper contained a condemnation yet more explicit: "He [the king of England] has waged cruel war against human nature itself; violating its most sacred rights of life and liberty in the persons of a distant people who never offended him; captivating and carrying them into slavery. . . . Determined to keep open a market where men should be bought and sold, he has prostituted his negative for suppressing every legislative attempt to prohibit or restrain this execrable commerce." This clause, says its author himself, "was struck out in compliance to South Carolina and Georgia, who had never attempted to restrain the importation of slaves, and who, on the contrary, still wished to continue it. Our Northern brethren also, I believe, felt a little tender under these censures; for though their people have very few slaves themselves, yet they had been pretty considerable carriers of them to others."

These were not the sentiments of a single enthusiastic young Republican. Dr. Rush, in the Continental Congress wished "the colonies to discourage slavery and encourage the increase of the free inhabitants." Another member of the American Congress declared, in 1779, "Men are by nature free;" "the right to be free can never be alienated." In 1776, Dr. Hopkins,

the head of the New England divines, declared that
" slavery is, in every instance wrong, unrighteous,
and oppressive; a very great and crying sin."

In the Articles of Confederation, adopted in 1778,
no provision is made for the support of slavery; none
for the delivery of fugitives. Slavery is not once
referred to in that document. The general government had nothing to do with it. " If any slave elopes
to those States where slaves are free," said Mr.
Madison in 1787, " he becomes emancipated by their
laws."

In the Convention of 1787, which drafted the
present Constitution of the United States, this matter
of slavery was abundantly discussed; it was the great
obstacle in the way of forming the Union, as now of
keeping it. But for the efforts of South Carolina,
it is probable slavery would have been abolished by the
Constitution. The South claimed the right of sending
representatives to Congress on account of their slaves.
Mr. Patterson, of New Jersey, contended that as the
slaves had no representative or vote at home, their
masters could not claim additional votes in Congress
on account of the slaves. Nearly all the speakers in
that Convention, except the members from South Carolina and Georgia, referred to the slave-trade with
horror. Mr. Gerry, of Massachusetts, declared in the
Convention, that it was " as humiliating to enter into
compact with the slaves of the Southern States, as
with the horses and mules of the North." It was contended that if slaves were men, then they should be
taxed as men, and have their vote as men; if mere
property, they should not entitle their owners to a
vote, more than other property. It might be proper
to tax slaves, " because it had a tendency to discour-

age slavery, but to take them into account in giving
representatives tended to encourage the slave-trade,
and to make it the interest of the States to continue
that infamous traffic." It was said, that "we had
just assumed a place among independent nations, in
consequence of our opposition to the attempts of
Great Britain to enslave us; that this opposition was
grounded upon the preservation of those rights to
which God and Nature had entitled us, not in particular, but in common with all the rest of mankind.
That we had appealed to the Supreme Being for His
assistance, as the God of heaven, who could not but ap-
prove our efforts to preserve the rights which he had
imparted to His creatures; that now, when we had
scarcely risen from our knees from supplicating His
aid and protection in forming our government over a
free people,— a government formed pretendedly on
the principles of liberty, and for its preservation,— in
that government to have a provision, not only putting
it out of its power to restrain or prevent the slave-
trade, even encouraging that most infamous traffic,
and giving States power and influence in the Union in
proportion as they cruelly and wantonly sport with
the rights of their fellow-creatures,— ought to be
considered as a solemn mockery of, and insult to, that
God whose protection we had then implored, and
could not fail to hold us up in detestation, and render
us contemptible to every true friend of liberty in the
world.

Luther Martin, the attorney-general of Maryland,
thought it "inconsistent with the principles of the
revolution, and dishonorable to the American character," to have the importation of slaves allowed by the
Constitution.

The Northern States, and some of the Southern, wished to abolish the slave-trade at once. Mr. Pinckney, of South Carolina, thought that State would "never accede to the Constitution, if it prohibits the slave-trade;" she would "not stop her importation of slaves in any short time." Said Mr. Rutledge, of South Carolina, "the people of the Carolinas and Georgia will never be such fools as to give up so important an interest." "Religion and humanity have nothing to do with this question. Interest alone is the governing principle with nations." In apportioning taxes, he thought three slaves ought to be counted as but one free man; while in apportioning representatives, his colleagues — Messrs. Butler and Pinckney — declared, "The blacks ought to stand on an equality with the whites." Mr. Pinckney would "make blacks equal to whites in the ratio of representation;" he went further,— he would have "some security against an emancipation of slaves;" and, says Mr. Madison, "seemed to wish some provision should be included [in the Constitution] in favor of property in slaves." "South Carolina and Georgia," said Mr. Pinckney, "cannot do without slaves." "The importation of slaves would be for the interest of the whole Union; the more slaves, the more produce to employ the carrying trade, the more consumption also."

On the other hand, Mr. Bedford of Delaware thought "South Carolina was puffed up with her wealth and her negroes." Mr. Madison, cool and far-sighted, always referring to first principles, was unwilling to allow the importation of slaves till 1808: — "So long a term will be more dishonorable to the American character than to say nothing about it in the Constitution."

Mr. Williamson of North Carolina, in 1783, thought "slaves an encumbrance to society" and was "both in opinion and practice against slavery." Col. Mann, of Virginia, in the Convention, called the slave-trade an "infernal traffic," and said that "slavery discourages arts and manufactures; the poor despise labor when performed by slaves." "They produce the most pernicious effect on manners. Every master of slaves is born a petty tyrant. They bring the judgment of Heaven on a country." Mr. Dickinson, of Delaware, thought it "inadmissible on every principle of honor and safety that the importation of slaves should be authorized." Gouverneur Morris, of Pennsylvania, "never would concur in upholding domestic slavery." It was a "nefarious institution;" "the curse of Heaven was on the States where it prevailed!" "Are the slaves men? Then make them citizens, and let them vote. Are they property? Why then is no other property included [in the ratio of representation]? The houses in this city [Philadelphia] are worth more than all the wretched slaves who cover the rice-swamps of South Carolina." Mr. Gerry declared we "ought to be careful not to give any sanction to it."

All the North was at first opposed to slavery and the slave-trade. Both parties seemed obstinate; the question of "taxes on exports" and of "navigation laws" remained to be decided. Gouverneur Morris recommended that the whole subject of slavery might be referred to a committee, "including the clauses relating to the taxes on exports and to the navigation laws. These things may form a bargain among the Northern and Southern States." Says Luther Martin, "I found the Eastern States, notwithstanding

their aversion to slavery, were very willing to indulge
the Southern States, at least with a temporary liberty
to prosecute the slave-trade, provided the Southern
States would in their turn gratify them by laying no
restriction on navigation acts." The North began to
understand if the contemplated navigation laws should
be enacted, that, as Mr. Grayson afterwards said, " all
the produce of the Southern States will be carried by
the Northern States on their own terms, which must
be high." Mr. Clymer, of Pennsylvania, declared,
" The Western and Middle States will be ruined, if not
enabled to defend themselves against foreign regula-
tions ; " will be ruined if they do not have some navigation laws giving Americans an advantage over foreign
vessels. Mr. Gorham of Massachusetts said, " The
Eastern States had no motives to union but a commercial one." The proffered compromise would favor
their commercial interests. It was for the commercial
interests of the South, said Mr. Pinckney, to have no
restrictions upon commerce, but " considering the loss
brought on the Eastern States by the revolution, and
their liberal conduct towards the views of South Carolina, [in consenting to allow slavery and the importation of slaves,] he thought that no fetters should be
imposed on the power of making commercial regula-
tions, and his constituents would be reconciled to the
liberality." So the North took the boon, and winked
at the " infernal traffic." When the question was put,
there were in favor of the importation of slaves,
Georgia, the two Carolinas, and Maryland, with New
Hampshire, Massachusetts, and Connecticut. Opposed to it were Pennsylvania, New Jersey, Delaware,
and Virginia! Subsequently Mr. Ames, in the Massachusetts Convention for the adoption of the Con-

stitution, said the Northern States "have great advantages by it in respect of navigation;" in the Virginia Convention Patrick Henry said, "Tobacco will always make our peace with them," for at that time cotton was imported from India, not having become a staple of the South. When the article which binds the free States to deliver up the fugitive slaves came to be voted on, it was a new feature in American legislation; not hinted at in the "Articles of Confederation;" hostile to the well-known principles of the common law of England — which always favors liberty — and the usages and principles of modern civilized nations. Yet new as it was and hostile, it seems not a word was said against it in the Convention. It "was agreed to, *nem. con.*" Yet "The Northern delegates," says Mr. Madison, "owing to their particular scruples on the subject of slavery, did not choose the word slave to be mentioned." In the Conventions of the several States it seems no remonstrance was made to this article.

Luther Martin returning home said to the House of Delegates in Maryland, "At this time we do not generally hold this commerce in so great abhorrence as we have done; when our liberties were at stake, we warmly felt for the common rights of men; the danger being thought to be past, we are daily growing more insensible to their rights."

When the several States came to adopt the Constitution, some hesitancy was shown at tolerating the slave-trade or even slavery itself. In the Massachusetts Convention, Mr. Neal would not "favor the making merchandise of the bodies of men." General Thompson exclaimed, "Shall it be said, that after we have established our own independence and freedom

we make slaves of others?" Washington has im-
mortalized himself, " but he holds those in slavery who
have as good a right to be free as he has." All parties
deprecated the slave-trade in most pointed terms.
" Slavery was generally detested." It was thought
that the new States could not claim the sad privilege
of their parents, that the South itself would soon hate
and abolish it. " Slavery is not smitten by an apo-
plexy," said Mr. Dawes, " yet it has received a mortal
wound, and will die of consumption." This reflection,
with the " tobacco " and " navigation laws," turned
the scale. Patrick Henry was no son of New England, but knew well on what hinges her political morality might turn, by what means and which way.

In the New York Convention, Mr. Smith could
" not see any rule by which slaves were to be included
in the ratio of representation, the very operation of it
was to give certain privileges to men who were so
wicked as to keep slaves;" to which Mr. Hamilton
replied, that " without this indulgence no union could
possibly have been formed. But . . . considering those peculiar advantages which we derived from
them, [the Southern States,]it is entirely just that
they should be gratified. The Southern States possess
certain staples, tobacco, rice, indigo, &c., which must
be capital objects in treaties of commerce with foreign
nations; and the advantage . . . will be felt in
all the States."

In the Pennsylvania Convention, Mr. Wilson considered that the Constitution laid the foundation for
abolishing slavery out of this country, though the
period was more distant than he could wish. Yet " the
new States . . . will be under the control of
Congress in this particular, and slavery will never be

introduced amongst them;" "yet the lapse of a few years, and Congress will have power to exterminate slavery from within our borders."

In the Virginia Convention Gov. Randolph regarded the slave trade as "infamous" and "detestable." Slavery was one of our vulnerable points. "Are we not weakened by the population of those whom we hold in slavery?" he asked. Col. Mason thought the trade "diabolical in itself and disgraceful to mankind." He would "not admit the Southern States [Georgia and the Carolinas] into the Union unless they agreed to the discontinuance of this disgraceful trade." Mr. Tyler thought "nothing could justify it." Patrick Henry, who contended for slavery, confessed "Slavery is detested,— we feel its fatal effects,— we deplore it with all the pity of humanity." "It would rejoice my very soul that every one of my fellow-beings was emancipated." Said Mr. Johnson, "Slavery has been the foundation of that impiety and dissipation which have been so much disseminated among our country-men. If it were totally abolished it would do much good."

In the North Carolina Convention, it was found necessary to apologize for the pro-slavery character of the Constitution. Mr. Iredell in defense said, the matter of slavery was "regulated with great difficulty, and by a spirit of concession which it would not be prudent to disturb for a good many years." "It is probable that all the members reprobated this inhuman traffic [in slaves], but those of South Carolina and Georgia would not consent to an immediate prohibition of it." "Were it practicable to put an end to the im-portation of slaves immediately, it would give him the greatest pleasure." "When the entire abolition of slavery takes place it will be an event which must be pleasing to every generous mind and every friend of human nature." Mr. McDowall looked upon the slave-trade " as a very objectionable part of the system." Mr. Goudy did not wish " to be represented with negroes."

In the South Carolina Convention, Gen. Pinckney admitted that the Carolinas and Georgia were so weak that they " could not form a union strong enough for the purpose of effectually protecting each other; " it was their policy therefore " to form a close union with the Eastern States who are strong; " the Eastern States had been the greatest sufferers in the revolution, they had " lost everything but their country and their freedom; " " we," the Carolinas and Georgia, " should let them, in some measure, partake of our prosperity." But the union could come only from a compromise; " we have secured an unlimited importation of negroes for twenty years." " We have obtained a right to recover our slaves in whatever part of America they shall take refuge, which is a right we had not before." " We have made the best terms for the security of this species of property it was in our power to make; we would have made better if we could, but on the whole I do not think them bad." No one in South Carolina, it seems, thought slavery an evil.

Thus the Constitution was assented to as " the result of accommodation," though containing clauses confessedly " founded on unjust principles." The North had been false to its avowed convictions, and in return " higher tonnage duties were imposed on foreign than on American bottoms," and goods imported in American vessels " paid ten per cent. less duty than the same

goods brought in those owned by foreigners." The
" navigation laws " and the " tobacco " wrought after
their kind; South Carolina and Georgia had their way.
The North, said Gouverneur Morris, in the national
Convention, for the " sacrifice of every principle of
right, of every impulse of humanity," had this compensation, " to bind themselves to march their militia
for the defense of the Southern States, for their defense against those very slaves of whom they complain.
They must supply vessels and seamen in case of
foreign attack. The legislature will have indefinite
power to tax them by excises and duties on imports."

Still, with many there lingered a vague belief that
slavery would soon perish. In the first Congress Mr.
Jackson, of Georgia, admitted that it was " an evil
habit." Mr. Gerry and Mr. Madison both thought
that Congress had " the right to regulate this business,"
and, " if they see proper, to make a proposal to purchase all the slaves." But the most obvious time for
ending the institution had passed by; the feeling of
hostility to it grew weaker and weaker as the nation
became united, powerful and rich; its " mortal wound "
was fast getting healed.

II. *Condition and Treatment of Slaves*

I will next consider the general condition and
treatment of the slaves themselves. The slave is not
theoretically considered as a person; he is only a thing,
as much so as an axe or a spade; accordingly he is
wholly subject to his master, and has no rights —
which are an attribute of persons only, not of things.
All that he enjoys therefore is but a privilege. He
may be damaged but not wronged. However ill
treated, he cannot of himself, in his own name and
VIII—4

right, bring a formal action in any court, no more
than an axe or a spade, though his master may bring
an action for damages. The slave cannot appear as
a witness when a freeman is on trial. His master can
beat, maim, mutilate, or mangle him, and the slave
has, theoretically, no complete and legal redress;
practically, no redress at all. The master may force
him to marry or forbid his marriage; can sell him away
from wife and children. He can force the lover to
beat his beloved; the husband his wife, the child his
parent. " A slave is one who is in the power of his
master, to whom he belongs. The master may sell him,
dispose of his person, his industry, and his labor; he
can do nothing, possess nothing, nor acquire anything
but what must belong to his master." No contract
between master and slave, however solemnly made and
attested, is binding on the master. Is the freeborn
child of the freeman likewise theoretically subject to
his father? — natural and instinctive affection prevent the abuse of that power. The connection between
father and child is one of guardianship and reciprocal
love, a mutual gain; that of master and slave is founded
only on the interest of the owner; the gain is only on
the master's side.

The relation of master and slave begins in violence;
it must be sustained by violence — the systematic
violence of general laws, or the irregular violence of
individual caprice. There is no other mode of conquering and subjugating a man. Regarding the
slave as a thing, " an instrument of husbandry," the
master gives him the least, and takes the most that is
possible. He takes all the result of the slave's toil,
leaving only enough to keep him in a profitable working condition. His work is the most he can be made to

do; his food, clothing, shelter, amusement, the least he can do with. "A Southern Planter," in his "Notes on Political Economy as applicable to the United States," says to his fellow slaveholders: "You own this labor, can regulate it, work it many or few hours in the day, accelerate it, stimulate it, control it, avoid turn-outs and combinations, and pay no wages. You can dress it plainly, feed it coarsely and cheap, lodge it, on simple forms, as the plantations do, house it in cabins costing little." "The slaves live without beds or houses worth so calling, or family cares, or luxuries, or parade or show; have no relaxations, or whims, or frolics, or dissipations; instead of sun to sun, in their hours are worked from daylight till nine o'clock at night. Where the freeman or laborer would require a hundred dollars a year for food and clothing alone, the slave can be supported for twenty dollars a year, and often is." "Let us bestow upon them the worst, the most unhealthy and degrading sort of duties and labor." Said Mr. Jefferson, "The whole commerce between master and slave is a perpetual exercise of the most boisterous passions, the most unremitting despotism on the one part, and degrading submission on the other."

The idea of slavery is to use a man as a thing, against his nature and in opposition to his interests. The consequences of such a principle it is impossible to escape; the results of this idea meet us at every step. Man is certainly not cruel by nature; even in the barbarous state. In our present civilization man is far from being brutal. There are many kind and considerate slaveholders whose aim is to make their slaves as comfortable and happy as it is possible while they are slaves; men who feel and know that slavery is

wrong, and would gladly be rid of it; who are not
consistent with the idea of slavery. Let us suppose,
in this argument, there are ten thousand such who
are heads of families in the United States, and ninety
thousand of a different stamp, men who have at least
the average of human selfishness.

Now under the mildest and most humane of masters,
slavery commonly brings intensity of suffering. The
slave feels that he is a man, a person, his own person,
born with all a man's unalienable rights; born with the
right to life, to liberty, and the pursuit of happiness.
He sees himself cut off from these rights, and that too
amid the wealth, the refinement, and culture of this
country and this age. He feels his degradation, born
a man to be treated as a thing, bought and sold, beaten
as a beast. Here and there is one with a feeble nature,
with affections disproportionately strong, attached to
an owner who never claimed all the legal authority of
master, and this man may not desire his freedom.
Some hear of the actual sufferings of the free blacks,
or exaggerated reports thereof, and fear that by becoming free in America they might exchange a well-
known evil for a greater or a worse. Others have
become so debased by their condition that the man is
mainly silenced in their consciousness, the animal alone
surviving, contented if well fed and not overworked,
and they do not wish to be free. Suppose that these
three classes, the feeble-minded, the timid, and the
men overwhelmed and crushed by their condition, are
as numerous as the humane portion of the masters,
are one-tenth of the whole, or 300,000. The rest are
conscious of the qualities of a man. They desire their
freedom, and are kept in slavery only by external
force — the systematic force of public law, the ir-

regular force of private will. The number of this
class will be about 2,700,000, a greater number than
the whole population of the colonies in 1776.

The condition of the majority of the slaves is indeed
terrible. They have no rights, and are to be treated
not as men, but only as things; this first principle involves continual violence and oppression, with all the
subordinate particulars of their condition, which shall
now be touched on as briefly as possible. A famous
man said in public, that his slaves were " sleek and
fat; " the best thing he could say in defense of his
keeping men in bondage. But even this is not always
true. Take the mass of slaves together, and an
abundance of testimony compels the conviction that
they are miserably clad, and suffer bitterly from
hunger. So far as food, clothing, and shelter are
concerned, the physical condition of the mass of field-
slaves is far worse than that of condemned criminals,
in the worst prison of the United States. House-
slaves and mechanics in large towns fare better; they
are under the eye of the public. Farm-slaves feel
most the poignant smart. The plantations are large,
the dwellings distant, the ear of the public hears not
the oppressor's violence. " The horse fattens on his
master's eye," says the proverb; but the farm-slaves
are committed mainly to overseers, the Swiss of
slavery,[3] whom Mr. Wirt calls " the most abject, degraded, and unprincipled race."

Let us pass over the matter of food, clothing,
shelter, and toil, to consider other features of their
condition. They are treated with great cruelty;
often branded with a red-hot iron on the breast, or
the shoulder, the arm, the forehead, or the cheek,
though the Roman law forbid it fifteen centuries ago.

They are disfigured and mutilated now by the madness of anger, then by the jealous malice of revenge; their back and sides scored with the lash, or bruised with the " paddle," bear marks of the violence needful to subdue manhood still smouldering in the ashes of the negro slave. Drive Nature out with whips and brands — she will come back. These abuses can be proved from descriptions of runaways in the newspapers of the South.

The slaveholder's temptation to cruelty is too much for common men. His power is irresponsible. 'Tis easy to find a stick if you would beat a dog. The lash is always at hand; if a slave disobeys, — the whip; if he is idle,— the whip; does he murmur,— the whip; is he sullen and silent,— the whip; is the female coy and reluctant,— the whip. Chains and dungeons also are at hand. The slave is a thing; judge and jury no friends to him. The condition of the weak is bad enough everywhere, in Old England and in New England. But when the strong owns the very bodies of the weak, making and executing the laws as he will — it is not hard to see to what excess their wrongs will amount, wrongs which cannot be told.

It is often said that the evils of slavery are exaggerated. This is said by the masters. But the story of the victim when told by his oppressor — it is well known what that is. The few slaves who can tell the story of their wrongs, show that slavery cannot easily be represented as worse than it is. Imagination halts behind the fact. The lives of Moses Roper, of Lunsford Lane, of Moses Grundy, Frederic Douglas, and W. W. Brown, are before the public, and prove what could easily be learned from the advertisements of Southern newspapers, conjectured from the laws of the

Southern States, or foretold outright from a knowledge of human nature itself : — that the sufferings of
three millions of slaves form a mass of misery which
the imagination can never realize, till the eye is
familiar with its terrible details.   Governor Giles, of
Virginia, calls slavery " a punishment of the highest
order."   And Mr. Preston says, " Happiness is incom-
patible with slavery."

In the most important of all relations, that of man
and wife, neither law nor custom gives protection to the
slave.   Their connection may at any moment be dissolved by the master's command, the parties be torn
asunder, separated for ever, husband and wife, child
and mother ; the infant may be taken from its mother's
breast, and sold away out of her sight and power.   The
wife torn from her husband's arms, forced to the lust
of another, for the slave is no person, but a thing.   For
the chastity of the female there is no defense ; no more
than for the chastity of sheep and swine.   Many are
ravished in tender years.   So is the last insult, and
outrage the most debasing, added to this race of Americans.   By the laws of Louisiana, all children born of
slaves are reckoned as " natural and illegitimate."
Marriage is " prostitution ; " sacred and permanent
neither in the eyes of the churches nor the law.   The
female slave is wholly in her master's power.   Mulattoes are more valuable than blacks.   So in the slave
States lust now leagues with cupidity, and now acts
with singleness of aim.   The South is full of mulattoes ;
its " best blood flows in the veins of the slaves"—
masters owning children white as themselves.   Girls,
the children of mulattoes, are sold at great price, as
food for private licentiousness, or public furniture in
houses of ill-fame.   Under the worst of the Roman em-

perors this outrage was forbidden, and the prefect of
the city gave such slaves their freedom. But Republican parents not rarely sell their own children for that
abuse.

After the formal and legal abolition of the African
slave trade, it became more profitable to breed slaves
for sale in the northern slaveholding States. Their
labor was of comparatively little value to the declining
agriculture of Delaware, Maryland, Virginia, and
North Carolina. From planting they have become,
to a great degree, slave-breeding States. The reputed
sons of the " Cavaliers " have found a new calling, and
the " chivalry of the Old Dominion " betakes itself,
not to manufactures, commerce, or agriculture,— but
to the breeding of slaves for the Southern market.
Kentucky and Tennessee have embarked largely in the
same adventure. It would be curious to ascertain the
exact annual amount of money brought into those
States from the sale of their children, but the facts are
not officially laid before the public, and a random conjecture, or even a shrewd estimate, is not now to the
purpose.

In the latter half of the last century Virginia displayed such an array of talent and statesmanship, of
eloquence, of intelligent and manly life in a noble form,
as few States with the same population could ever
equal; certainly none in America. There were Randolph and Mason, Wythe, Henry, Madison, Jefferson,
Marshall, Washington; her very " tobacco " could purchase the peace of New England and New York. Now
Virginia is eminent as a nursery of slaves, bred and be-
gotten for the Southern market. Ohio sends abroad
the produce of her soil — flour, oxen, and swine;
Massachusetts the produce of her mills and manual

craft — cottons and woolens, hardware and shoes; while Virginia, chivalrous Virginia, the "Old Dominion," sells in the world's market the produce of her own loins — men-servants and maidens; her choicest exports are her sons and daughters. She has borne for the nation five presidents, three of them conspicuous men, famous all over the world; and God knows how many slaves to till the soil of the devouring South. In 1832, it was shown in her legislature that slaves were "all the productive capacity," and "constitute the entire available wealth of eastern Virginia." The president of William and Mary's College says, "Virginia is a negro-raising State for other States." Thomas Jefferson Randolph pronounced it "one grand menagerie where men are raised for the market like oxen for the shambles." In 1831, it was maintained in her legislature by Mr. Gholson, that "the owner of land had a reasonable right to its annual profits; the owner of orchards to their annual fruits; the owner of brood-mares to their products, and the owner of female slaves to their increase."

Is any man born a slave? The Declaration of Independence says, all men are born "equal;" their natural rights "unalienable." It is absurd to say a man was born free in Africa, and his son born a slave in Virginia. The child born in Africa is made a slave by actual theft and personal violence; by what other process can he be made a slave in America? The fact that his father was stolen before him makes no difference. By the law of the United States it is piracy to enslave a man born in Africa; by the law of justice is it less piracy to enslave him when born in Baltimore?

The domestic slave trade is carried on continually in all the great cities of the South; the capital of the

Union, called after " the father of his country," is a
great slave mart.   Droves of slaves, chained together,
may often be seen in the streets of Washington; the
advertisements of the dealers are in the journals of
that city.   There the great demagogues and the great
drovers of slaves meet together, and one city is common to them all.   If there be degrees in such wrong-
doing, it seems worse to steal a baby in America than
a man in Guinea; worse to keep a gang of women in
Virginia, breeding children as swine for market, than
to steal grown men in Guinea; it is cowardly no less
than inhuman.   But so long ago as 1829, it was said
in the Baltimore Reporter, " Dealing in slaves has
become a large business, establishments are made in
several places in Maryland, at which they are sold like
cattle; these places of deposit are strongly built, and
well supplied with iron thumb-screws and gags, and
ornamented with cowskins and other whips, often
bloody."

The African slave-trader perhaps even now is not
unknown at Baltimore or New Orleans, but he is a
pirate; he shuffles and hides, goes sneaking and cringes
to get along amongst men, while the American slave-
trader goes openly to work, advertises " the increase
of his female slaves," erects his jail, and when that is
insufficient, has those of the nation thrown open for his
use, and all the States solemnly pledge to deliver up the
fugitives who escape from his hands.   He marches his
coffles where he will.   The laws are on his side, " public
sentiment " and the " majesty of the Constitution."
He looks in at the door of the Capitol and is not
ashamed.

There are mean men engaged in that traffic who " are
generally despised even in the slave-holding States,"

but men of property and standing are also concerned in
this trade.   Mr. Erwin, the son-in-law of Mr. Clay, it
is said, laid the foundation of a large fortune by dealing in slaves; General Jackson was a dealer in slaves,
and so late as 1811, bought a coffle and drove them to
Louisiana for sale.

In this transfer of slaves, the most cruel separation
of families takes place.   In the slave-breeding States it
is a common thing to sell a boy or a girl while the
mother is kept as a " breeder."   Does she complain of
the robbery? — There is the scourge, there are chains
and collars.   Will the husband and father resent the
wrong? — There are handcuffs and jails; the law of
the United States, the Constitution, the Army and
Navy, all the able-bodied men of the free States, are
legally bound to come, if need be, and put down the
insurrection.   Yet, more than fifteen hundred years
ago, a Roman emperor forbade the separation of families of slaves, and ordered all which had been separated
to be reunited.   " Who can bear," said the Emperor
to his heathen subjects, " who can bear that children
should be separated from their parents, sisters from
their brothers, wives from their husbands? "

In 1836, the Presbyterian Synod of Kentucky said
to the world: " Brothers and sisters, parents and
children, husbands and wives, are torn asunder and permitted to see each other no more.   These acts are daily
occurring in the midst of us.   There is not a neighborhood where these heart-rending scenes are not displayed.
There is not a village or road which does not behold
the sad procession of manacled outcasts, whose chains
and mournful countenances tell that they are exiled
by force from all that their hearts held dear."   The
affections are proportionally stronger in the negro than

the American; his family his all. The terror of being
sold and thus separated from the companion of his sad
misfortune, hangs over the slave for ever, at least till
too old for service in that way. The most able-minded
are of course the most turbulent, the most difficult to
manage, and therefore the most commonly sold. But
the angel of death — to them the only angel of mercy
— benignantly visits these poor Ishmaels in the hot
swamps of Georgia and Alabama. Thou-God-seest-me,
were fitting inscription over the spot where the servant
thus becomes free from his master and the weary is at
rest.

III. *Effects of Slavery on Industry*

Let us examine the effects of slavery on industry in
all its forms. In the South, manual labor is considered
menial and degrading; it is the business of slaves. In
the free States the majority work with their hands,
counting it the natural business of a man, not a reproach, but a duty and a dignity. Thus in Boston —
the richest city of its population in America, and perhaps in the world — out of 19,037 private families in
1845, there were 15,744 who kept no servant, and only
1069 who had more than one assistant to perform their
household labor. In the South the freeman shuns
labor; " in a slave country every freeman is an aristo-
crat," and of course labor is avoided by such. Where
work is disgraceful, men of spirit will not submit to it.
So the high-minded but independent freemen are continually getting worse off, or else emigrating out of the
slave States into the new free States,— not as the enterprising adventurer goes from New England, because
he wants more room, but because his condition is a
reproach.

Most of the productive work of the South is done by slaves. But the slave has no stimulus; the natural instinct of production is materially checked. The master has the mouth which consumes, the slave only the hand which earns. He labors not for himself, but for another; for another who continually wrongs him. His aim, therefore, is to do the least he can get along with. He will practise no economy; no thrift; he breaks his tools. He will not think for his master; it is all hand-work, for he only gives what the master can force from him, and he cannot conceal; there is no head-work. There is no invention in the slave; little among the masters, for their business is to act on men, not directly on things. This circumstance may fit the slaveholder for politics — of a certain character; it unfits him for the great operations of productive industry. They and all labor-saving contrivances come from the North. In 1846 there were seventy-six patents granted by the national office for inventions made in fourteen slave States, with a population of 7,334,431, or one for each 96,505 persons; at the same time there were 564 granted to the free States with a population of 9,728,922, or one for each 17,249 persons. Maryland, by her position, partakes more of the character of the free States than most of her sisters, and accordingly made twenty-one inventions — more than a fourth part of all made in the South. But Massachusetts had made sixty-two; and New York, with a population of only 2,428,921, had received two hundred and forty-seven patent-rights — more than three times as many as the whole South. Works which require intelligence and skill require also the hand of the freeman. The South can grow timber, it is the North which builds the ships. The South can rear cotton, the free intelligence of the North must weave it into cloth.

In the North the freeman acts directly upon things by his own will; in the South, only through the medium of men reduced to the rank of things, and they act on material objects against their will. Half the moral and intellectual effect of labor is thereby lost; half the productive power of the labor itself. All the great movements of industry decline where the aristocracy own the bodies of the laboring class. No fertility of soil or loveliness of climate can ever make up for the want of industry, invention, and thrift in the laboring population itself. Agriculture will not thrive as under the freeman's hand. Slave labor can only be profitably employed in the coarse operations of field-work. It was so in Italy 2000 years ago; the rich gardens of Latium, Alba, Tuscany, were the work of freemen. When their owners were reduced to slavery by the Roman conqueror, those gardens became only pastures for buffaloes and swine. Only coarse staples, sugar, cotton, rice, corn, tobacco, can be successfully raised by the slave of America. His rude tillage impoverishes the soil; the process of tilth " consists in killing the land." They who will keep slavery as a " patriarchal institution," must adopt the barbarism of the patriarchs, become nomadic, and wander from the land they have exhausted to some virgin soil. The freeman's fertilizing hand enriches the land the longer he labors.

In Maryland, Virginia, and the Carolinas, the soil is getting exhausted; the old land less valuable than the new. In 1787, said Gouverneur Morris, in the national Convention, " Compare the free regions of the Middle States, where a rich and noble cultivation marks the prosperity and happiness of the people, with the misery

and poverty which overspread the barren wastes of
Virginia, Maryland, and the other States having slaves.
Travel through the whole Continent, and you behold
the prospect continually varying with the appearance
and disappearance of slavery. The moment you leave
the Eastern States and enter New York, the effects of
the institution become visible. Passing through the
Jerseys and entering Pennsylvania, every criterion of
superior improvement witnesses the change. Proceed
southwardly, and every step you take through the great
regions of slaves, presents a desert increasing with the
increasing proportion of these wretched beings." At
this day, sixty years later, the contrast is yet more
striking, as will presently appear. Slavery has
wrought after its way. Every tree bears its own fruit.

Slavery discourages the immigration of able but poor
men from the free States. They go elsewhere to sell
their labor; all the Southern States afford proof of this.
The freeman from the North will not put himself and his
intelligent industry on a level with the slave, degraded
and despised. In the free States the farmer buys his
land and his cattle; hires men to aid him in his work
— he buys their labor. Both parties are served —
this with labor, that with employment. There is no
degradation, but reciprocal gain. In a few years the
men who at first sold their labor will themselves become
proprietors, and hire others desirous of selling their
services. It requires little capital to start with. So
the number of proprietors rapidly increases, and the
amount of cultivated land, of wealth, of population,
of comfort. In the South the proprietor must also
buy his workmen; the poor man who seeks a market
for his work, not his person, must apply elsewhere.

This cause has long impeded the agriculture of the

South; it will also hinder the advance of manufactures. At Lowell the manfacturer builds his mill, buys his cotton, and reserves a sufficient sum for his " floating capital; " he hires five hundred men and women to work his machinery, paying them from week to week for the labor he has bought.   In South Carolina he must buy his operatives also; five hundred slaves at $600 each amount to $300,000.   This additional sum is needed before a wheel can turn.   To start, it requires large capital; but capital is what is not so easily obtained in a slave State, where there is no natural stimulus urging the laboring mass to production.   Men of small capital are kept out of the field; business is mainly in the hands of the rich; property tends to accumulate in few hands.

Compare a slave and a free State; in the free population of the former there is less enterprise; less activity of body and mind; less intelligence; less production; less comfort, and less welfare.   In the free States an enterprising man whose own hands are not enough for him to work out his thoughts with, can trade in human labor, buying men's work and seeing the result of that work.   That is the business of the merchant-manufacturer in all departments.   In the present state of society both parties are gainers by the operation.   In the South, such a man must buy the laborers before he can use their work, but intelligent labor he cannot thus buy.

Men are born with different tastes and tendencies — some for agriculture, others for commerce, navigation, manufactures, for science, letters, the arts, useful or elegant.   The master is able to command the muscles, not to develop the mind.   He directs labor mainly to the coarser operations of husbandry, and makes work monotonous. Uniformity of labor involves a great loss. Political economists know well the misery which happens to Ireland from this source — not to mention others and worse.

In Connecticut, every farmer and day-laborer, in his family or person, is a consumer not only of the productions of his own farm or handiwork, but also of tea, coffee, sugar, rice, molasses, salt, and spices; of cotton, woolen, and silk goods, ribbons and bonnets; of shoes and hats; of beds and other furniture; of hardware, tinware, and cutlery; of crockery and glassware; of clocks and jewelry; of books, paper, and the like. His wants stimulate the mechanic and the merchant; they stimulate him in return, all grow up together; each has a market at home, a market continually enlarging and giving vent to superior wares. The young man can turn his hand to the art he likes best. Industry, activity, intelligence, and comfort are the result.

In a slave population the reverse of all this takes place. The " Southern planter " thinks $20 adequate for the yearly support of a slave. Add twenty-five per cent. to his estimate, making the sum $25; then the 3,000,000 slaves are consumers to the amount of $75,000,000 a year. In 1845 the annual earnings of the State of Massachusetts were $114,492,636. This does not include the improvements made on the soil, nor bridges, nor railroads, highways, houses, shops, stores, and factories that were built — these things form a permanent investment for future years. It cannot reasonably be supposed that, in addition, so large a sum as fourteen per cent. of the annual earnings is saved and laid by. But on that supposition, the 737,699 inhabitants of Massachusetts are consumers to the amount of $100,000,000 a year; that is, $25,-000,000 more than four times that number of slaves would consume. The amount of additional energy, comfort, and happiness is but poorly indicated even by these figures.

In the present age, slavery can compete successfully with free labor only under rare circumstances. The population must be sparse; perhaps not exceeding fifty persons to the square mile. But in the nice labor and minute division of employment, in the economy and the improved methods of cultivation, consequent on a dense population, slavery ceases to be profitable; the slave will not pay for rearing. It must be on a soil extraordinarily fertile, which the barbarous tillage of the slave cannot exhaust. Some of the rich lands of Georgia, Alabama, Louisiana, and Mississippi are of this character. Then it must have the monopoly of some favorite staple which cannot be produced elsewhere. A combination of those three conditions may render slavery profitable even at this day, yet by no means so profitable as the work of the freeman. Mr. Rutledge was not far from right in 1787, when he contended that, in direct taxation, a slave should pay but one third as much as a freeman, his labor being only of one third the value of a freeman's.

In the Northern States, the freeman comes directly in contact with the material things which he wishes to convert to his purpose. To shorten his labor he makes his head save his hands. He invents machines. The productive capacity of the free States is extended by their use of wind, water, and steam for the purposes of human labor. That is a solid gain to mankind. Windmills, water-mills, steam-engines, are the servants of the North; homebred slaves born in their house, the increase of fertile heads. These are an important element in the power and wealth of a nation. While South Carolina has taken men from Africa, and made slaves, New England has taken possession of the winds, of the waters; she has kidnapped the Merrimack, the Connecticut, the Androscoggin, the Kennebeck, the Penobscot, and a hundred smaller streams. She has caught the lakes of New Hampshire, and holds them in thrall. She has seized fire and water, joined them with an iron yoke, and made an army of slaves, powerful, but pliant. Consider the machinery moved by such agents in New England, New York, Pennsylvania; compare that with the human machines of the South, and which is the better drudge? The " Patriarchal Institution of slavery " and the economic institution of machinery stand side by side,— this representing the nineteenth century before Christ, and that the nineteenth century after Christ. They run for the same goal, though slavery started first and had the smoother road. It is safe to say that the machinery of the free States has greater productive ability than the 3,000,000 bondmen of the South. While slavery continues, the machinery will not appear. Steam-engines and slaves come of a different stock.

The foreign trade of the South consists mainly in the export of the productions of the farm and the forest; the domestic trade, in collecting those staples and distributing the articles to be consumed at home. Much of the domestic trade is in the hands of Northern men — though mainly " with Southern principles." The foreign trade is almost wholly in the hands of foreigners, or men from the North, and is conducted by their ships. In the South, little is demanded for home consumption; so the great staples of Southern production find their market chiefly in the North, or in foreign ports. The shipping is mainly owned by the North. Of the Atlantic States seven have no slaves: Maine, New Hampshire, Massachusetts, Rhode Island, Connecticut, New York, and New Jersey; in 1846, they with Pennsylvania, had 2,160,501 tons of shipping. In all the slave States which lie on the seaboard, there are owned but 401,583 tons of shipping. In 1846, the young State of Ohio, two thousand miles from the sea, had 39,917 tons; the State of South Carolina, 32,588. Even Virginia, full of bays and harbors, had but 53,441 tons. The single district of the city of New York had 572,522 tons, or 70,939 more than all the Southern States united.

The difference in the internal improvements of the two sections is quite as remarkable. In general, the public highways in the slaveholding States are far inferior to those of the North, both in extent and character. If the estimates made are correct, in 1846 there were, omitting the fractions, 5663 miles of railroad actually in operation in the United States. In all the slave States together there were 2090 miles. Taking the cost of such as are described in trustworthy sources, and estimating the value of those not so described by the general cost per mile of railroads in the same State, then the slave States have invested $43,910,183 in this property. In the free States there were 3573 miles of railroad, which had cost $112,914,465. Thus the free States have 1483 miles of railroad more than the South, the value of which is $69,004,282 above the value of all the railroads of the slave States. The railroads in Pennsylvania have cost $43,426,385; within less than half a million of the value of all the railroads in all the slave States. Maryland, from her position, resembles

the free States in many respects. Besides those of
this State, all the railroads of the South are worth only
$27,717,835, while those of Massachusetts alone have
cost $30,341,444, and are now, on the average, five or
six per cent. above par. The State of South Carolina
has only paid $5,671,452 for her railroad stock. I
will not undertake to estimate its present value. Nor
need I stop to inquire how many miles of the Southern
roads have been planned by Northern skill, paid for by
the capital of the free States, and are owned by their
citizens!

Let us next consider the increase of the value of the
landed property in the free and the slave States. In
1798, the value of all the houses and lands in the eight
slave States, that is, Delaware, Maryland, Virginia,
North and South Carolina, Georgia, Kentucky, and
Tennessee, was estimated at $197,742,557; that of the
houses and lands in the eight free States — New Hampshire, Vermont, Massachusetts, Connecticut, Rhode
Island, New Jersey, New York, and Pennsylvania —
was $422,235,780. It is not easy to ascertain exactly
the value of real property in all these States at this
moment. But in 1834-6, the government of New
York, and in 1839, that of Virginia, made a new valu-
ation of all the real property in their respective States.
In 1798, all the real estate in Virginia was worth
$71,225,127; in 1839, $211,930,538. In 1798, all
the real property in the State of New York was worth
$100,380,707; in 1835, $430,751,273. In Virginia
there had been an increase of 195.7 per cent. in forty-
one years; in New York, an increase of 329.9 per cent,
in thirty-seven years.

For convenience' sake let us suppose each of the
eight Southern States has gained as rapidly as Vir-

ginia, and each of those eight Northern, in the same ratio with New York — and what follows? In 1798, the real estate in South Carolina was valued at $17,-465,013; that of Rhode Island at $11,066,358. By the above ratios, the real estate in South Carolina was worth $51,958,393 in 1839; and in 1835, that of Rhode Island was worth $47,574,288. Thus the real property in the leading slave State of the Union, with a population of 594,398, was worth but $4,384,105 more than the real property of Rhode Island, with a population of only 108,830. In 1840 the aggregate real property in the city of Boston was valued at $60,-424,200, and in 1847 at $97,764,500,— $45,271,120 more than the computed value of all the real estate in South Carolina. In 1798, the value of the aggregate real property of the eight slave States was $197,742,-557; of the eight free, $422,235,780; in 1839, by the above ratios, the real estate of the Southern States would be worth $588,289,107, and that of the Northern $1,715,201,618. Thus the real property of these eight free States would be almost three times more valuable than the eight slave States, yet the free contain but 170,150 square miles, while the slave States contain 212,920. But this, in part, is a matter of calculation only, and liable to some uncertainty, as the ratio of Virginia and New York may not represent the increase of any either South or North. Let us come to public and notorious facts.

In 1839, the value of all the annual agricultural products of the South, as valued by the last census, was $312,380,151; that of the free States $342,007,-446. Yet in the South there were 1,984,866 persons engaged in agriculture, and in the North only 1,735,-086, and the South has the advantage of raising tropical productions, which cannot be grown in Europe. The agricultural products of the South which find their way to foreign lands, are mainly cotton, sugar, rice, and tobacco. The entire value of these articles raised in the fifteen slave States in that year, was $74,866,310; while the agricultural productions, the single State of New York amounted in the year to $108,275,281.

The value of articles manufactured in the South was $42,178,184; in the free States $197,658,040. In the slave States there were, in various manufactories, 246,601 spindles; in Rhode Island, the smallest of the free States, 518,817. The aggregate annual earnings of all the slave States was $403,429,718; of the free, $658,705,108. The annual earnings of six slave States — North Carolina, South Carolina, Georgia, Alabama, Mississippi, and Louisiana, amount to $189,-321,719; those of the State of New York to $193,806,-433, more than $4,000,000 above the income of six famous States. The annual earnings of Massachusetts alone are more than $9,000,000 greater than the united earnings of three slave States,— South Carolina, Georgia, and Florida. The earnings of South Carolina, with her population of 594,398, about equals that of the county of Essex, in Massachusetts, with less than 95,000.

In 1839, in the South there were built houses to the value of $14,421,441; and in the North, to the value of $27,496,560. The ships built by the South that year were valued at $704,289; by the North, at $6,301,-805.

In 1846, the absolute debt of all the free States was $109,176,527. The actual productive State-property of those States, including the school fund, was $96,-

630,285,— leaving the actual indebtedness above their State-property only $10,546,242. The absolute debt of the slave States was $55,948,373; their productive State-property, including their school funds, $30,294,-428 — leaving their actual indebtedness above their State-property $25,653,945, more than twice the corresponding indebtedness of the North.

Besides this, it must be remembered that in the free States there are 45,569 men engaged in the learned professions, while in the slave States there are but 20,292. In addition to that, in all the free States there are many employed in teaching common schools. Thus, in 1847, in Massachusetts, there were 7,582 engaged in the common schools. In the slave States this class is much smaller. Still more, in all the free States there are many, not ranked in the learned professions, who devote themselves to science, literature, and the fine arts; in the South but few. In the South, the female slaves are occupied in hard field-labor, which is almost unheard-of in the free States. Thus the difference in the earnings of the two, great as it is, is not an adequate emblem of the actual difference or productive capacity, or even of the production, in the two sections of the country.

IV. *Effects of Slavery on Population*

Let us next consider the effects of slavery on the increase of numbers, as shown by the great movements of the population in the North and South.

In 1790, the present free States — New England, New York, New Jersey, and Pennsylvania — contained 1,968,455 persons; the slave States 1,961,372. In 1840 the same slave States — Delaware, Maryland, Virginia, North Carolina, South Carolina, Georgia,

Kentucky — contained 5,479,860; the same free States, 6,767,082. In 50 years those slave States had increased 179 per cent.; those free States 243 per cent., or with 64 per cent. greater rapidity.

In 1790 the entire population of all the slave States was 1,961,372; in 1840, including the new slave States, 7,334,431; while the population of the free States — including the new ones — was 9,728,922. The slave States had increased 279 per cent.; the free, 394, the latter increasing with a rapidity 115 per cent. greater than the former.

In 1810 the new slave States — Louisiana, Mississippi, Alabama, Arkansas, Tennessee, Missouri, and Kentucky — contained 805,991 persons; the new free States — Ohio, Indiana, Illinois, Michigan — contained but 272,324. But in 1840 those new slave States, with the addition of Florida, contained 3,409,132, while the population of the new free States — with the addition of Wisconsin and Iowa — contained 2,967,840. In 50 years the new slave States had increased 323 per cent., and the new free States 1090 per cent.

In 1790, the whole free population of the present free States was 1,930,125; the free population of the present slave States and territories was 1,394,847. The difference in the number of free persons in the North and South was only 535,278. But in 1840 the free population of the free States and territories was 9,727,893; the free population of the slave States and territories only 4,848,105; the difference between the two was 4,879,788. In 50 years the free persons in the slave States had increased 247 per cent.; the free persons of the free States 404 per cent. It is true something has been added to the North by immigrations from abroad, but the accessions which the South has received by the purchase of Louisiana and Florida, by the immigration of enterprising men from the North, and by the importation of slaves, is perhaps more than adequate to balance the Northern increase by foreign immigration.

The Southern States have great advantages over the Northern in soil, climate, and situation; they have a monopoly of the tropical productions so greatly sought by all northern nations; they have superior facilities for the acquisition of wealth, and through that for the rapid increase of population. In some countries the advance of both is retarded by oppressive legislation. Of this the South cannot complain, as it will by and by appear. The new land lay nearer to the old Southern States than the old free States, and that not "infested with Indians" to the same extent with the soil since conquered and colonized by the emigrants from the Northern States. The difference of the increase of the two in wealth and numbers is to be ascribed, therefore, to the different institutions of the two sections of the land.

V.   *Effects of Slavery on Education*

Let us now look at the effects of slavery on the intellectual, moral, and religious development of the people. The effect on the intellectual, moral, and religious condition of the slave is easily understood. He is only continued in slavery by restraining him from the civilization of mankind in this age. His mind, conscience, soul — all his nobler powers — must be kept in a state of inferior development, otherwise he will not be a slave in the nineteenth century, and in the United States. In comparison with the intellectual culture of their masters the slaves are a mass of barbarians; still more emphatically, when compared with the free institutions of the North, they are savages. This is not a mere matter of inference, the fact is substantiated by the notorious testimony of slaveholders themselves. In 1834 the Synod of South Carolina and Georgia reported that the slaves " may justly be considered the heathen of this country, and will bear comparison with the heathen of any part of the world." " They are destitute of the privileges of the Gospel and ever will be, under the present state of things." " In all the slave States," says the Synod, " there are not twelve men exclusively devoted to the religious instruction of the negroes." Of the regular ministers " but a very small portion pay any attention to them." " We know of but five churches in the slaveholding States built exclusively for their use," and " there is no sufficient room for them in the white churches for their accommodation." " They are unable to read, as custom, or law, and generally both, prohibit their instruction. They have no Bible — no family altars; and when in affliction, sickness, or death, they have no minister to address to them the consolation of the Gospel, nor to bury them with solemn and appropriate services." They may sometimes be petted and caressed as children and toys, they are never treated as men.[4]

" Heathenism," says another Southern authority, " is as real in the slave States as in the South Sea Islands." " Chastity is no virtue among them [the slaves]; its violation neither injures female character in their own estimation nor that of their mistress." Where there is no marriage recognized by the State or Church as legal or permanent between slaves; where the female slave is wholly in her master's power — how can it be

otherwise? Said the Roman proverb, " Nothing is unlawful for the master to his slave." When men are
counted as things, instruments of husbandry, separable
limbs of the master, and retained in subjugation by
external force and the prohibition of all manly culture,
the effect of slavery on its victim is so obvious that no
more need be said thereof.

The effect of slavery on the intellectual, moral, and
religious condition of the free population of the South
is not so obvious perhaps at first sight. But a comparison with the free States will render that also plain.

All attempts at the improvement of the humbler and
more exposed portions of society, the perishing and
dangerous classes thereof, originate in the free States.
It is there that men originate societies for the reform
of prisons, the prevention of crime, pauperism, intemperance, licentiousness, and ignorance. There spring
up education societies, Bible societies, peace societies,
societies for teaching Christianity in foreign and barbarous lands. There, too, are the learned and philosophical societies for the study of science, letters, and
art. Whence come the men of superior education who
occupy the pulpits, exercise the professions of law and
medicine, or fill the chairs of the professors in the
colleges of the Union? Almost all from the North,
from the free States. There is preaching everywhere.
But search the whole Southern States for the last seven-
and-forty years, and it were hard to show a single
preacher of any eminence in any pulpit of a slaveholding State; a single clergyman remarkable for ability in his calling, for great ideas, for eloquence, elsewhere so cheap — or even for learning! Even exposi-
tions and commentaries on the Bible, the most common
clerical productions, are the work of the North alone.

Whence come the distinguished authors of America?
the poets — Bryant, Longfellow, Whittier; historians
— Sparks, Prescott, Bancroft; jurists — Parsons,
Wheaton, Story, Kent? Whence Irving, Channing,
Emerson; — whence all the scientific men, the men of
thought, who represent the nation's loftier conscious-
ness? All from the free States; north of Mason and
Dixon's line!

Few works of any literary or scientific value have
been written in this country in any of the slave States;
few even get reprinted there. Compare the works which
issue from the press of New Orleans, Savannah,
Charleston, Norfolk, Baltimore, with such as come from
Philadelphia, New York, and Boston — even from
Lowell and Cincinnati; compare but the booksellers'
stock in those several cities, and the difference between
the cultivation of the more educated classes of the
South and North is apparent at a glance.

But leaving general considerations of this sort, let
us look at facts. In 1671, Sir William Berkely, Governor of Virginia, said, " I thank God that there are
no free schools nor printing-presses [in Virginia], and
I hope we shall not have them these hundred years."
In 1840, in the fifteen slave States and territories there
were at the various primary schools 201,085 scholars;
at the various primary schools of the free States 1,626,-
028. The State of Ohio alone had 218,609 scholars
at her primary schools, 17,524 more than all the fifteen
slave States. South Carolina had 12,520 such scholars,
and Rhode Island 17,355. New York alone had
502,367.

In the higher schools there were in the South, 35,935
" scholars at the public charge," as they are called in
the census; in the North, 432,388 similar scholars.

Virginia, the largest of the slave States, had 9791 such scholars; Rhode Island, the smallest of the free States, 10,749. Massachusetts alone had 158,351, more than four times as many as all the slave States.

In the slave States, at academies, and grammar schools, there were 52,906 scholars; in the free States, 97,174. But the difference in numbers here does not represent the difference of fact, for most of the academies and grammar schools of the South are inferior to the " schools at public charge " of the North; far inferior to the better portion of the northern " district schools."

In 1840 there were at the various colleges in the South, 7106 pupils, and in the free States, 8927. Here, too, the figures fail to indicate the actual difference in the numbers of such as receive a superior education; for the greater part of the eighty-seven universities and colleges of the South are much inferior to the better academies and high schools of the North.

In the libraries of all the universities and colleges of the South there are 223,416 volumes; in those of the North, 593,897. The libraries of the theological schools of the South contain 22,800 volumes; those of the North 102,080. The difference in the character and value of these volumes does not appear in the returns.

In the slave States there are 1,368,325 free white children between the ages of five and twenty; in the free States 3,536,689 such children. In the slave States, at schools and colleges, there are 301,172 pupils; in the free States, 2,212,444 pupils, at schools or colleges. Thus, in the slave States, out of twenty-five free white children between five and twenty, there are not quite five at any school or college; while out of twenty-five such children in the free States, there are more than fifteen at school or college.

In the slave States, of the free white population that is over twenty years of age, there is almost one tenth part that are unable to read and write; while in the free States there is not quite one in one hundred and fifty-six who is deficient to that degree.

In New England there are but few born therein and more than twenty years of age, who are unable to read and write; but many foreigners arrive there with no education, and thus swell the number of the illiterate, and diminish the apparent effect of her free institutions. The South has few such emigrants; the ignorance of the Southern States therefore is to be ascribed to other causes. The Northern men who settle in the slaveholding States, have perhaps about the average culture of the North, and more than that of the South. The South therefore gains educationally from immigration as the North loses.

Among the Northern States, Connecticut, and among the Southern States, South Carolina, are to a great degree free from disturbing influences of this character. A comparison between the two will show the relative effects of the respective institutions of the North and South. In Connecticut, there are 163,843 free persons over twenty years of age; in South Carolina but 111,663. In Connecticut, there are but 526 persons over twenty who are unable to read and write, while in South Carolina there are 20,615 free white persons over twenty years of age unable to read and write. In South Carolina, out of each 626 free whites more than twenty years of age, there are more than 58 wholly unable to read or write; out of that number of such persons in Connecticut, not quite two! More

than the sixth part of the adult freeman of South
Carolina are unable to read the vote which will be de-
posited at the next election. It is but fair to infer
that at least one third of the adults of South Carolina,
if not of much of the South, are unable to read and
understand even a newspaper. Indeed, in one of the
slave States, this is not a matter of mere inference,
for in 1837 Gov. Clarke, of Kentucky, declared, in
his message to the legislature, that " one third of the
adult population were unable to write their names ; "
yet Kentucky has a " school-fund," valued at $1,221,-
819, while South Carolina has none.

One sign of this want of ability even to read, in the
slave States, is too striking to be passed by. The
staple reading of the least cultivated Americans is the
newspapers, one of the lowest forms of literature, though
one of the most powerful, read even by men who read
nothing else. In the slave States there are published
but 377 newspapers, and in the free 1135. These
numbers do not express the entire difference in the
case, for as a general rule the circulation of the
Southern newspapers is 50 to 75 per cent. less than
that of the North. Suppose, however, that each
Southern newspaper has two thirds the circulation of a
Northern journal, we have then but 225 newspapers
for the slave States! The more valuable journals —
the monthlies and quarterlies — are published almost
entirely in the free States.

The number of churches, the number and character
of the clergy who labor for these churches, are other
measures of the intellectual and moral condition of the
people. The scientific character of the Southern clergy
has been already touched on. Let us compare the
more external facts.

In 1830, South Carolina had a population of 581,-185 souls; Connecticut, 297,675. In 1836, South Carolina had 364 ministers; Connecticut, 498.

In 1834, there were in the slave States but 82,532 scholars in the Sunday schools; in the free States 504,835; in the single State of New York, 161,768.

A cause which keeps 3,000,000 men in bondage in America and in the nineteenth century, has more subtle influences than those just now considered. It not only prevents the extension of education among the people, but affects the doctrines taught them, even the doctrines taught in the name of God. Christianity is nominally the public religion of America; not of the Government, which extends protection alike to all modes of worship, of the Indian, the Mormon, and the Jew, but of the people. I will not touch the doctrines of the sects, in which Christian differs from Christian, but come to what is general among Christians — a part of the universal religion implied also in human nature itself. All sects, as such, theoretically agree that the most important practical doctrine of Christianity is love to men; to all men, of all ages, races and conditions. As the Christian idea of God rises far above the heathen or Hebrew conception thereof, so the Christian idea of man's relation to man far transcends the popular notions of human duty which formerly had prevailed. God is " our Father," the God of love; Man our brother, whom we are bound to love as ourselves, and treat as we would be treated. Christian piety, or love of God, involves Christian morality, or love of man.

I lay aside the peculiar theoretical doctrines of the sects, that are preached everywhere, and ask: Can the Christian relations of human brotherhood, the Chris-

VIII—6

tian duty of love to men, be practically preached in the slave States? I only publish an open secret in saying it is impossible. The forms of Christianity may be preached, not its piety, not its morality, not even its philosophy, or its history. If a man holds slaves in practice and justifies the deed in theory, how can he address an audience of slaveholders and teach them the duty of loving others as themselves? He cannot consistently teach that doctrine, nor they consistently hear.

The doctrines of the public religion are always modified by national habits, history, institutions, and ideas. Christianity, as taught in New England, has modifications unknown in Old England. The great national and peculiar ideas of America — of which I shall soon speak — are among the truths of Christianity. We began our national career by declaring all men born with equal rights. In such a people we might look for a better and more universal development of Christianity, than in a nation which knows no unalienable rights, or equality of all men, but robs the many of their rights, to squander privileges on the few.

In some lands monarchy, aristocracy, prelacy, appear in the public teaching as parts of Christianity. In America it is not so. But it is taught that slavery in an ordinance of God,— justified by Christianity. Thus as the public religion is elsewhere made to subserve the private purposes of kings, nobles, priests — so here is it made to prove the justice of holding men in bondage. There are no claims like those wrought in the name of God, and welded upon their victim by the teachers of religion.

Most of the churches in the United States exercise the power of excluding a man from their communion for such offenses as they see fit; for any unpopular breach of the moral law — for murder, robbery, theft, public drunkenness, seduction, licentiousness, for heresy. Even dancing is an offense for which the churches sometimes deal with their children. But, with the exception of the Quakers and the United Brethren, no religious bodies in the United States now regard slaveholding or slave-dealing as an ecclesiastical offense. Church-members and clergymen are owners of slaves. Even churches themselves in some instances have, in their corporate capacity, been owners of men. In Turkey, when a man becomes a Mahometan, he ceases to be a slave. But in America a clergymen may own a member of his own church, beat him, sell him, and grow rich on " the increase of his female slaves."

Few productions of the Southern clergy find their way to the North. Conspicuous among those few are sermons in defense of slavery; attempts to show that if Christ were now on earth he might consistently hold property in men!

The teachings of the Southern pulpit become more and more favorable to slavery. Oppressed, America promulgated the theory of freedom; — free, she established the practice of oppression. In 1780 the Methodist Episcopal Church declared " slavery is contrary to the laws of God," and " hurtful to society; " in 1784 it refused to admit slaveholders to its communion — passing a vote to exclude all such. But in 1836 the general conference voted " not to interfere in the civil and political relations between master and slave," and exhorted its ministers " to abstain from all abolition movements." The general conference since declared that American slavery " is not a moral evil." The conference of South Carolina has made a similar declaration.

In 1794 the Presbyterian Church added a note to the eighth commandment, bringing slavery under that prohibition, declaring it manstealing and a sin. Yet, though often entreated, it did not excommunicate for that offense. In 1816, by a public decree, the note was erased. Numerous presbyteries and synods have passed resolutions like these: " Slavery is not opposed to the will of God; " " It is compatible with the most fraternal regard to the best good of those servants whom God may have committed to our charge." Even the Catholic Church in the United States forms no exception to the general rule. The late lamented Dr. England, the Catholic bishop of Charleston, South Carolina, undertook in public to prove that the Catholic Church had always been the uncompromising friend of slaveholding, not defending the slaves' right, but the usurped privilege of the masters. What a difference between the present Christian Pope of Rome, and the bishop of a Democratic State in a Christian republic!

It has been currently taught in the most popular churches of the land, that slavery is a " Christian institution," sustained by the apostles, and sanctioned by Christ himself. None of the theological parties has been so little connected with slavery as the Unitarians — perhaps from the smallness of the sect itself, and its northern latitude — but, for years, one of its vice-presidents was a slaveholder.

While the Southern churches teach that slavery is Christian, the Northern join in the belief. Here and there a few voices in the North have been lifted up against it; seldom an eminent voice in an eminent place, then to be met with obloquy and shame. Almost all the churches in the land seem joined in opposing such as draw public attention to the fact that a Christian republic holds millions of men in bondage. Not long since a clergyman of the South, who boasted that he owned thirty slaves, and "would wade knee-deep in blood" to defend his right to them, was received by the Northern churches, and, as himself has said, "invited on every hand to pulpits," with no rebuke, but only welcome from the large and powerful denomination to which he belonged. He returned, as he says, "leaving the hot-beds of abolitionism, without having been once foiled. God be praised for sustaining me. I give Him all the glory, for without Him I am nothing." Even in Boston there is a church of the same denomination, in which no colored man is allowed to purchase a seat. Colored men at the North are excluded from colleges and high schools, from theological seminaries and from respectable churches — even from the town hall and the ballot. Doctrines and outward deeds are but signs of sentiments and ideas which rule the life.

The sons of the North, when they settle in the South, as merchants, ministers, lawyers, planters, when they stand in the Congress of the nation, when they fill important offices in the Federal Government — what testimony do they bear to the declaration that "all men are created equal"? I should blush to refresh your memories with Northern shame.

If the clergy find slavery "ordained" in the Bible, and established amongst the "Christian institutions," did not the laymen first find it in the Bible of Rousseau? Important men at the South have taught that slavery is "a moral and humane institution, productive of the greatest political and social advantages;" "the corner-stone of our republican edifice:" "It is the most sure and stable edifice for free institutions in the world." The doctrine that "all men are created equal" in rights is declared "ridiculously absurd." Democratic Mr. Calhoun declares that where "common labor is performed by members of the political community a dangerous element is obviously introduced into the body politic." A pagan had taught it two thousand years before.

Thus powerful is the influence of slavery in its action on the intellectual, moral, and religious development of the people at the South; thus subtly does it steal upon the North. As one of your most illustrious citizens, old but not idle, has said, the spirit of slavery "has crept into the philosophical chairs of the schools. Its cloven foot has ascended the pulpits of the churches. Professors of colleges teach it as a lesson of morals; ministers of the gospel seek and profess to find sanctions for it in the Word of God."

The effect of slavery on the industrial, numerical, intellectual, and moral developments of the people may be best shown by a comparison of the condition and history of the two largest States, one slave, the other free. Virginia contains more than 64,000 square miles, or 13,370 more than England. The climate is delightful. The State is intersected by "the finest bay in the world," watered by long and abundant rivers; this inviting navigation, and allowing numerous and easy communications with the interior; that waiting to turn the wheels of the manufacturer, to weave and spin. The soil is rich in minerals. Iron, lead, and limestone are abundant. Nitre is found in her caverns. Salt abounds on the Great Kanawha and the Holston. Fields of coal, anthracite and bituminous, are numerous, rich, and of easy access. The soil is fertile, the

sky genial, the air salubrious.   She is the oldest State
in the Union; long the most important in wealth,
population, and political power.   The noble array of
talent and virtue found there in the last century has
already been mentioned.   Abundantly blessed with
bays, harbors, rivers, mines, no State in the Union had
such natural advantages as Virginia in 1790.   New
York has 49,000 square miles, and was settled somewhat later than Virginia, and under circumstances less
propitious.   Numerous causes retarded her growth before   the   Revolution.   Though   favored   with   an
excellent harbor, she has but one natural channel of
communication with the interior.   In 1790 Virginia
contained 748,348 inhabitants; New York but 340,120.
In 1840 Virginia had 1,239,797; New York 2,428,921,
and in 1845, 2,604,495.   In fifty years Virginia had
not doubled her population, while New York had increased more than fourfold.   In 1790, Virginia had
more than eleven inhabitants to each square mile, and
New York not quite eight; but in 1840, Virginia had
only nineteen, and New York fifty-three persons to the
square mile.   In 1798, the houses and lands of Virginia
were valued at $71,225,127, those of New York at
$100,380,707; in 1839 the real estate in Virginia was
worth but $211,930,538, while that of New York had
increased to $430,751,273.   In 1840 the annual
earnings of Virginia were $76,769,032; of New York
$193,806,433.   The population of New York is not
quite double that of Virginia, but her annual earnings
nearly three times as great.   In 1840, at her various
colleges and schools, Virginia had 57,302 scholars, and
also 58,787 adult free whites unable to read and write
— 1484 more than the entire number of her children at
school or college.   New York had 44,452 illiterate

adults, and 565,442 children at school or college. Besides that, in Virginia there were 448,987 slaves, with no literary culture at all, shut out from communication with the intelligence of the age. In 1844, in New York, 709,156 children, between four and sixteen, attended the common public schools of the State, and the common school libraries contained over a million of volumes; while in Virginia there was over 100,000 free white children between four and sixteen, who attended no school at all, perpetual vagrants from learning, year out and year in. Shall it always be so? The effect follows the cause. A man loses half his manhood by slavery, said Homer, and it is as true of a State as a man.

VI. *Effect of Slavery on Law and Politics*

I now call your attention to the influence of slavery on law and politics, its local effect on the slave States in special, its general effect on the politics of the Union.

In the settlement of America only the people came over. Nobility and royalty did not migrate. The people, the third estate, of course brought the institutions and laws of their native land — these are the national habits, so to say. But they brought also political sentiments and ideas not represented by the institutions or laws; sentiments and ideas hostile thereto, and which could not be made real in England, but were destined — as are all such ideas — to form institutions and make laws in their own image. There are three such political ideas which have already found a theoretical expression, and have more or less been made facts and become incarnate in institutions and laws. These are, first, the idea, that in virtue of his manhood,

each man has unalienable rights, not derived from men
or revocable thereby, but derived only from God;
second, that in respect to these rights all men are
created equal; third, that the sole design of political
government is to place every man in the entire possession of all his unalienable rights.

The priesthood, nobility, royalty, did not share these
ideas — nor the sentiments which led to them. These
ideas were of the people; they must form a democracy,
the government of all, for all, and by all — a commonwealth with no privileged class — a state without nobles
or kings, a church without prelate or priest.

These ideas, in becoming facts and founding
political institutions to represent themselves, modified
also the ancient and common law. "The laws of
England," said Sir John Fortescue, in the fifteenth
century, "the laws of England favor liberty in every
case;" "let him who favors not liberty be judged
impious and cruel." After the national and solemn
expression of the above democratic ideas, the laws must
favor liberty yet more, and new institutions likewise
come into being. Accordingly, in the free States of the
North, where these ideas have always had the fullest
practical exposition, ever since the Revolution there has
been a continual advance in legislation — laws becoming more humane, universal principles getting established, and traditional exceptions becoming annulled.
In law — the theory of these ideas — so far as expressed in institutions and habits; and in society —
the practice thereof, so far as they have passed into
actual life,— there is a constant levelling upward; the
low are raised — the slave, the servant, the non-free-
holder, the lofty not degraded. In the constitutions of
nearly all the free States it is distinctly stated that all

men are created equal in rights, and in all it is implied. They are all advancing towards a realization of that idea — slowly, but constantly. They have lost none of the justice embodied in the common law of their ancestors — but gained new justice, and embodied it in their own forms.

This idea of the natural equality of all men in rights is inconsistent with slavery; accordingly it is expressed in the constitutions of but one slave State — Virginia. It is consistently rejected by the politicians of the South. This difference of ideas must appear in all the institutions of the North and South, and produce continual and conflicting modifications of the common law of England, which they both inherit; if the one idea adds justice thereto, the other takes it away.

Now among the institutions inherited from England were the trial by a jury of twelve men in all matters affecting liberty and life; the presumption in favor of life, liberty, and innocence; the right of every man under restraint to have a legal reason publicly shown for his confinement, by a writ of habeas corpus. The form of the latter is indeed modern, but its substance old, and of uncertain date. These three have long been regarded as the great safeguards of public justice, and in the legislation of the free States remain undisturbed in their beneficent action, extending to every person therein. In the slave States the whole class of bondmen is in fact mainly deprived of them all.

By the customs of England and her law, while villainage obtained there, the rule was that the child followed the condition of its father: *Filius sequitur patrem.* Hence the issue of a freeman, though born of a servile mother, was always free. In virtue of this maxim, and the legal presumption in favor of liberty, a presumption extending to all classes of men, the child of a female slave, which was born out of wedlock, was of course free.   It was possible the father was a freeman.   The child gained nothing but existence from his unknown father, and the law would not make that a curse.   The child of a slave father, but born before the father was proved a slave, retained his freedom for ever.

If a freeman married a female slave, she became free during the life of her husband, and the children of course were free.

The slave, under certain circumstances, could possess property, acquired by devise, by gift, or other means. It was so as a general rule through all the north of Europe; the more cruel maxims of the Roman slave-code never prevailed with the Teutonic race.

The slave could make a contract with his lord, binding as that between peer and peer.   He could in his own name bring an action against any one; in some cases even against his master.   He could, in all cases and in his own name, demand a trial by jury in a court of record, to determine if he were born a slave, or free. To determine against him, it was necessary not only to show in general that he was a slave, but that he was the slave of some one person in special.   If it was simply shown that the man was a slave, but was not shown to the jury's satisfaction that he was the slave of the particular man who claimed him, the slave received his freedom at once, as one derelict by his master, and if legally claimed by nobody, he naturally belonged to himself.

He could be a witness in any court even when his master was an adverse party; though not possessed of all the privileges of a citizen — *legalis homo* — not admitted to hold office or serve on a jury, yet he could testify on oath even in criminal cases, as any other man.

If a slave ran away, and the master for one year neglected to pursue him with public outcry and prosecution of his claim, the slave was free by adverse possession of himself. While he was in flight, and in actual possession of freedom, the master could not seize on his children or on his possessions. He must legally possess the principal, the substance, before he could touch the subordinate and accident thereof. Did the slave flee to another borough or shire, a jury of that place — except in certain cases, when the trial must take place in another county — must not only convict him as a slave before the master could recover his body, but must convict him of being the slave of that special claimant.

If a slave took orders in the church, or became a monk, he was free from his master, though this was an exception to the law in most Catholic countries. If violence were offered to a female slave by her master, she had redress as a free woman. Slaves had all the personal rights of freemen except in regard to their own respective masters, and in some cases even then. There was no hindrance to manumission.

In America the laws relating to slavery are in many respects more severe than the English laws, since the Norman conquest, respecting villains — *regardant* or *in gross*. The child's condition follows that of the mother. This American departure from the common law was early made by statute, and the opposite maxim, the rule of the civil law, extended over the slave States; — *Partus sequitur ventrem*. Illegitimate children of female slaves were of course slaves for ever, though the father was free. But for this alteration, many thousands of men now slaves would have been free.

Contrary to the old common law of England, but in obedience to the Roman code, the American slave, in law, is regarded merely as a thing; " doomed," as Judge Ruffin, of North Carolina, sorrowfully declares, " to live without knowledge and without the capacity to make anything his own, and to toil that another may reap the fruits." In some of the slave States trial by jury is allowed to him in all capital cases; sometimes with the concurrence of a grand jury, sometimes without. Sometimes he is allowed to challenge the jurors " for cause," though not peremptorily. But in South Carolina, Virginia, and Louisiana, the slave is not allowed a jury trial, even when his life is in peril. In some others he has the protection of a jury when arraigned for inferior offenses. But in every slave State he may be beaten to the extent of " thirty-nine lashes well laid on," without the verdict of a jury, but by the decision of a body of justices of the peace, varying in number from two to five. In all cases he is tried by men who regard him only as a thing, never by a jury of his peers — not even by a mixed jury of slaveholders and slaves. Some States have made humane provisions to guard against popular excitement, removing the trial to another county; now and then humane decisions are made in their favor by just men. But these are exceptional spots of humanity amidst the general gloom of the slave-code. There is some difference in the legislation of the several States, justifying the remark long ago made in Europe, that the condition of slaves was mildest in the North — hardest in the South.

Since the slave is a thing, he is not allowed his oath;
sometimes he may give legal evidence for or against
another slave, though without any form of solemn
affirmation. There are laws in all the slave States
designed to restrain the master from excessive cruelty,
still they afford but incomplete protection to the slave;
he cannot bring an action against the oppressor in his
own name—for, as a thing, he has no rights. No
slave, free negro, or mulatto to the fourth degree of descent is allowed to testify against a white man; as if
this were not enough in South Carolina and Louisiana,
if a slave is injured or killed when only one white person is present — and the presumption of guilt fall on
the one white man, he is allowed by statute " to clear
or exculpate himself by his own oath." This law is
worse than the code of the Romans, " whose history
was written in the blood of vanquished nations."

The slave has no legal right of self-defense against
his master's assault and battery; the female none
against brutal violation. The law of Georgia directs
that " if any slave shall presume to strike any white
man, such slave shall, for the first offense, suffer such
punishment as the justice or justices shall see fit, not
extending to life or limb; and, for the second offense,
suffer death." In South Carolina, on his owner's
account, he is allowed to strike even a white man, and
the offense is capital only when twice repeated. In
Kentucky, the penalty is less severe, but applied to freemen of color as well as slaves.

A slave cannot be party to a civil suit. Indeed, when
his condition is doubtful, he may apply to a court, and
the court authorize some man to act as " guardian,"
and bring an action in the slave's behalf, and have
investigation made of his servitude. But the burden

of proof remains on the slave's shoulders — to show
that he is free.   The presumption that he is a slave —
presumptio malæ partis — prevails in all the South except North Carolina,— where the slave-code is perhaps more humane than elsewhere,— and is thus declared by statute in South Carolina and Georgia: "It
shall always be presumed that every negro, Indian,
mulatto, and mestizo is a slave."   No adverse possession of himself, however long, makes a negro free, or
his offspring born while he is in that state.   In Mississippi, every negro or mulatto, not able to prove that he
is free, may be sold by order of the court, as a slave
for ever.   If an applicant for freedom is cast in his
suit, the court is " fully empowered to inflict such punishment not extending to life and limb, as they should
think fit ; " the " guardian " shall pay the costs ; and in
South Carolina, double those costs with damages to the
owner of the slave.   In Virginia, such a guardian, if
defeated in his application, may be fined $100.   In
such a trial in Maryland, the master is allowed to
challenge peremptorily twelve jurors.   How difficult
to find a " guardian " willing to incur the risk ! how
more than difficult to secure justice when a negro is
wrongfully claimed as a slave !   Yet notwithstanding
the general spirit displayed by such legislation, some
decisions have been made in the Southern States remarkable for the nicety of legal distinction and the
exactness of their justice even to the slave.

Since the slave is a thing in many States, a condi-
tional contract which the master has solemnly made
with a slave, is not binding on the master, even after
the slave has fulfilled the contract in spirit and letter.
This is notoriously the law in South Carolina, and even
in Virginia.   A contract made with a spade or a mule

binds no man — with a slave no more; the court cannot proceed to "enforce a contract between master and slave, even though the contract should be fully complied with on the part of the slave." This is a departure from the common law of England, and even from the customs of the Saxons and Germans.

The common law of England jealously defends the little property of the slave; — his *peculium.* By the common law of villainage, in England and Germany, he could acquire property as it was said above, and could transmit it to his heirs. Something of the sort was allowed even at Rome. But in all the slave States this is strictly forbidden. A slave cannot hold property solemnly devised to him by testament, even by that of his master. This provision, enforced by statute in Virginia, North Carolina, South Carolina, Georgia, Mississippi, Kentucky, and Tennessee, and perhaps all the slave States, is more rigorous even than the black codes of the Spanish and Portuguese colonies.

By the common law, the marriage of a slave was sacred as that of a peer of the realm. The customs of Turkey regard it as inviolable. Even the Roman code respected that, and the common law, by making marriage a sacrament, rendered it perpetual. "Neither bond nor free may be separated from the sacraments of the Church," said the Decretal of Gregory; "the marriages among slaves must not be hindered, and though contracted against their master's will, ought not, on that account, to be dissolved." But in the American law the slave cannot contract marriage. In North Carolina no marriage is legal between whites and persons of color, including in the latter term all descended from a negro to the fourth generation.

In some States it is a penal offense to teach slaves the elements of common learning. By the recent code of Virginia, any one who undertakes to teach reading or writing to slaves, or even free colored persons, may be fined from $10 to $100. The same is forbidden in Georgia. In Alabama, the punishment in a fine from $250 to $500; in Mississippi imprisonment for one year. Louisiana forbids the teaching of slaves to read or write, and prohibits any one from using language in public discourse or private conversation, having a tendency to produce discontent among the free colored population. The latter offense is punishable " with imprisonment or death, at the discretion of the court." This antipathy to the education of the colored race extends even to the free States. It is not unknown in New England. The State of Ohio estabblished schools in 1829 for " the white youth of every class and grade without distinction."

According to the alleged precept of Mahomet, slaves are supposed to be bound by feebler social and civil obligations than freemen, and thus common offenses receive but half the punishment of the free. Such, it is said, is the common law of Mahometans in Turkey and the East. In Virginia there are six capital offenses for a freeman, seventy-one for a slave. In Mississippi there are thirty-eight offenses for which a slave must be punished with death,— not one of which is a capital crime in a free white man. In some States the law is milder, but in none does the Christian Republican of Anglo-Saxon descent imitate the humanity of the Mussulman, and legally favor the weaker part — correcting slaves as the children of the State.

Many offenses for which a slave is severely punished are not wrongs by nature, sins against the universal

VIII—7

and divine law, but only crimes by statute. Thus in Mississippi, if a slave be found "fire-hunting" he is punishable "with thirty-nine lashes, well laid on his bare back." In the same State, if a slave be found out of the limits of the town or off the plantation where he usually works, " any one may apprehend and punish him with whipping on the bare back, not exceeding twenty lashes." If he refuses to submit to the examination of any white person, "such white person may apprehend and moderately correct him, and if he shall assault and strike such white person, he may be lawfully killed." Louisiana has a similar law, and also punishes any slave or free colored person exercising the functions of a minister of the Gospel, with thirty-nine lashes. In Virginia a slave or free colored person may be beaten with twenty lashes for being found at any school for teaching reading and writing. In South Carolina he is forbidden to wear any but the coarsest garments.

The Roman code allowed emancipation; the customs of England and Germany favored it. The Christian Church often favored and recommended it. In the Roman Empire, the advance of humanity continually rendered it easy and common. A slave sick, and derelict of his master, recovering, claimed legally his freedom for salvage of himself. But in America the laws constantly throw obstacles in its way. In South Carolina, Georgia, Alabama, and Mississippi no man can emancipate any slave, except by authority of the legislature, granted by a special enactment conveying the power. In Georgia, a will, setting free a slave, is so far null and void, and any person attempting to execute it shall be fined $1000. In Kentucky, Missouri, Virginia, Maryland, it is less difficult; but even there no man is allowed

to emancipate a slave to the prejudice of his creditors;
— or in Virginia, Mississippi, and Kentucky, to the
lessening of his widow's dower, the common law favors
three things — life, liberty, and dower; — the law of
these three States sacrifices the liberty of slaves to the
dower of a widow. Emancipation must be made with
most formal and technical minuteness, or the act is
void. Does the master solemnly covenant with his
slave to emancipate him? The contract can be revoked
at the master's will. No extraordinary service of the
slave, except in North Carolina, would be held " a good
consideration " and sufficient to bind the bargain. In
some States, as Maryland and Virginia, in fact — no
person under thirty nor over five-and-forty can be
emancipated.

Take all the slave-laws of the United States together,
consider the race that has made them, their religion,
the political ideas of their government, that it is in the
nineteenth century after Christ, and they form the
most revolting work of legislation to be found in the
annals of any pacific people. The codes of the Barbarians who sat on the ruins of the Roman Empire —
the Burgundians, Bavarians, the Allemanni, with the
Visigoths and their northern kin — have left enactments certainly more terrible in themselves. But the
darkness of that period shrouds all those barbarian legislations in a general and homogeneous
gloom; and here, it is " the freest and most enlightened
nation of the world," who keeps, extends, and intensi-
fies the dreadful statutes which make men only things,
binds them and sells them as brute cattle. In 1102, the
council of London decreed that " hereafter no one shall
presume to carry on the nefarious business in which,
hitherto, men in England are wont to be sold as brute

beasts." The churches of America have no voice of rebuke — no word of entreaty — when Christian clergymen sell their brothers in the market. The flag of America and the majesty of the law defend that "business," which the Anglo-Saxon bishops, seven hundred and forty-five years ago, looked on as "nefarious," *nefarium negotium.* M. de Tocqueville regarded the American slave-code as "Legislation stained by unparalleled atrocities; a despotism directed against the human mind; legislation which forbids the slaves to be taught to read and write, and which aims to sink them as nearly as possible to the level of the brutes."

The effect of slavery appears in the general legislation of the South. In wisdom and humanity it is far behind the North. It is there that laws are most bloody; punishments most barbarous and vindictive, that irregular violence takes most often the place of legal procedure; that equity is least sure even for the free whites themselves. One end of the slave's chain is round the master's neck. "Justice," says a proverb, "has feet of wool but iron hands." The slave-driver's whip and the bowie-knife of the American have a near relation.

Some of the Southern States have enacted remarkable laws to this effect: That when any free negro or person of color arrives in any vessel at a Southern port, he shall be shut up in prison until the departure of the vessel, the owner of the vessel paying the costs. By this law the free citizens of the free States are continually imprisoned in South Carolina and Louisiana. This is not only a violation of the Constitution of the United States, but it is contrary to the common customs of Christian nations; a law without a parallel in their codes; a result which Gouverneur

Morris did not anticipate in 1787, when he made his satirical calculation of the value of the Union to the North.

The iniquity of the code of the slave States has passed into some enactments of the general government of the Union. In 1793, a law was made by Congress to this effect: A fugitive slave escaping into a free State — and consequently any man claimed to be such — may be seized by the master or his agent, and carried back to slavery without the intervention of a trial by jury to determine whether the man is a slave — simply by a trial before " any judge of the circuit or district courts of the United States residing or being within the State, or before any magistrate of the county, city, or town corporate where such seizure or arrest shall be made." The proof required that the man is a slave is by " oral testimony or affidavit " of the parties interested in the man's capture. This is a departure from the customs of your fathers; a departure which the common law of England would not justify at any time since the Norman conquest. The trial by jury has been regarded the great safeguard of personal freedom; even in the dark ages of English law it was the right of every man, of every fugitive slave, when his person was in peril. Had a slave escaped with his children, and remained some time a freeman — *statu liber;* did the master find the children and not the father, he could not hold them till he caught the father, and by a jury-trial proved his claim. In the United States the laws do not favor liberty in case of men born with African blood in their veins.

The power of the general government has been continually exercised against this class of Americans.

It pursues them after they have taken refuge with the Indians; it has sullied the American name by vainly asking the monarch of England to deliver up fugitive American slaves who had fled to Canada and sought freedom under her flag.

The Federal Government established slavery in the District of Columbia, in various territories, and approved the constitutions of eight new States which aim to perpetuate the institution.

For a long time the House of Representatives refused to receive " all petitions, memorials, resolutions, and propositions relating in any way or to any extent whatever to the subject of slavery." Thus have the " unalienable rights " of man been trampled under foot by the government of the most powerful Republic in the world. But last summer, in the city of Washington two women were sold as slaves, on account of the United States of America, by her marshal, at public auction!

But let us look at the political effect of slavery. The existence of 3,000,000 slaves in the heart of the nation, with interests hostile to their masters, weakens the effective force of the nation in a time of war. It was found to be so in the Revolution, and in the late war. The slave States offer a most vulnerable point of attack. Let an enemy offer freedom to all the slaves who would join the standard — they will find " in every negro a decided friend," and the South could not stand with millions of foes scattered through all parts of her territory.[5] Have the slaves arms? There are firebrands on every hearth. During the Revolution many thousands escaped from South Carolina alone. At the conclusion of the last war with England she offered to pay $1,204,000 as the value of the slaves who, in a brief period, had taken shelter beneath her flag. What if England had armed them as soldiers — to revenge the country and burn the towns? Will a future enemy be so reluctant? The feeling of the civilized world revolts at our inhumanity. The English, for reasons no longer existing, took little pains to avail themselves of the weapon thus thrust into their hands. In the time of our troubles with France, when war was expected, General Washington had serious apprehensions from this source. Even in 1756, during the French war, Governor Dinwiddie of Virginia did not " dare venture to part with any of our white men any distance, as we must have a watchful eye over our negro slaves."

The Revolutionary War showed the respective military abilities of North and South, and their respective devotion to their country's cause. It is not easy, perhaps not possible, to ascertain the sums of money furnished by the particular States, for the purposes of that war; the number of men it is easy to learn. Taking the census of 1790 as the standard, the six slave States had a free population of 1,852,504, or, including Kentucky and Tennessee, 1,961,372. Let us suppose that during the Revolution, from 1775 to 1783, the number was but two-thirds as great, or 1,307,549. In those States there were 657,527 slaves, all the other States had likewise slaves; but in New England there were but 3886, their influence quite inconsiderable in military affairs. Let us therefore compare the number of men furnished for the war by New England and the six slave States. In 1790 the population of New England was 1,009,823. But let us suppose, as before, that from 1775 to 1783, it was, on an average, but two-thirds as large, or 673,215.

During the nine years of the Revolutionary War,
New England furnished for the continental army
119,305 men; while the slave States, with a free population of 1,307,549, furnished but 59,336 men for the
continental army. Besides that, the slave States
furnished 10,123 militia men, and New England
29,324.

Let us compare a slave State, and a free one, of
about equal population. In 1790, South Carolina
contained 249,073 persons; Connecticut, 238,141.
Supposing the population during the war only two-
thirds as great as in 1790, then South Carolina contained 166,018, and Connecticut 158,760 persons.
During the nine years of the war, South Carolina sent
6417 soldiers to the continental army, and Connecticut
32,039. In 1790, Massachusetts contained 475,257
souls; during the Revolution, according to the above
ratio, 316,838. While the six slave States, with their
free population of 1,307,549, furnished but 59,336
soldiers for the continental army, and 10,123 militia
men, Massachusetts alone sent 68,007 soldiers to the
continental army, and 15,155 militia. Thus shoulder
to shoulder, Massachusetts and South Carolina went
through the Revolution, and felt the great arm of
Washington lean on them both for support.

By the Constitution of the United States, in the apportionment of representatives to Congress, five slaves
count the same as three freemen. This is a provision
unknown in former national codes, resting on a principle un-democratic, detrimental to liberty, and hitherto unheard of: the principle of allowing parts of
a nation political power in proportion to the number
of men which they hold in bondage. It would have
astonished the heathen democracy of Athens long cen-

turies ago. By this arrangement, from 1789 to 1792, the South gained seven representatives in the first Congress; from 1795 to 1813 — fourteen; from 1813 to 1823 — nineteen; from 1823 to 1833 — twenty-two; from 1833 to 1843 — twenty-five. By the last apportionment bill, one representative is allowed for 70,680 freemen, or a proportionate number of slaves. By this arrangement, in a house of only 225 members, the South gains twenty representatives on account of her slaves — more than one-twelfth part of the whole.

At present the North has 138 representatives for 9,728,922 souls; or 9,727,893 freemen; one representative for each 70,492 freemen. The South has 87 representatives. There are within the slave States 4,848,105 freemen; they have one representative for each 55,725 free persons.

In the next Presidential election the North will have 166 electoral votes; the South 117. The North has an electoral vote for each 52,576 freemen; the South one for each 41,436. Part of this difference is due to the fact that in the South there are several small States. But twenty electoral votes are given by the South, on account of her property in slaves. But if slaves are merely property, there is no reason why Southern negroes should be represented in Congress more than the spindles of the North.

But the South pays direct taxes for her slaves in the same proportion. A direct tax has been resorted to only four times since 1789 by the General Government, viz. in 1798, 1813, 1814, and 1816. The whole amount assessed is $14,000,000. Of this about $12,-750,000 was actually paid into the treasury of the United States, though part in a depreciated currency. Of that the South paid for her slaves, if the computation be correct, only $1,256,553.

In 1837 the surplus revenue of the Union, amounting to $37,468,859.97, was distributed among the several States in proportion to their electoral votes. By the census of 1830, the North had 7,008,451 free persons, and the South but 3,823,289. The free States received $21,410,777.12, and the slave States $16,058,082.85. Each freeman of the North received but $3.05, while each freeman of the South received $4.20 in that division.

At that time the South had one hundred and twenty-six electoral votes, of which twenty-five were on account of her slave-representation. She therefore received by that arrangement $3,186,127.50 on account of the representation of her slaves. From that if we deduct the $1,256,553 paid by her as direct taxes on her slaves, there is left $1,929,574.50, as the bonus which the South has received from the treasury of the nation on account of the representation of slaves — Southern property represented in Congress. To this we must add $57,556, which the South received in 1842 from the sale of public land on account of her slaves, the sum is $1,987,130.50. Mr. Pinckney was right when he said the terms were not bad for the South.

Slavery diverts the freeman from industry, from science, from letters and the elegant arts. It has been said to qualify him for politics. As political matters have been managed in the United States in this century, the remark seems justified by the facts. Elections are not accidents. Of the eight presidents elected in the nineteenth century, six were born in the South — children of the slave States. No Northern man has ever twice been elected to the highest office of the nation. A similar result appears in the appointment of important officers by the President himself. From 1789 to 1845, one hundred and seventy appointments were made of ministers and charges to foreign powers; of these, seventy-eight were filled from the North, ninety-two from the South. Of the seventy-four ministers plenipotentiary sent to Europe before 1846, forty-three were from the slave States. There have been fifteen judges of the supreme court from the North; eighteen from the South. The office of attorney-general has been four times filled by Northern men, fourteen times by men from the slave States. Out of thirty Congresses, eleven only have had a speaker from the North. These are significant facts, and plainly show the aptitude of Southern men to manage the political affairs of America. There are pilots for fair weather; pilots also only trusted in a storm.

VII. *Slavery Considered as a Wrong*

I am now to speak of slavery considered as a wrong, an offense against the natural and eternal laws of God. You all know it is wrong — a crime against humanity, a sin before Almighty God. The great men who call slavery — right and just; — do they not know better? The little and humble men who listen to their speech — do not we all know better? Yes, we all know that slavery is a sin before God; — is the union of many sins. On this theme I will say but a word.

The Roman code declares liberty the natural estate of man, but calls slavery an institution of positive law, by which one man is made subject to another, contrary to nature. By the Hebrew law it was a capital offense to steal a man and sell him, or hold him as a slave.

Now if that doctrine be true which the American people once solemnly declared self-evident — that all

men are created with equal rights — then every slave
in the United States is stolen. Then slavery is a
continual and aggravated theft. It matters not that
the slave's mother was stolen before. To take the
child of a slave must be theft as much as to take the
child of a freeman; it is stealing mankind. He that
murders a child has no defense in the fact that he
first murdered the sire.

When we hear that the Emperor of Russia or
Austria, for some political opinion, shuts a man in the
Spielberg, or sends him to Siberia, for life — we pity
the victim of such despotic power, thinking his natural
rights debarred. But the defense is that the man had
shown himself dangerous to the welfare of the State,
and so had justly forfeited his rights. When we reduce a man to a slave, making him a thing — we can
plead no extenuation of the offense. The slave is
only " guilty of a skin not colored like our own,"—
guilty of the misfortune to be weak and unprotected.
For this he is deprived of his liberty; he and his
children.

Slavery is against nature. It has no foundation in
the permanent nature of man, in the nature of things,
none in the eternal law of God, as reason and conscience declare that law. Its foundation is the selfishness, the tyranny of strong men. We all know it is
so — the little and the great. Better say it at once,
and with Mr. Rutledge declare that religion and
humanity have nothing to do with the matter, than
make the miserable pretense that it is consistent with
reason and accordant with Christianity; even the boys
know better.

In the last century your fathers cried out to God
against the oppressions laid on them by England, justly

cried out. Yet those oppressions were but little things
— a tax on sugar, parchment, paper, tea; nothing
but a tax, allowing no voice in the granting thereof
or its spending. They went to war for an abstraction
— the great doctrine of human rights. They declared
themselves free, free by right of birth, free because born
men and children of God. For the justice of their
cause they made solemn appeal to God Most High.
What was the oppression the fathers suffered, to this
their sons commit? It is no longer a question about
taxes and representatives, a duty on sugar, parchment,
paper, tea, but the liberty, the persons, the lives of
three millions of men are in question. You have taken
their liberty, their persons, and rendered their lives
bitter by oppression. Was it right in your fathers to
draw the sword and slay the oppressors, who taxed
them for his own purpose, taking but their money, nor
much of that? Were your fathers noble men for their
resistance? When they fell in battle did they fall " in
the sacred cause of God and their country? " Do you
build monuments to their memory and write thereon,
" Sacred to liberty and the rights of mankind? " Do
you speak of Lexington and Bunker Hill as spots most
dear in the soil of the New World, the Zion of freedom,
the Thermopylæ of universal right? Do you honor
the name of Washington far beyond all political names
of conqueror or king? How then can you justify
your oppression? How refuse to admit that the bondmen of the United States have the same right, and a
far stronger inducement to draw the sword and smite
at your very life? Surely you cannot do so, not in
America; never till Lexington and Bunker Hill are
wiped out of the earth; never till the history of your
own Revolution is forgot; never till the names of the

Adamses, of Jefferson, of Washington, are expunged from the memory of men.

When the rude African who rules over Dahomey or the Gaboon country burns a village and plunders the shrieking children of his fellow-barbarians to sell them away into bondage for ever, far from their humble but happy homes and their luxuriant soil, their bread-fruit and their palms, far from father and mother, from child and lover, from all the human heart clings to with tenderest longing — you are filled with horror at the deed.[6] "What! steal a man," say you; "Great God," you ask, "is the Gaboon chieftain a man, or but a taller beast, with mind more cunning and far-reaching claws?" That chieftain is a barbarian. He knows not your letters, your laws, the tenets of your religion. The nobler nature of the man sleeps in his savage breast. His only plea is — his degradation. His defense before the world and before God is this: He is a savage, he knows no law but force, no right but only might alone. For that plea and defense the civilized man must excuse him, perhaps God holds him guiltless.

But when a civilized nation comes, with all the art and science which mankind has learned in the whole lifetime of the race, and steals the children of the defenseless, stimulating the savage to plunder his brothers and make them slaves, the offense has no such excuse; it is a conscious crime; a wrong before the judgment of the nations; a sin before God.

In your case it is worse still; the autocrat of all the Russias may have no theory of man's unalienable rights adverse to the slavery he aims to abolish on his broad estates and wide-spread realm; the Bey of Tunis deals not in abstractions, in universal laws, knows noth-

ing of unalienable rights and the inborn equality of man.
But you, the people of the United States; you, a nation
of freemen, who owe allegiance to none; you, a republic, one of the foremost nations of the earth; you
with your theories of human, universal justice; you
who earliest made national proclamation to mankind of
human right, and those three political ideas whereon
the great American commonwealth now stands and rests;
you who profess to form a government not on force,
but law, not on national traditions, but abstract justice
— the nation's constant and perpetual will to give to
every one his constant and perpetual right; you who
would found a state not on cannon balls, but universal
laws, thoughts of God,— what plea can you put forth
in your defense?

You call yourselves Christians. It is your boast.
" Christianity," say the courts, " is the common law of
the land." You have a religion which tells that God
is the Father, equal, just, and loving to all mankind,—
the red man, whom you murdered, and the black man,
whom you have laid in iron, hurting his feet with
fetters. It tells you, all are brothers, African, American, red man, and black, and white. It tells you,
as your highest duty to love God with all your heart;
to love His justice, love His mercy, love His love; to
love that brother as yourself — the more he needs, to
love him still the more; that without such love for men
there is no love for God. The sacred books of the
nation — read in all pulpits, sworn over in all courts
of justice, borne even in your war-ships, and sheltered
by the battle-flag of your armies — the sacred books
of the nation tell that Jesus, the highest, dearest
revelation of God to man, who loved them all, that
he laid down his life for them, for all; and bade you

follow him! What is a natural action in the savage, a mere mistake in the despot of Turkey or of Russia, with you becomes a conscious and fearful wrong. For you to hold your brothers in bondage, to keep them from all chance of culture, growth in mind, or heart, or soul; for you to breed them as swine, and beat them as oxen; to treat them as mere things, without soul, or rights,— why, what was a mistake in political economy, a wrong before your ideas of government, becomes a sin foul and heinous before your ideas of man, and Christ, and God.

When you remember the intelligence of this age, its accumulated stores of knowledge, science, art, and wealth of matter and of mind, its knowledge of justice and eternal right; when you consider that in political ideas you stand the first people in the vanguard of mankind, now moving towards new and peaceful conquests for the human race; when you reflect on the great doctrine of universal right set forth in so many forms amongst you by the senator and the school-boy; when you bring home to your bosoms the religion whose sacred words are taught in that Bible, laid up in your churches, reverently kept in your courts of justice, carried under the folds of your flag over land and sea — that Bible, by millions multiplied and spread throughout the peopled world in every barbarous and stammering tongue,— and then remember that slavery is here; that three million men are now by Christian Republican America held in bondage worse then Egyptian, hopeless as hell,— you must take this matter to heart, and confess that American slavery is the greatest, foulest wrong which man ever did to man; the most hideous and detested sin a nation has ever committed before the just, all-bounteous God — a wrong and a sin wholly without excuse.[7]

Conclusion

FELLOW-CITIZENS OF AMERICA,

You see some of the effects of slavery in your land. It costs you millions of dollars each year. If there had been no slaves in America for forty years, it is within bounds to say, your annual earnings would be three hundred million dollars more than now. It has cost you also millions of men. But for this curse, Virginia had been as populous as New York, as rich in wealth and intelligence; without this the freemen of the South must have increased as rapidly as in the North, and at this day, perhaps five-and-twenty million men would rejoice at their welfare in the United States. Slavery retards industry in all its forms; the education of the people in all its forms, intellectual, moral, and religious. It hinders the application of those great political ideas of America; hinders the development of mankind, the organization of the rights of man in a worthy state, society, or church. Such effects are the divine sentence against the cause thereof.[8]

It is not for me to point out the remedy for the evil, and show how it can be applied; that is work for those men you dignify with place and power. I pretend not to give counsel here, only to tell the warning truth. Will you say that in the free States also there is oppression, ignorance, and want and crime? 'Tis true. But an excuse, specious and popular, for its continuance, is this: that the evils of slavery are so much worse, men will not meddle with the less till the greater is removed. Men are so wonted to this monstrous wrong, they cannot see the little wrongs with which modern society is full; evils which are little only when compared to that. When this shame of the nation is

VIII—8

wiped off, it will be easy, seeing more clearly, to redress the minor ills of ignorance and want and crime. But there is one bright thing connected with this wrong. I mean the heroism which wars against it with pure hands; historic times have seen no chivalry so heroic.

Not long ago Europe and the whole Christian world rang with indignation at the outrage said to be offered by the Russian government to some Polish nuns who were torn from their home, driven from place to place, brutally beaten, and vexed with continual torments. Be the story false or true, the ears of men tingled at the tale. But not one of the nuns was sold. Those wrongs committed against a few defenseless women are doubled, trebled in America, and here continually applied to thousands of American women. This is no fiction; a plain fact, and notorious; but whose ears tingle? Is it worse to abuse a few white women in Russia, than a nation of black women in America? Is that worse for a European than this for the democratic republicans of America? The truth must be spoken; the voice of the bondman's blood cries out to God against us; His justice shall make reply. How can America ask mercy, who has never shown it there?

Civilization extends everywhere: the Russian and the Hottentot feel its influence. Christian men send the Bible to every island in the Pacific sea. Plenty becomes general; famine but rare. The arts advance, the useful, the beautiful, with rapid steps. Machines begin to dispense with human drudgery. Comfort gets distributed through their influence, more widely than ancient benefactors dared to dream. What were luxuries to our fathers, attainable only by the rich, now find their way to the humble home. War — the old demon which once possessed each strong nation,

making it deaf and blind, but yet exceeding fierce, so
that no feebler one could pass near and be safe — war
is losing his hold of the human race, the devil getting
cast out by the finger of God. The day of peace
begins to dawn upon mankind, wandering so long in
darkness, and watching for that happy star. Science,
letters, religion, break down the barriers betwixt man
and man, 'twixt class and class. The obstacles which
severed nations once now join them. Trade mediates
between land and land — the gold entering where steel
could never force its way. New powers are developed
to hasten the humanizing work; they post o'er land
and ocean without rest, or serve our bidding while they
stand and wait. The very lightning comes down, is
caught, and made the errand-boy of the nations.
Steamships are shooting across the ocean, weaving
East and West in one united web. The soldier yields
to the merchant. The man-child of the Old World,
young but strong, carries bread to his father in the
hour of need. The ambassadors of science, letters, and
the arts, come from the Old World to reside near the
court of the New, telling truth for the common welfare
of all. The genius of America sends also its first-fruits
and a scion of its own green tree, a token of future
blessings, to the parent land. These things help the
great synthesis of the human race, the reign of peace
on earth, of good-will amongst all men.

Everywhere in the Old World the poor, the ignorant,
and the oppressed, get looked after as never before.
The hero of force is falling behind the times; the hero
of thought, of love, is felt to deserve the homage of
mankind. The Pope of Rome himself essays the reformation of Italy; the King of Denmark sets free the
slaves in his dominions, East and West; the Russian

Emperor liberates his serfs from the milder bondage of the Sclavonian race; his brother monarch of Turkey will have no slave-market in the Mahometan metropolis, no shambles there for human flesh; the Bey of Tunis cannot bear a slave; it grieves his Islamitish heart, swarthy African though he be.

Yet amid all this continual advance, America, the first of the foremost nations to proclaim equality, and human rights inborn with all; the first confessedly to form a state on nature's law — America restores barbarism; will still hold slaves. More despotic than Russia, more barbarous than the chieftain of Barbary, she establishes ferocity by federal law. There is suffering enough amongst the weak and poor in the cities of the free laborious North. England has her misery patent to the eye, and Ireland her looped and windowed raggedness, her lean and brutal want. So it is everywhere; there is sadness amid all the splendors of modern science and civilization, though far less than ever before. But amidst the ills of Christendom, the saddest and most ghastly spectacle on earth is American slavery. The misery of the Old World grows less and less; the monster-vice of America, to make itself more awful yet, must drag your cannon to invade new lands.

I have addressed you as citizens, members of the State. I cannot forget that you are men; are members of the great brotherhood of man, children of the one and blessed God, whose equal love has only made to bless us all, who will not suffer wrong to pass without its due. Think of the nation's deed, done continually and afresh. God shall hear the voice of your brother's blood, long crying from the ground; His justice asks you even now, "America, where is thy brother?"

This is the answer which America must give: "Lo, he is there in the rice-swamps of the South, in her fields teeming with cotton and the luxuriant cane. He was weak and I seized him; naked and I bound him; ignorant, poor and savage, and I over-mastered him. I laid on his feebler shoulders my grievous yoke. I have chained him with my fetters; beat him with my whip. Other tyrants had dominion over him, but my finger was thicker than their loins. I have branded the mark of my power, with red-hot iron, upon his human flesh. I am fed with his toil; fat, voluptuous on his sweat, and tears, and blood. I stole the father, stole also the sons, and set them to toil; his wife and daughters are a pleasant spoil to me. Behold the children also of thy servant and his handmaidens — sons swarthier than their sire. Askest Thou for the African? I found him a barbarian. I have made him a beast. Lo, there Thou hast what is Thine."

That voice shall speak again: "America, why dost thou use him thus — thine equal, born with rights the same as thine?"

America may answer: "Lord, I knew not the negro had a right to freedom. I rejoiced to eat the labors of the slave; my great men, North and South, they told me slavery was no wrong; I knew no better, but believed their word, for they are great, O Lord, and excellent."

That same voice may answer yet again, quoting the nation's earliest and most patriotic words: "'All men are created equal, and endowed by their Creator with unalienable rights — the right to life, to liberty, and the pursuit of happiness.' America, what further falsehood wilt thou speak?"

The Nation may reply again: "True, Lord, all

that is written in the nation's creed, writ by my greatest
spirits in their greatest hour. But since then, why,
holy men have come and told me in Thy name that
slavery was good; was right; that Thou thyself didst
once establish it on earth, and he who spoke Thy words
spoke nought against this thing. I have believed these
men, for they are holy men, O Lord, and excellent."

Then may that Judge of all the earth take down
the Gospel from the pulpit's desk, and read these few
plain words: "Thou shalt love the Lord thy God
with all thy heart; and thou shalt love thy neighbor
as thyself. Whatsoever ye would that others should
do to you, do also even so to them."

Further might He speak and say: "While the
poor Mussulman, whom thou call'st pagan and shut'st
out from heaven, sets free all men, how much more
art thou thyself condemned; yea, by the Bible which
thou sendest to the outcasts of the world?"

Across the stage of time the nations pass in the
solemn pomp of their historical procession; what kingly
forms sweep by, leading the nations of the past, the
present age! Let them pass — their mingled good
and ill. A great people now comes forth, the newest
born of nations, the latest hope of mankind, the heir
of sixty centuries — the bridegroom of the virgin
West. First come those Pilgrims, few and far between, who knelt on the sands of a wilderness, whose
depth they knew not, nor yet its prophecy, who meekly
trusting in their God, in want and war, but wanting
not in faith, laid with their prayers the deep foundations of the State and Church. Then follow more
majestic men, bringing great truths for all mankind,
seized from the heaven of thought, or caught, ground-
lightning, rushing from the earth; and on their ban-

ners have they writ these words: " Equality and in-born rights." Then comes the one with venerable face, who ruled alike the Senate and the camp, and at whose feet the attendant years spread garlands, laurel-wreaths, calling him first in war, and first in peace, and first in his country's heart, as it in his. Then follow men bearing the first-fruits of our toil, the wealth of the sea and land, the labors of the loom, the stores of commerce and the arts. A happy people comes, some with shut Bibles in their hands, some with nation's laws, some uttering those mighty truths which God has writ on man, and men have copied into golden words. Then comes, to close this long historic pomp, — the panorama of the world. — the NEGRO SLAVE, bought, branded, beat.

I remain your fellow-citizen and friend,

THEODORE PARKER.

Boston, December 22, 1847.

IV

THE DESTINATION OF AMERICA

Every nation has a peculiar character, in which it differs from all others that have been, that are, and possibly from all that are to come; for it does not yet appear that the Divine Father of the nations ever repeats Himself and creates either two nations or two men exactly alike. However, as nations, like men, agree in more things than they differ, and in obvious things too, the special peculiarity of any one tribe does not always appear at first sight. But if we look through the history of some nation which has passed off from the stage of action, we find certain prevailing traits which continually reappear in the language and laws thereof; in its arts, literature, manners, modes of religion — in short, in the whole life of the people. The most prominent thing in the history of the Hebrews is their continual trust in God, and this marks them from their first appearance to the present day. They have accordingly done little for art, science, philosophy, little for commerce and the useful arts of life, but much for religion; and the psalms they sang two or three thousand years ago are at this day the hymns and prayers of the whole Christian world. Three great historical forms of religion, Judaism, Christianity, and Mahometanism, all have proceeded from them.

He that looks at the Ionian Greeks, finds in their story always the same prominent characteristic, a devotion to what is beautiful. This appears often to

the neglect of what is true, right, and therefore holy.
Hence, while they have done little for religion, their
literature, architecture, sculpture, furnish us with
models never surpassed, and perhaps not equaled. Yet
they lack the ideal aspiration after religion that appears
in the literature and art and even language of some
other people, quite inferior to the Greeks in elegance
and refinement. Science, also, is most largely indebted
to these beauty-loving Greeks, for truth is one form
of loveliness.

If we take the Romans, from Romulus their first
king, to Augustulus, the last of the Cæsars, the same
traits of national character appear, only the complexion and dress thereof changed by circumstances.
There is always the same hardness and materialism the
same skill in organizing men, the same turn for affairs
and genius for legislation. Rome borrowed her theology and liturgical forms; her art, science, literature,
philosophy, and eloquence; even her art of war was an
imitation. But law sprang up indigenous in her soil;
her laws are the best gift she offers to the human race,
— the "monument more lasting than brass," which
she has left behind her.

We may take another nation, which has by no
means completed its history, the Saxon race, from
Hengist and Horsa to Sir Robert Peel; there also is
a permanent peculiarity in the tribe. They are yet
the same bold, handy, practical people as when their
bark first touched the savage shores of Britain; not
over religious; less pious than moral; not so much
upright before God, as downright before men; servants
of the understanding more than children of reason;
not following the guidance of an intuition, and the
light of an idea, but rather trusting to experiment,

facts, precedents, and usages; not philosophical, but
commercial; warlike through strength and courage,
not from love of war or its glory; material, obstinate,
and grasping, with the same admiration of horses,
dogs, oxen, and strong drink; the same willingness to
tread down any obstacle, material, human, or divine,
which stands in their way; the same impatient lust of
wealth and power; the same disposition to colonize
and re-annex other lands; the same love of liberty and
love of law; the same readiness in forming political
confederations.

In each of these four instances, the Hebrews, the
Ionians, the Romans, and the Anglo-Saxon race, have
had nationality so strong, that while they have mingled
with other nations in commerce and in war, as victors
and vanquished, they have stoutly held their character
through all; they have thus modified feebler nations
joined with them.   To take the last, neither the Britons
nor the Danes affected very much the character of the
Anglo-Saxon; they never turned it out of its course.
The Normans gave the Saxon manners, refinement,
letters, elegance.   The Anglo-Saxon bishop of the
eleventh century, dressed in untanned sheep-skins, " the
woolly side out and the fleshy side in; " he ate cheese
and flesh, drank milk and mead.   The Norman taught
him to wear cloth, to eat also bread and roots, to drink
wine.   But in other respects the Norman left him as
he found him.   England has received her kings and
her nobles from Normandy, Anjou, the Provence,
Scotland, Holland, Hanover, often seeing a foreigner
ascend her throne; yet the sturdy Anglo-Saxon character held its own, spite of the new element infused
into its blood: change the ministries, change the dynasties often as they will, John Bull is obstinate as

ever, and himself changes not; no philosophy or religion makes him less material. No nation but the English could have produced a Hobbes, a Hume, a Paley, or a Bentham; they are all instantial and not exceptional men in that race.

Now this idiosyncrasy of a nation is a sacred gift; like the genius of a Burns, a Thorwaldsen, a Franklin, or a Bowditch, it is given for some divine purpose, to be sacredly cherished and patiently unfolded. The cause of the peculiarities of a nation or an individual man we cannot fully determine as yet, and so we refer it to the chain of causes which we call Providence. But the national persistency in a common type is easily explained. The qualities of father and mother are commonly transmitted to their children, but not always, for peculiarities may lie latent in a family for generations, and reappear in the genius or the folly of a child —often in the complexion and features: and, besides, father and mother are often no match. But such exceptions are rare, and the qualities of a race are always thus reproduced, the deficiency of one man getting counterbalanced by the redundancy of the next: the marriages of a whole tribe are not far from normal.

Some nations, it seems, perish through defect of this national character, as individuals fail of success through excess or deficiency in their character. Thus the Celts — that great flood of a nation which once swept over Germany, France, England, and, casting its spray far over the Alps, at one time threatened destruction to Rome itself — seems to have been so filled with love of individual independence that they could never accept a minute organization of human rights and duties; and so their children would not group themselves into a city, as other races, and submit to a strong central power which should curb individual will enough to insure national unity of action. Perhaps this was once the excellence of the Celts, and thereby they broke the trammels and escaped from the theocratic or despotic traditions of earlier and more savage times, developing the power of the individual for a time, and the energy of a nation loosely bound; but when they came in contact with the Romans, Franks, and Saxons, they melted away as snow in April — only, like that, remnants thereof yet lingering in the mountains and islands of Europe. No external pressure of famine or political oppression now holds the Celts in Ireland together, or gives them national unity of action enough to resist the Saxon foe. Doubtless in other days this very peculiarity of the Irish has done the world some service. Nations succeed each other as races of animals in the geological epochs, and, like them also, perish when their work is done.

The peculiar character of a nation does not appear nakedly, without relief and shadow. As the waters of the Rhone, in coming from the mountains, have caught a stain from the soils they have traversed which mars the cerulean tinge of the mountain snow that gave them birth, so the peculiarities of each nation become modified by the circumstances to which it is exposed, though the fundamental character of a nation, it seems, has never been changed. Only when the blood of the nation is changed by additions from another stock is the idiosyncrasy altered.

Now, while each nation has its peculiar genius or character which does not change, it has also and accordingly a particular work to perform in the economy of the world, a certain fundamental idea to unfold and develop. This is its national task, for in God's world,

as in a shop, there is a regular division of labor.
Sometimes it is a limited work, and when it is done
the nation may be dismissed, and go to its repose.
Non omnia possumus omnes is as true of nations as
of men; one has a genius for one thing, another
for something different, and the idea of each nation
and its special work will depend on the genius of the
nation. Men do not gather grapes of thorns.

In addition to this specific genius of the nation and
its corresponding work, there are also various accidental or subordinate qualities which change with
circumstances, and so vary the nation's aspect that its
peculiar genius and peculiar duty are often hid from
its own consciousness, and even obscured to that of
the philosophic looker-on. These subordinate peculiarities will depend first on the peculiar genius, idea and
work of the nation, and next on the transient circumstances, geographical, climatic, historical and
secular, to which the nation has been exposed. The
past helped form the circumstances of the present age,
and they the character of the men now living. Thus
new modifications of the national type continually take
place; new variations are played, but on the same old
strings and of the same old tune. Once circumstances
made the Hebrews entirely pastoral, now as completely
commercial; but the same trust in God, the same
national exclusiveness, appear as of old. As one looks
at the history of the Ionians, Romans, Saxons, he sees
unity of national character, a continuity of idea and of
work; but it appears in the midst of variety, for while
these remained ever the same to complete the economy
of the world, subordinate qualities — sentiments, ideas,
actions — changed to suit the passing hour. The
nation's *course* was laid towards a certain point, but

they stood to the right hand or the left, they sailed
with much canvas or little, and swift or slow, as the
winds and waves compelled: nay, sometimes the national
ship "heaves to," and lies with her "head to the
wind," regardless of her destination; but when the
storm is overblown resumes her course. Men will care-
lessly think the ship has no certain aim, but only
drifts.

The most marked characteristic of the American
nation is love of freedom; of man's natural rights.
This is so plain to a student of American history, or
of American politics, that the point requires no argu-
ing. We have a genius for liberty: the American
idea is freedom, natural rights. Accordingly, the
work providentially laid out for us to do seems this,—
to organize the rights of man. This is a problem
hitherto unattempted on a national scale, in human
history. Often enough attempts have been made to
organize the powers of priests, kings, nobles, in a
theocracy, monarchy, oligarchy, powers which had no
foundation in human duties or human rights, but solely
in the selfishness of strong men. Often enough have
the mights of men been organized, but not the rights
of man. Surely there has never been an attempt made
on a national scale to organize the rights of man as
man; rights resting on the nature of things; rights
derived from no conventional compact of men with
men; not inherited from past generations, nor received from parliaments and kings, nor secured by
their parchments; but rights that are derived straightway from God, the Author of duty and the Source
of right, and which are secured in the great charter
of our being.

At first view it will be said, the peculiar genius of

America is not such, nor such her fundamental idea, nor that her destined work. It is true that much of the national conduct seems exceptional when measured by that standard, and the nation's course as crooked as the Rio Grande; it is true that America sometimes seems to spurn liberty, and sells the freedom of three million men for less than three million annual bales of cotton; true, she often tramples, knowingly, consciously, tramples on the most unquestionable and sacred rights. Yet, when one looks through the whole character and history of America, spite of the exceptions, nothing comes out with such relief as this love of freedom, this idea of liberty, this attempt to organize rights. There are numerous subordinate qualities which conflict with the nation's idea and work, coming from our circumstances, not our soul, as well as many others which help the nation perform her providential work. They are signs of the times, and it is important to look carefully among the most prominent of them, where, indeed, one finds striking contradictions.

The first is an impatience of authority. Every thing must render its reason, and show cause for its being. We will not be commanded, at least only by such as we choose to obey. Does some one say, " Thou shalt," or " Thou shalt not," we ask, " Who are you? " Hence comes a seeming irreverence. The shovel hat, the symbol of authority, which awed our fathers, is not respected unless it covers a man, and then it is the man we honor, and no longer the shovel hat. " I will complain of you to the government! " said a Prussian nobleman to a Yankee stage-driver, who uncivilly threw the nobleman's trunk to the top of the coach. " Tell the government to go to the devil! " was the symbolical reply.

Old precedents will not suffice us, for we want something anterior to all precedents; we go beyond what is written, asking the cause of the precedent and the reason of the writing. "Our fathers did so," says some one. "What of that?" say we. "Our fathers — they were giants, were they? Not at all, only great boys, and we are not only taller than they, but mounted on their shoulders to boot, and see twice as far. My dear wise man, or wiseacre, it is we that are the ancients, and have forgotten more than all our fathers knew. We will take their wisdom joyfully, and thank God for it, but not their authority, we know better; of their nonsense not a word. It was very well that they lived, and it is very well that they are dead. Let them keep decently buried, for respectable dead men never walk."

Tradition does not satisfy us. The American scholar has no folios in his library. The antiquary unrolls his codex, hid for eighteen hundred years in the ashes of Herculaneum, deciphers its fossil wisdom, telling us what great men thought in the bay of Naples, and two thousand years ago. "What do you tell of that for?" is the answer to his learning. "What has Pythagoras to do with the price of cotton? You may be a very learned man; you can read the hieroglyphics of Egypt, I dare say, and know so much about the Pharaohs, it is a pity you had not lived in their time, when you might have been good for something; but you are too old-fashioned for our business, and may return to your dust." An eminent American, a student of Egyptian history, with a scholarly indignation declared, "There is not a man who cares to know whether Shoophoo lived one thousand years before Christ, or three."

The example of other and ancient States does not terrify or instruct us. If slavery were a curse to Athens, the corruption of Corinth, the undoing of Rome, and all history shows it was so, we will learn no lesson from that experience, for we say, "We are not Athenians, men of Corinth, nor pagan Romans, thank God, but free Republicans, Christians of America. We live in the nineteenth century, and though slavery worked all that mischief then and there, we know how to make money out of it, twelve hundred millions of dollars, as Mr. Clay counts the cash." [1]

The example of contemporary nations furnishes us little warning or guidance. We will set our own precedents, and do not like to be told that the Prussians or the Dutch have learned some things in the education of the people before us, which we shall do well to learn after them. So when a good man tells us of their schools and their colleges, " patriotic " schoolmasters exclaim, " It is not true; our schools are the best in the world! But if it were true, it is unpatriotic to say so; it aids and comforts the enemy." Jonathan knows little of war; he has heard his grandfather talk of Lexington and Saratoga; he thinks he should like to have a little touch of battle on his own acount: so when there is difficulty in setting up the fence betwixt his estate and his neighbor's, he blusters for awhile, talks big, and threatens to strike his father; but, not having quite the stomach for that experiment, falls to beating his other neighbor, who happens to be poor, weak, and of a sickly constitution; and when he beats her at every step,—

> " For 'tis no war, as each one knows,
> When only one side deals the blows,
> And t'other bears 'em,"—

VIII—9

Jonathan thinks he has covered himself with "imperishable honors," and sets up his general for a great king. Poor Jonathan — he does not know the misery, the tears, the blood, the shame, the wickedness, and the sin he has set a-going, and which one day he is to account for with God, who forgets nothing!

Yet while we are so unwilling to accept the good principles, to be warned by the fate, or guided by the success, of other nations, we gladly and servilely copy their faults, their follies, their vice and sin. Like all upstarts, we pique ourselves on our imitation of aristocratic ways. How many a blusterer in Congress, — for there are two denominations of blusterers, differing only in degree, your great blusterer in Congress and your little blusterer in a bar-room,— has roared away hours long against aristocratic influence, in favor of the "pure democracy," while he played the oligarch in his native village, the tyrant over his hired help, and though no man knows who his grandfather was, spite of the herald's office, conjures up some trumpery coat of arms! Like a clown, who, by pinching his appetite, has bought a gaudy cloak for Sabbath wearing, we chuckle inwardly at our brave apery of foreign absurdities, hoping that strangers will be astonished at us — which, sure enough, comes to pass. Jonathan is as vain as he is conceited, and expects that the Fiddlers, and the Trollopes, and others who visit us periodically as the swallows, and likewise for what they can catch, shall only extol, or at least stand aghast at the brave spectacle we offer, of "the freest and most enlightened nation in the world;" and if they tell us that we are an ill-mannered set, raw and clownish, that we pick our teeth with a fork, loll back in our chairs, and make our countenance

hateful with tobacco, and that with all our excellences
we are a nation of " rowdies," — why, we are offended,
and our feelings are hurt.   There was an African
chief, long ago, who ruled over a few miserable cabins,
and one day received a French traveller from Paris,
under a tree.   With the exception of a pair of shoes,
our chief was as naked as a pestle, but with great
complacency he asked the traveller, " What do they
say of me at Paris? "

Such is our dread of authority, that we like not old
things; hence we are always a-changing.   Our house
must be new, and our book, and even our church.   So
we choose a material that soon wears out, though it
often outlasts our patience.   The wooden house is an
apt emblem of this sign of the times.   But this love
of change appears not less in important matters.   We
think " Of old things all are over old, of new things
none are new enough."   So the age asks of all institutions their right to be: What right has the
government to existence?   Who gave the majority a
right to control the minority, to restrict trade, levy
taxes, make laws, and all that?   If the nation goes
into a committee of the whole and makes laws, some
little man goes into a committee of one and passes his
counter resolves.   The State of South Carolina is a
nice example of this self-reliance, and this questioning
of all authority.   That little brazen State, which contains only about half so many free white inhabitants
as the single city of New York, but which none the
less claims to have monopolized most of the chivalry
of the nation, and its patriotism, as well as political
wisdom — that chivalrous little State says, " If the
nation does not make laws to suit us; if it does not
allow us to imprison all black seamen from the North;

if it prevents the extension of Slavery wherever we wish to carry it — then the State of South Carolina will nullify, and leave the other nine-and-twenty States to go to ruin!"

Men ask what right have the churches to the shadow of authority which clings to them — to make creeds, and to bind and to loose! So it is a thing which has happened, that when a church excommunicates a young stripling for heresy, he turns round, fulminates his edict, and excommunicates the church. Said a sly Jesuit to an American Protestant at Rome: "But the rites and customs and doctrines of the Catholic church go back to the second century, the age after the apostles!" "No doubt of it," said the American, who had also read the Fathers, "they go back to the times of the apostles themselves; but that proves nothing, for there were as great fools in the first century as the last. A fool or a folly is no better because it is an old folly or an old fool. There are fools enough now, in all conscience. Pray don't go back to prove their apostolical succession."

There are always some men who are born out of due season, men of past ages, stragglers of former generations, who ought to have been born before Dr. Faustus invented printing, but who are unfortunately born now, or, if born long ago, have been fraudulently and illegally concealed by their mothers, and are now, for the first time, brought to light. The age lifts such aged juveniles from the ground, and bids them live, but they are sadly to seek in this day; they are old-fashioned boys; their authority is called in question; their traditions and old-wives' fables are laughed at, at any rate disbelieved; they get profanely elbowed in the crowd — men not knowing their great age and consequent venerableness; the shovel hat though apparently born on their head, is treated with disrespect. The very boys laugh pertly in their face when they speak, and even old men can scarce forbear a smile, though it may be a smile of pity. The age affords such men a place, for it is a catholic age, large-minded, and tolerant,— such a place as it gives to ancient armor, Indian Bibles, and fossil bones of the mastodon; it puts them by in some room seldom used, with other old furniture, and allows them to mumble their anilities by themselves; now and then takes off its hat; looks in, charitably, to keep the mediæval relics in good heart, and pretends to listen, as they discourse of what comes of nothing and goes to it; but in matters which the age cares about, commerce, manufactures, politics, which it cares much for, even in education, which it cares far too little about, it trusts no such counsellors, nor tolerates nor ever affects to listen.

Then there is a philosophical tendency, distinctly visible; a groping after ultimate facts, first principles, and universal ideas. We wish to know first the fact, next the law of that fact, and then the reason of the law. A sign of this tendency is noticeable in the titles of books; we have no longer " treatises " on the eye, the ear, sleep, and so forth, but in their place we find works professing to treat of the " philosophy " of vision, of sound, of sleep. Even in the pulpits, men speak about the " philosophy " of religion; we have philosophical lectures, delivered to men of little culture, which would have amazed our grandfathers, who thought a shoemaker should never go beyond his last, even to seek for the philosophy of shoes. " What a pity," said a grave Scotchman, in the beginning of this century, "to teach the beautiful science of geometry to weavers and cobblers." Here nothing is too good or high for any one tall and good enough to get hold of it. What audiences attended the Lowell lectures in Boston — two or three thousand men, listening to twelve lectures on the philosophy of fish! It would not bring a dollar or a vote, only thought to their minds! Young ladies are well versed in the philosophy of the affections, and understand the theory of attraction, while their grandmothers, good easy souls, were satisfied with the possession of the fact. The circumstance that philosophical lectures get delivered by men like Walker, Agassiz, Emerson, and their coadjutors, men who do not spare abstruseness, get listened to, and even understood, in town and village, by large crowds of men of only the most common culture; this indicates a philosophical tendency, unknown in any other land or age. Our circle of professed scholars, men of culture and learning, is a very small one, while our circle of thinking men is disproportionately large. The best thought of France and Germany finds a readier welcome here than in our parent land: nay, the newest and the best thought of England finds its earliest and warmest welcome in America. It was a little remarkable that Bacon and Newton should be reprinted here, and La Place should have found his translator and expositor coming out of an insurance office in Salem! Men of no great pretensions object to an accomplished and eloquent politician: "That is all very well; he made us cry and laugh, but the discourse was not philosophical; he never tells us the reason of the thing; he seems not only not to know it, but not to know that there *is* a reason for the thing, and if not, what is the use of this

bobbing on the surface?" Young maidens complain
of the minister, that he has no philosophy in his sermons, nothing but precepts, which they could read in
the Bibles as well as he; perhaps in heathen Seneca.
He does not feed their souls.

One finds this tendency where it is least expected:
there is a philosophical party in politics, a very small
party it may be, but an actual one.   They aim to get
at everlasting ideas and universal laws, not made by
man, but by God, and for man, who only finds them;
and from them they aim to deduce all particular enactments, so that each statute in the code shall represent
a fact in the universe; a point of thought in God;
so, indeed, that legislation shall be divine in the same
sense that a true system of astronomy is divine — or the
Christian religion — the law corresponding to a fact.
Men of this party, in New England, have more ideas
than precedents, are spontaneous more than logical;
have intuitions, rather than intellectual convictions,
arrived at by the process of reasoning.   They think it
is not philosophical to take a young scoundrel and
shut him up with a party of old ones, for his amendment; not philosophical to leave children with no
culture, intellectual, moral, or religious, exposed to the
temptations of a high and corrupt civilization, and
then, when they go astray — as such barbarians needs
must, in such temptations — to hang them by the neck
for the example's sake.   They doubt if war is a more
philosophical mode of getting justice between two nations, than blows to settle a quarrel between two men.
In either case they do not see how it follows that he
who can strike the hardest blow is always in the right.
In short, they think that judicial murder, which is
hanging, and national murder, which is war, are not

more philosophical than homicide, which one man commits on his own private account.

Theological sects are always the last to feel any popular movement. Yet all of them, from the Episcopalians to the Quakers, have each a philosophical party, which bids fair to outgrow the party which rests on precedent and usage, to overshadow and destroy it. The Catholic church itself, though far astern of all the sects, in regard to the great movements of the age, shares this spirit, and abroad, if not here, is well nigh rent asunder by the potent medicine which this new Daniel of philosophy has put into its mouth. Everywhere in the American churches there are signs of a tendency to drop all that rests merely on tradition and hearsay, to cling only to such facts as bide the test of critical search, and such doctrines as can be verified in human consciousness here and to-day. Doctors of divinity destroy the faith they once preached.

True, there are antagonistic tendencies; for, soon as one pole is developed, the other appears; objections are made to philosophy, the old cry is raised —" Infidelity," " Denial," " Free-thinking." It is said that philosophy will corrupt the young men, will spoil the old ones, and deceive the very elect. " Authority and tradition," say some, " are all we need consult; reason must be put down, or she will soon ask terrible questions." There is good cause for these men warring against reason and philosophy; it is purely in self-defense. But this counsel and that cry come from those quarters before mentioned, where the men of past ages have their place, where the forgotten is re-collected, the obsolete preserved, and the useless held in esteem. The counsel is not dangerous; the bird of night, who

overstays his hour, is only troublesome to himself, and
was never known to hurt a dovelet or a mouseling
after sunrise.   In the night only is the owl destructive.
Some of those who thus cry out against this tendency,
are excellent men in their way, and highly useful, valuable as conveyancers of opinions.   So long as there are
men who take opinions as real estate, " to have and
to hold for themselves and their heirs for ever," why
should there not be such conveyancers of opinions, as
well as of land?   And as it is not the duty of the latter
functionary to ascertain the quality or the value of the
land, but only its metes and bounds, its appurtenances,
and the title thereto; to see if the grantor is regularly
seized and possessed thereof, and has good right to
convey and devise the same, and to make sure that the
whole conveyance is regularly made out — so is it with
these conveyancers of opinion; so should it be, and
they are valuable men.   It is a good thing to know
that we hold, under Scotus, and Ramus, and Albertus
Magnus, who were regularly seized of this or that
opinion.   It gives an absurdity the dignity of a relic.
Sometimes these worthies, who thus oppose reason and
her kin, seem to have a good deal in them, and, when
one examines, he finds more than he looked for.   They
are like a nest of boxes from Hingham and Nurem-
burg, you open one, and behold another; that, and lo!
a third.   So you go on, opening and opening, and
finding and finding, till at last you come to the heart
of the matter, and then you find a box that is very
little, and entirely empty.

Yet, with all this tendency — and it is now so strong
that it cannot be put down, nor even howled down,
much as it may be howled over — there is a lamentable
want of first principles, well known and established;

we have rejected the authority of tradition, but not yet accepted the authority of truth and justice. We will not be treated as striplings, and are not old enough to go alone as men. Accordingly, nothing seems fixed. There is a perpetual see-sawing of opposite principles. Somebody said ministers ought to be ordained on horseback, because they are to remain so short a time in one place. It would be as emblematic to inaugurate American politicians, by swearing them on a weathercock. The great men of the land have as many turns in their course as the Euripus or the Missouri. Even the facts given in the spiritual nature of man are called in question. An eminent Unitarian divine regards the existence of God as a matter of opinion, thinks it cannot be demonstrated, and publicly declares that it is " not a certainty." Some American Protestants no longer take the Bible as the standard of ultimate appeal, yet venture not to set up in that place reason, conscience, the soul getting help of God; others, who affect to accept the Scripture as the last authority, yet, when questioned as to their belief in the miraculous and divine birth of Jesus of Nazareth, are found unable to say yes or no, not having made up their minds.

In politics, it is not yet decided whether it is best to leave men to buy where they can buy cheapest, and sell where they can sell dearest, or to restrict that matter.

It was a clear case to our fathers, in '76, that all men were " created equal," each with " unalienable rights." That seemed so clear, that reasoning would not make it appear more reasonable; it was taken for granted, as a self-evident proposition. The whole nation said so. Now, it is no strange thing to find it said that negroes are not "created equal" in unalienable rights with white men. Nay, in the Senate of the United States, a famous man declares all this talk a dangerous mistake. The practical decision of the nation looks the same way. So, to make our theory accord with our practice, we ought to recommit the Declaration to the hands which drafted that great State paper, and instruct Mr. Jefferson to amend the document, and declare that "All men are created equal, and endowed by their Creator with certain unalienable rights, if born of white mothers; but if not, not."

In this lack of first principles, it is not settled in the popular consciousness that there is such a thing as an absolute right, a great law of God, which we are to keep, come what will come. So the nation is not upright, but goes stooping. Hence, in private affairs, law takes the place of conscience, and, in public, might of right. So the bankrupt pays his shilling in the pound, and gets his discharge, but afterwards, becoming rich, does not think of paying the other nineteen shillings. He will tell you the law is his conscience; if that be satisfied, so is he. But you will yet find him letting money at one or two per cent. a month, contrary to law; and then he will tell you that paying a debt is a matter of law, while letting money is only a matter of conscience. So he rides either indifferently — now the public hack, and now his own private nag, according as it serves his turn.

So a rich State borrows money and "repudiates" the debt, satisfying its political conscience, as the bankrupt his commercial conscience, with the notion that there is no absolute right; that expediency is the only justice, and that King People can do no wrong.

No calm voice of indignation cries out from the pulpit and the press, and the heart of the people, to shame the repudiators into decent morals; because it is not settled in the popular mind that there is any absolute right. Then, because we are strong and the Mexicans weak, because we want their land for a slave-pasture, and they cannot keep us out of it, we think that is reason enough for waging an infamous war of plunder. Grave men do not ask about "the natural justice" of such an undertaking, only about its cost. Have we not seen an American Congress vote a plain lie, with only sixteen dissenting voices in the whole body; has not the head of the nation continually repeated that lie; and do not both parties, even at this day, sustain the vote?

Now and then there rises up an honest man, with a great Christian heart in his bosom, and sets free a score or two of slaves inherited from his father; watches over and tends them in their new-found freedom: or another, who, when legally released from payment of his debts, restores the uttermost farthing. We talk of this and praise it, as an extraordinary thing. Indeed it is so; justice is an unusual thing, and such men deserve the honor they thus win. But such praise shows that such honesty is a rare honesty. The Northern man, born on the battle-ground of freedom, goes to the South and becomes the most tyrannical of slave-drivers. The son of the Puritan, bred up in austere ways, is sent to Congress to stand up for truth and right, but he turns out a "dough-face," and betrays the duty he went to serve. Yet he does not lose his place, for every dough-faced representative has a dough-faced constituency to back him.

It is a great mischief that comes from lacking first

principles, and the worst part of it comes from lacking first principles in morals. Thereby our eyes are holden so that we see not the great social evils all about us. We attempt to justify slavery, even to do it in the name of Jesus Christ. The Whig party of the North loves slavery; the Democratic party does not even seek to conceal its affection therefor. A great politician declares the Mexican War wicked, and then urges men to go and fight it; he thinks a famous general not fit to be nominated for President, but then invites men to elect him. Politics are national morals, the morals of Thomas and Jeremiah, multiplied by millions. But it is not decided yet that honesty is the best policy for a politician; it is thought that the best policy is honesty; at least as near it as the times will allow. Many politicians seem undecided how to turn, and so sit on the fence between honesty and dishonesty. Mr. Facing-bothways is a popular politician in America just now, sitting on the fence between honesty and dishonesty, and, like the blank leaf between the Old and New Testaments, belonging to neither dispensation. It is a little amusing to a trifler to hear a man's fitness for the Presidency defended on the ground that he has no definite convictions or ideas!

There was once a man who said he always told a lie when it would serve his special turn. It is a pity he went to his own place long ago. He seemed born for a party politician in America. He would have had a large party, for he made a great many converts before he died, and left a numerous kindred busy in the editing of newspapers, writing addresses for the people, and passing " resolutions."

It must strike a stranger as a little odd that a republic should have a slaveholder for President five-sixths of the time, and most of the important offices be monopolized by other slaveholders; a little surprising that all the pulpits and most of the presses should be in favor of slavery, at least not against it. But such is the fact. Everybody knows the character of the American government for some years past, and of the American parties in politics. " Like master, like man," used to be a true proverb in old England, and " like people, like ruler," is a true proverb in America; true now. Did a decided people ever choose dough-faces? — a people that loved God and man, choose representatives that cared for neither truth nor justice? Now and then, for dust gets into the brightest eyes; but did they ever choose such men continually? The people are always fairly represented; our representatives do actually represent us, and in more senses than they are paid for. Congress and the Cabinet are only two thermometers hung up in the capital, to show the temperature of the national morals.

But amid this general uncertainty there are two capital maxims which prevail amongst our hucksters of politics: to love your party better than your country, and yourself better than your party. There are, it is true, real statesmen amongst us, men who love justice and do the right; but they seem lost in the mob of vulgar politicians and the dust of party editors.

Since the nation loves freedom above all things, the name democracy is a favorite name. No party could live a twelvemonth that should declare itself anti-democratic. Saint and sinner, statesman and politician, alike love the name. So it comes to pass that there are two things which bear that name; each has

its type and its motto. The motto of one is, " You
are as good as I, and let us help one another." That
represents the democracy of the Declaration of Independence, and of the New Testament; its type is
a free school, where children of all ranks meet under the
guidance of intelligent and Christian men, to be educated in mind, and heart, and soul. The other has for
its motto, " I am as good as you, so get out of my way."
Its type is the bar-room of a tavern — dirty, offensive,
stained with tobacco, and full of drunken, noisy,
quarrelsome " rowdies," just returned from the
Mexican War, and ready for a " buffalo hunt," for
privateering, or to go and plunder any one who is
better off than themselves, especially if also better.
That is not exactly the democracy of the Declaration,
or of the New Testament; but of — no matter whom.

Then, again, there is a great intensity of life and
purpose. This displays itself in our actions and
speeches; in our speculations; in the " revivals " of the
more serious sects; in the excitements of trade; in the
general character of the people. All that we do we
overdo. It appears in our hopefulness; we are the
most aspiring of nations. Not content with half the
continent, we wish the other half. We have this
characteristic of genius: we are dissatisfied with all
that we have done. Somebody once said we were too
vain to be proud. It is not wholly so; the national
idea is so far above us that any achievement seems
little and low. The American soul passes away from
its work soon as it is finished. So the soul of each
great artist refuses to dwell in his finished work, for
that seems little to his dream. Our fathers deemed the
Revolution a great work; it was once thought a surprising thing to found that little colony on the shores

of New England; but young America looks to other revolutions, and thinks she has many a Plymouth colony in her bosom. If other nations wonder at our achievements, we are a disappointment to ourselves, and wonder we have not done more. Our national idea out-travels our experience, and all experience. We began our national career by setting all history at defiance — for that said, " A republic on a large scale cannot exist." Our progress since has shown that we were right in refusing to be limited by the past. The political ideas of the nation are transcendant, not empirical. Human history could not justify the Declaration of Independence and its large statements of the new idea: the nation went behind human history and appealed to human nature.

We are more spontaneous than logical; we have ideas, rather than facts or precedents. We dream more than we remember, and so have many orators and poets, or poetasters, with but few antiquaries and general scholars. We are not so reflective as forecasting. We are the most intuitive of modern nations. The very party in politics which has the least culture, is richest in ideas which will one day become facts. Great truths — political, philosophical, religious — lie a-burning in many a young heart which cannot legitimate nor prove them true, but none the less feels, and feels them true. A man full of new truths finds a ready audience with us. Many things which come disguised as truths under such circumstances pass current for a time, but by and by their bray discovers them. The hope which comes from this intensity of life and intuition of truths is a national characteristic. It gives courage, enterprise, and strength. They can who think they can. We are confident in our star;

other nations may see it or not, we know it is there
above the clouds.   We do not hesitate at rash experiments — sending fifty thousand soldiers to conquer a
nation with eight or nine millions of people.   We are
up to everything, and think ourselves a match for anything.   The young man is rash, for he only hopes, having little to remember; he is excitable, and loves excitement; change of work is his repose; he is hot and
noisy, sanguine and fearless with the courage that
comes from warm blood and ignorance of dangers;
he does not know what a hard, tough, sour old world
he·is born into.   We are a nation of young men.   We
talked of annexing Texas and northern Mexico, and
did both; now we grasp at Cuba, Central America,—
all the continent,— and speak of a railroad to the
Pacific as a trifle for us to accomplish.   Our national
deeds are certainly great, but our hope and promise
far outbrags them all.

If this intensity of life and hope has its good side,
it has also its evil; with much of the excellence of
youth we have its faults — rashness, haste, and superficiality.   Our work is seldom well done.   In English manufactures there is a certain solid honesty of
performance; in the French a certain air of elegance
and refinement: one misses both these in American
works.   It is said America invents the most machines,
but England builds them best.   We lack the phlegmatic
patience of older nations.   We are always in a hurry,
morning, noon, and night.   We are impatient of the
process, but greedy of the result; so that we make
short experiments but long reports, and talk much
though we say little.   We forget that a sober method
is a short way of coming to the end, and that he who,
before he sets out, ascertains where he is going and
VIII—10

the way thither, ends his journey more prosperously than one who settles these matters by the way. Quickness is a great desideratum with us. It is said an American ship is known far off at sea by the quantity of canvas she carries. Rough and ready is a popular attribute. Quick and off would be a symbolic motto for the nation at this day, representing one phase of our character. We are sudden in deliberation; the "one-hour rule" works well in Congress. A committee of the British Parliament spends twice or thrice our time in collecting facts, understanding and making them intelligible, but less than our time in speech-making after the report; speeches there commonly being for the purpose of facilitating the business, while here one sometimes is half ready to think, notwithstanding our earnestness, that the business is to facilitate the speaking. A State revises her statutes with a rapidity that astonishes a European. Yet each revision brings some amendment, and what is found good in the constitution or laws of one State gets speedily imitated by the rest; each new State of the North becoming more democratic than its predecessor.

We are so intent on our purpose that we have no time for amusement. We have but one or two festivals in the year, and even then we are serious and reformatory. Jonathan thinks it a very solemn thing to be merry. A Frenchman said we have but two amusements in America — theology for the women and politics for the men; preaching and voting. If this be true, it may help to explain the fact that most men take their theology from their wives, and women politics from their husbands. No nation ever tried the experiment of such abstinence from amusement.

We have no time for sport, and so lose much of the
poetry of life.   All work and no play does not always
make a dull boy, but it commonly makes a hard man.[2]

We rush from school into business early; we hurry
while in business; we aim to be rich quickly, making
a fortune at a stroke, making or losing it twice or
thrice in a lifetime.   " Soft and fair, goes safe and
far," is no proverb to our taste.   We are the most
restless of people.   How we crowd into cars and
steamboats; a locomotive would well typify our fum-
ing, fizzing spirit.   In our large towns life seems to
be only a scamper.   Not satisfied with bustling about
all day, when night comes we cannot sit still, but alone
of all nations have added rockers to our chairs.

All is haste, from the tanning of leather to the
education of a boy, and the old saw holds its edge good
as ever —" the more haste the worse speed."   The
young stripling, innocent of all manner of lore, whom
a judicious father has barreled down in a college, or
law-school, or theological seminary, till his beard be
grown, mourns over the few years he must spend there
awaiting that operation.   His rule is, " to make a
spoon or spoil a horn;" he longs to be out in the
world " making a fortune," or " doing good," as he
calls what his father better names " making noisy work
for repentance, and doing mischief."   So he rushes
into life not fitted, and would fly towards heaven, this
young Icarus, his wings not half fledged.   There
seems little taste for thoroughness.   In our schools as
our farms, we pass over much ground, but pass over it
poorly.

In education the aim is not to get the most we can,
but the least we can get along with.   A ship with over-
much canvas and over-little ballast were no bad

emblem of many amongst us.   In no country is it so
easy to get a reputation for learning — accumulated
thought, because so few devote themselves to that ac-
cumulation.   In this respect our standard is low.   So
a man of one attainment is sure to be honored, but a
man of many and varied abilities is in danger of being
undervalued.   A Spurzheim would be warmly welcomed, while a Humboldt would be suspected of
superficiality, as we have not the standard to judge
him by.   Yet in no country in the world is it so difficult
to get a reputation for eloquence, as many speak, and
that well.   It is surprising with what natural strength
and beauty the young American addresses himself to
speak.   Some hatter's apprentice, or shoemaker's
journeyman, at a temperance or anti-slavery meeting,
will speak words like the blows of an axe, that cut
clean and deep.   The country swarms with orators,
more abundantly where education is least esteemed —
in the West or South.

   We have secured national unity of action for the
white citizens without much curtailing individual
variety of action, so we have at the North pretty well
solved that problem which other nations have so often
boggled over ; we have balanced the centripetal power,
the government and laws, with the centrifugal
power, the mass of individuals, into harmonious pro-
portions.   If one were to leave out of sight the three
million slaves, one-sixth part of the population, the
problem might be regarded as very happily solved.
As the consequences of this, in no country is there more
talent, or so much awake and active.   In the South
this unity is attained by sacrificing all the rights of
three million slaves, and almost all the rights of the
other colored population.   In despotic countries this

unity is brought about by the sacrifice of freedom, individual variety of action, in all except the despot and his favorites; so, much of the nation's energy is stifled in the chains of the State, while here it is friendly to institutions which are friendly to it, goes to its work, and approves itself in the vast increase of wealth and comfort throughout the North, where there is no class of men which is so oppressed that it cannot rise. One is amazed at the amount of ready skill and general ability which he finds in all the North, where each man has a little culture, takes his newspaper, manages his own business, and talks with some intelligence of many things — especially of politics and theology. In respect to this general intellectual ability and power of self-help, the mass of people seem far in advance of any other nation. But at the same time our scholars, who always represent the nation's higher modes of consciousness, will not bear comparison with the scholars of England, France, and Germany, men thoroughly furnished for their work. This is a great reproach and mischief to us, for we need most accomplished leaders, who by their thought can direct this national intensity of life. Our literature does not furnish them; we have no great men there; Irving, Channing, Cooper, are not names to conjure with in literature. One reads thick volumes devoted to the poets of America, or her prose writers, and finds many names which he wonders he never heard of before; but when he turns over their works, he finds consolation and recovers his composure.

American literature may be divided into two departments: the permanent literature, which gets printed in books, that sometimes reach more than one edition; and the evanescent literature, which appears only in

the form of speeches, pamphlets, reviews, newspaper
articles, and the like extempore productions. Now our
permanent literature, as a general thing, is superficial,
tame, and weak; it is not American; it has not our
ideas, our contempt of authority, our philosophical
turn, nor even our uncertainty as to first principles,
still less our national intensity, our hope, and fresh
intuitive perceptions of truth. It is a miserable imitation. Love of freedom is not there. The real
national literature is found almost wholly in speeches,
pamphlets, and newspapers. The latter are pretty
thoroughly American: mirrors in which we see no very
flattering likeness of our morals or our manners.
Yet the picture is true: that vulgarity, that rant, that
bragging violence, that recklessness of truth and
justice, that disregard of right and duty, are a part
of the nation's everyday life. Our newspapers are
low and " wicked to a fault;" only in this weakness
are they un-American. Yet they exhibit, and
abundantly, the four qualities we have mentioned as
belonging to the signs of our times. As a general
rule, our orators are also American, with our good
and ill. Now and then one rises who has studied
Demosthenes in Leland or Francis, and got a second-
hand acquaintance with old models: a man who uses
literary commonplaces, and thinks himself original
and classic because he can quote a line or so of Horace,
in a western House of Representatives, without
getting so many words wrong as his reporter; but
such men are rare, and after making due abatement
for them, our orators all over the land are pretty
thoroughly American, a little turgid, hot, sometimes
brilliant, hopeful, intuitive, abounding in half truths,
full of great ideas, often inconsequent; sometimes

coarse; patriotic, vain, self-confident, rash, strong, and
young-mannish. Of course the most of our speeches
are vulgar, ranting, and worthless; but we have produced some magnificient specimens of oratory, which
are fresh, original, American, and brand-new.

The more studied, polished, and elegant literature is
not so; that is mainly an imitation. It seems not a
thing of native growth. Sometimes, as in Channing,
the thought and the hope are American, but the form
and the coloring old and foreign. We dare not be
original; our American pine must be cut to the trim
pattern of the English yew, though the pine bleed at
every clip. This poet tunes his lyre at the harp of
Goethe, Milton, Pope, or Tennyson. His songs might
be better sung on the Rhine than the Kennebec. They
are not American in form or feeling; they have not
the breath of our air; the smell of our ground is not
in them. Hence our poet seems cold and poor. He
loves the old mythology; talks about Pluto — the
Greek devil, the fates and furies — witches of old time
in Greece, but would blush to use our mythology, or
breathe the name in verse of our devil, or our own
witches, lest he should be thought to believe what he
wrote. The mother and sisters, who with many a
pinch and pain sent the hopeful boy to college, must
turn over the classical dictionary before they can find
out what the youth would be at in his rhymes. Our
poet is not deep enough to see that Aphrodite came
from the ordinary waters, that Homer only hitched
into rhythm and furnished the accomplishment of
verse to street-talk, nursery tales, and old men's gossip
in the Ionian towns; he thinks what is common is
unclean. So he sings of Corinth and Athens, which he
never saw, but has not a word to say of Boston, and

Fall River, and Baltimore, and New York, which are just as meet for song. He raves of Thermopylæ and Marathon, with never a word for Lexington and Bunker Hill, for Cowpens, and Lundy's Lane, and Bemis's Heights. He loves to tell of the Ilyssus, of "smooth-sliding Mincius, crowned with vocal reeds," yet sings not of the Petapsco, the Susquehanna, the Aroostook, and the Willimantick. He prates of the narcissus and the daisy, never of American dandelions and blue-eyed grass; he dwells on the lark and the nightingale, but has not a thought for the brown thrasher and the bobolink who every morning in June rain down such showers of melody on his affected head. What a lesson Burns teaches us, addressing his "rough bur-thistle," his daisy, "wee crimson tippit thing," and finding marvellous poetry in the mouse whose nest his plough turned over! Nay, how beautifully has even our sweet poet sung of our own Green river, our waterfowl, of the blue and fringed gentian, the glory of autumnal days.

Hitherto, spite of the great reading public, we have no permanent literature which corresponds to the American idea. Perhaps it is not time for that; it must be organized in deeds before it becomes classic in words; but as yet we have no such literature which reflects even the surface of American life, certainly nothing which protrays our intensity of life, our hope, or even our daily doings and drivings, as the Odyssey paints old Greek life, or Don Quixote and Gil Blas portray Spanish life. Literary men are commonly timid; ours know they are but poorly fledged as yet, so dare not fly away from the parent tree, but hop timidly from branch to branch. Our writers love to creep about in the shadow of some old renown, not

venturing to soar away into the unwinged air, to sing
of things here and now, making our life classic. So,
without the grace of high culture, and the energy of
American thought, they become weak, cold, and poor;
are " curious, not knowing, not exact, but nice."
Too fastidious to be wise, too unlettered to be elegant,
too critical to create, they prefer a dull saying that
is old to a novel form of speech, or a natural expression of a new truth. In a single American work,—
and a famous one too,— there are over sixty similes,
not one original, and all poor. A few men, conscious
of this defect, this sin against the holy spirit of
literature, go to the opposite extreme, and are
American-mad; they wilfully talk rude, write in-
numerous verse, and play their harps all jangling, out
of tune. A yet fewer few are American without
madness. One such must not here be passed by, alike
philosopher and bard, in whose writings " ancient wisdom shines with new-born beauty," and who has en-
riched a genius thoroughly American in the best sense,
with a cosmopolitan culture and literary skill, which
were wonderful in any land. But of American literature in general and of him in special, more shall be
said at another time.[3]

Another remarkable feature is our excessive love of
material things. This is more than a utilitarianism, a
preference of the useful over the beautiful. The
Puritan at Plymouth had a corn-field, a cabbage-
garden, and a patch of potatoes, a school-house, and
a church, before he sat down to play the fiddle. He
would have been a fool to reverse this process. It
were poor economy and worse taste to have painters,
sculptors, and musicians, while the rude wants of the
body are uncared for. But our fault in this respect

is that we place too much the charm of life in mere material things,— houses, lands, well-spread tables, and elegant furniture,— not enough in man, in virtue, wisdom, genius, religion, greatness of soul, and nobleness of life. We mistake a perfection of the means of manliness for the end — manhood itself. Yet the housekeeping of a Shakspeare, Milton, Franklin, had only one thing worth boasting of. Strange to say, that was the master of the house. A rich and vulgar man once sported a coach and four, and at its first turn out rode into the great commercial street of a large town in New England. "How fine you must feel with your new coach and four," said one of his old friends, though not quite so rich. "Yes," was the reply, "as fine as a beetle in a gold snuff-box." All of his kindred are not so nice and discriminating in their self-consciousness.

This practical materialism is a great affliction to us. We think a man cannot be poor and great also. So we see a great man sell himself for a little money, and it is thought "a good operation." A conspicuous man, in praise of a certain painter, summed up his judgment with this: "Why, sir, he has made twenty thousand dollars by his pictures." "A good deal more than Michael Angelo, Leonardo, and Raphael together," might have been the reply. But it is easier to weigh purses than artistic skill. It was a characteristic praise bestowed in Boston on a distinguished American writer, that his book brought him more money than any man had ever realized for an original work in this country. "Commerce," said Mr. Pitt, "having got into both houses of Parliament, privilege must be done away,"— the privilege of wit and genius, not less than rank. Clergymen estimate their own and their brothers' importance, not by their apostolical gifts, or even apostolic succession, but by the value of the living.

All other nations have this same fault, it may be said. But there is this difference: in other nations the things of a man are put before the man himself; so a materialism which exalts the accidents of the man — rank, wealth, birth, and the like — above the man, is not inconsistent with the general idea of England or Austria. In America it is a contradiction. Besides, in most civilized countries, there is a class of men living on inherited wealth, who devote their lives to politics, art, science, letters, and so are above the mere material elegance which surrounds them. That class has often inflicted a deep wound on society, which festers long and leads to serious trouble in the system, but at the same time it redeems a nation from the reproach of mere material vulgarity; it has been the source of refinement, and has warmed into life much of the wisdom and beauty which have thence spread over all the world. In America there is no such class. Young men inheriting wealth very rarely turn to anything noble; they either convert their talents into gold, or their gold into furniture, wines, and confectionary. A young man of wealth does not know what to do with himself or it; a rich young woman seems to have no resource but marriage! Yet it must be confessed, that at least in one part of the United States wealth flows freely for the support of public institutions of education.

Here it is difficult for a man of science to live by his thought. Was Bowditch one of the first mathematicians of his age? He must be at the head of an annuity office. If Socrates should set up as a dealer

in money, and outwit the brokers as formerly the
Sophists, and shave notes as skilfully as of old, we
should think him a great man. But if he adopted his
old plan, what should we say of him?

　　Manliness is postponed and wealth preferred.
" What a fine house is this," one often says: " what
furniture; what feasting. But the master of the
house! — why, every stone out of the wall laughs at
him. He spent all of himself in getting this pretty
show together, and now it is empty, and mocks its
owner. He is the emblematic coffin at the Egyptian
feast." " Oh, man!" says the looker-on, " why not
furnish thyself with a mind, and conscience, a heart
and a soul, before getting all this brass and mahogany
together; this beef and these wines?" The poor
wight would answer,—" Why, sir, there were none
such in the market!" The young man does not say,
" I will first of all things be a man, and so being, will
have this thing and the other," putting the agreeable
after the essential. But he says, " First of all, by
hook or by crook, I will have money, the manhood may
take care of itself." He has it,— for tough and hard
as the old world is, it is somewhat fluid before a strong
man who resolutely grapples with difficulty and will
swim through; it can be made to serve his turn. He
has money, but the man has evaporated in the process;
when you look he is not there. True, other nations
have done the same thing, and we only repeat their experiment. The old devil of conformity says to our
American Adam and Eve, " Do this and you shall be
as gods," a promise as likely to hold good as the devil's
did in the beginning. A man was meant for something more than a tassel to a large estate, and a woman
to be more than a rich housekeeper.

With this offensive materialism we copy the vices of feudal aristocracy abroad, making our vulgarity still more ridiculous. We are ambitious or proud of wealth, which is but labor stored up, and at the same time are ashamed of labor, which is wealth in process. With all our talk about democracy, labor is thought less honorable in Boston than in Berlin and Leipsic. Thriving men are afraid their children will be shoemakers, or ply some such honorable and useful craft. Yet little pains are taken to elevate the condition or improve the manners and morals of those who do all the manual work of society. The strong man takes care that his children and himself escape that condition. We do not believe that all stations are alike honorable if honorably filled; we have little desire to equalize the burdens of life, so that there shall be no degraded class; none cursed with work, none with idleness. It is popular to endow a college; vulgar to take an interest in common schools. Liberty is a fact, equality a word, and fraternity, we do not think of yet.

In this struggle for material wealth and the social rank which is based thereon, it is amusing to see the shifting of the scenes; the social aspirations of one, and the contempt with which another rebuts the aspirant. An old man can remember when the most exclusive of men, and the most golden, had scarce a penny in their purse, and grumbled at not finding a place where they would. Now the successful man is ashamed of the steps he rose by. The gentleman who came to Boston half a century ago, with all his worldly goods tied up in a cotton handkerchief, and that not of so large a pattern as are made now-a-days, is ashamed to recollect that his father was a currier, or a blacksmith, or a skipper at Barnstable or Beverly; ashamed, also, of his forty or fifty country cousins, remarkable for nothing but their large hands and their excellent memory. Nay, he is ashamed of his own humble beginnings, and sneers at men starting as he once started. The generation of English " Snobs " came in with the Conqueror, and migrated to America at an early day, where they continue to thrive marvelously — the chief " conservative party " in the land.

Through this contempt for labor, a certain affectation runs through a good deal of American society, and makes our aristocracy vulgar and contemptible. What if Burns had been ashamed of his plough, and Franklin had lost his recollection of the candle-moulds and the composing stick? Mr. Chubbs, who got rich to-day, imitates Mr. Swipes, who got rich yesterday, buys the same furniture, gives similar entertainments, and counts himself " as good a man as Swipes, any day." Nay, he goes a little beyond him, puts his servants in livery, with the " Chubbs' arms " on the button; but the new-found family arms are not descriptive of the character of the Chubbses, or of their origin and history — only of their vanity. Then Mr. Swipes looks down on poor Chubbs, and curls his lip with scorn; calls him a " parvenu," " an upstart," " a plebeian;" speaks of him as one of " that sort of people," " one of your ordinary men;" " thrifty and well off in the world, but a little vulgar." At the same time Mr. Swipes looks up to Mr. Bung, who got rich the day before yesterday, as a gentleman of old family and quite distinguished, and receives from that quarter the same treatment he bestows on his left-hand neighbor. The real gentleman is the same all the

world over. Such are by no means lacking here, while
the pretended gentlemen swarm in America. Chaucer
said a good word long ago:

> " — This is not mine intendément
> To clepen no wight in no age
> Only gentle for his lineáge;
> But whoso that is virtuous,
> And in his port not outragéous:
> When such one thou see'st thee beforn,
> Though he be not gentle born,
> Thou mayest well see this in soth,
> That he is gentle, because he doth
> As 'longeth to a gentleman;
> Of them none other deem I can;
> For certainly withouten drede,
> A churl is deeméd by his deed,
> Of high or low, as ye may see,
> Or of what kindred that he be."

It is no wonder vulgar men, who travel here and
eat our dinners, laugh at this form of vulgarity.
Wiser men see its cause, and prophesy its speedy de-
cay. Every nation has its aristocracy, or controlling
class: in some lands it is permanent, an aristocracy of
blood; men that are descended from distinguished
warriors, from the pirates and freebooters of a rude
age. The nobility of England are proud of their
fathers' deeds, and emblazon the symbols thereof in
their family arms, emblems of barbarism. Ours is an
aristocracy of wealth, not got by plunder, but by toil,
thrift, enterprise; of course it is a movable aristocracy: the first families of the last century are now
forgot, and their successors will give place to new
names. Now earning is nobler than robbing, and
work is before war; but we are ashamed of both, and
seek to conceal the noble source of our wealth. An
aristocracy of gold is far preferable to the old and

immovable nobility of blood, but it has also its peculiar vices: it has the effrontery of an upstart, despises its own ladder, is heartless and lacks noble principle, vulgar and cursing. This lust of wealth, however, does us a service, and gives the whole nation a stimulus which it needs, and, low as the motive is, drives us to continual advancement. It is a great merit for a nation to secure the largest amount of useful and comfortable and beautiful things which can be honestly earned, and used with profit to the body and soul of man. Only when wealth becomes an idol, and material abundance is made the end, not the means, does the love of it become an evil. No nation was ever too rich, or over-thrifty, though many a nation has lost its soul by living wholly for the senses.

Now and then we see noble men living apart from this vulgarity and scramble; some rich, some poor, but both content to live for noble aims, to pinch and spare for virtue, religion, for truth and right. Such men never fail from any age or land, but everywhere they are the exceptional men. Still they serve to keep alive the sacred fire in the hearts of young men, rising amid the common mob as oaks surpass the brambles or the fern.

In these secondary qualities of the people which mark the special signs of the times, there are many contradictions, quality contending with quality; all by no means balanced into harmonious relations. Here are great faults not less than great virtues. Can the national faults be corrected? Most certainly; they are but accidental, coming from our circumstances, our history, our position as a people — heterogeneous, new, and placed on a new and untamed continent. They come not from the nation's soul; they do not belong to our fundamental idea, but are hostile to it. One day our impatience of authority, our philosophical tendency, will lead us to a right method, that to fixed principles, and then we shall have a continuity of national action. Considering the pains taken by the fathers of the better portion of America to promote religion here, remembering how dear is Christianity to the heart of all, conservative and radical — though men often name as Christian what is not — and seeing how truth and right are sure to win at last,— it becomes pretty plain that we shall arrive at true principles, laws of the universe, ideas of God; then we shall be in unison also with it and Him. When that great defect — lack of first principles — is corrected, our intensity of life, with the hope and confidence it inspires, will do a great work for us. We have already secured an abundance of material comforts hitherto unknown; no land was ever so full of corn and cattle, clothing, comfortable houses, and all things needed for the flesh. The desire of those things, even the excessive desire thereof, performs an important part in the divine economy of the human race; nowhere is its good effect more conspicuous than in America, where in two generations the wild Irishman becomes a decent citizen, orderly, temperate, and intelligent. This done or even a-doing, as it is now, we shall go forth to realize our great national idea, and accomplish the great work of organizing into institutions the unalienable rights of man. The great obstacle in the way of that is African slavery — the great exception in the nation's history; the national sin. When that is removed, as soon it must be, lesser but kindred evils will easily be done away; the truth which the land-reformers, which the associationists,

VIII—11

the free-traders and others have seen, dimly or clearly,
can readily be carried out. But while this monster
vice continues, there is little hope of any great and
permanent national reform. The positive things which
we chiefly need for this work, are first, education,
next, education, and then education, a vigorous development of the mind, conscience, affections, religious
power of the whole nation. The method and the
means for that I shall not now discuss.

The organization of human rights, the performance
of human duties, is an unlimited work. If there shall
ever be a time when it is all done, then the race will
have finished its course. Shall the American nation
go on in this work, or pause, turn off, fall, and perish?
To me it seems almost treason to doubt that a glorious
future awaits us. Young as we are, and wicked, we
have yet done something which the world will not let
perish. One day we shall attend more emphatically
to the rights of the hand, and organize labor and skill;
then to the rights of the head, looking after education,
science, literature, and art; and again to the rights of
the heart, building up the State with its laws, society
with its families, the church with its goodness and
piety. One day we shall see that it is a shame, and a
loss, and a wrong, to have a criminal, or an ignorant
man, or a pauper, or an idler, in the land; that the
jail, and the gallows, and the almshouse are a reproach
which need not be. Out of new sentiments and ideas,
not seen as yet, new forms of society will come, free
from the antagonism of races, classes, men — representing the American idea in its length, breadth, depth,
and height, its beauty, and its truth, and then the old
civilization of our time shall seem barbarous and even
savage. There will be an American art commensurate

with our idea and akin to this great continent; not an imitation, but a fresh, new growth. An American literature also must come with democratic freedom, democratic thought, democratic power — for we are not always to be pensioners of other lands, doing nothing but import and quote; a literature with all of German philosophic depth, with English solid sense, with French vivacity and wit, Italian fire of sentiment and soul, with all of Grecian elegance of form, and more than Hebrew piety and faith in God. We must not look for the maiden's ringlets on the baby's brow; we are yet but a girl; the nameless grace of maturity, and womanhood's majestic charm, are still to come. At length we must have a system of education, which shall uplift the humblest, rudest, worst born child in all the land; which shall bring forth and bring up noble men.

An American State is a thing that must also be; a State of free men who give over brawling, resting on industry, justice, love, not on war, cunning, and violence — a State where liberty, equality, and fraternity are deeds as well as words. In its time the American Church must also appear, with liberty, holiness, and love for its watchwords, cultivating reason, conscience, affection, faith, and leading the world's way in justice, peace, and love. The Roman Church has been all men know what and how; the American Church, with freedom for the mind, freedom for the heart, freedom for the soul, is yet to be, sundering no chord of the human harp, but tuning all to harmony. This also must come; but hitherto no one has risen with genius fit to plan its holy walls, conceive its columns, project its towers, or lay its corner-stone. Is it too much to hope all this? Look

at the arena before us — look at our past history.
Hark! there is the sound of many million men, the
trampling of their freeborn feet, the murmuring of
their voice; a nation born of this land that God re-
served so long a virgin earth, in a high day married to
the human race,— rising, and swelling, and rolling on,
strong and certain as the Atlantic tide; they come
numerous as ocean waves when east winds blow, their
destination commensurate with the continent, with
ideas vast as the Mississippi, strong as the Alleghanies,
and awful as Niagara; they come murmuring little of
the past, but, moving in the brightness of their great
idea, and casting its light far on to other lands and
distant days — come to the world's great work, to
organize the rights of man.

V

THE ABOLITION OF SLAVERY BY THE FRENCH REPUBLIC

Mr. Chairman,— The gentleman before me [1] has made an allusion to Rome. Let me also turn to that same city. Underneath the Rome of the emperors, there was another Rome; not seen by the sun, known only to a few men. Above, in the sunlight, stood Rome of the Cæsars, with her markets and her armies, her theaters, her temples, and her palaces, glorious and of marble. A million men went through her brazen gates. The imperial city, she stood there, beautiful and admired, the queen of nations. But underneath all that, in caverns of the earth, in the tombs of dead men, in quarries whence the upper city had been slowly hewn, there was another population, another Rome, with other thoughts; yes, a devout body of men who swore not by the public altars; men whose prayers were forbidden; their worship disallowed, their ideas prohibited, their very lives illegal. Time passed on; and gradually Rome of the pagans disappeared, and Rome of the Christians sat there in her place, on the Seven Hills, and stretched out her scepter over the nations.

So underneath the laws and the institutions of each modern nation, underneath the monarchy and the republic there is another and unseen state, with sentiments not yet become popular, and with ideas not yet confirmed in actions, not organized into institutions, ideas scarcely legal, certainly not respectable. Slowly

165

from its depths comes up this ideal state, the state of the future; and slowly to the eternal deep sinks down the actual state, the state of the present. But sometimes an earthquake of the nations degrades of a sudden the actual; and speedily starts up the ideal kingdom of the future. Such a thing has just come to pass. In France, within five-and-forty days, a new state has arisen from underneath the old. Men, whose words were suppressed, and their ideas reckoned illegal but two months ago, now hold the scepter of five-and-thirty millions of grateful citizens, hold it in clean and powerful hands. A great revolution has taken place; one which will produce effects that we cannot foresee. It is itself the greatest act of this century. God only knows what it will lead to. We are here to express the sympathy of Republicans for a new republic. We are here to rejoice over the rising hopes of the new state, not to exult over the fallen fortunes of the Bourbons. Louis Philippe has done much which we may thank him for. He has kept mainly at peace the fiercest nation in the world; has kept the peace of Europe for seventeen years. Let us thank him for that. He has consolidated the French nation, helped to give them a new unity of thought and unity of action, which they had not before. Perhaps he did not intend all this. Since he has brought it about, let us thank him for it, even if his conduct transcended his intention. But, most of all, I would thank this "Citizen King" for another thing. His greatest lesson is his last. He has shown that five-and-thirty millions of Frenchmen, in this nineteenth century, are only to be ruled by justice and the eternal law of right. We have seen this crafty king, often wise and always cunning, driven from his throne. He was the richest man in Europe, and the embodiment of the idea of modern wealth.   He had an army the best disciplined, probably, in the world, and, as he thought, completely in his power.   He had a Chamber of Peers of his own appointment; a Chamber of Deputies almost of his own election.   He ruled a nation that contained three hundred thousand office-holders, appointed by himself, and only two hundred and forty thousand voters! Who sat so safe as the " Citizen King " on his throne, surrounded by Republican institutions!   So confident was he, as the journals tell, that he bade a friend stop a day or two, "and see how I will put down the people! "   For once, this shrewd calculator reckoned without his host.

Well, we have seen this man, this citizen monarch, who married his children only to kings, rush from his place; his peers and his deputies were unavailing; his office-holders could not sustain him; his army " fraternized with the people;" and he, forgetful of his own children, ignominiously is hustled out of the kingdom, in a street cab, with nothing but a five-franc piece in his pocket.   For the lesson thus taught, let us thank him most of all.

Men tell us it is too soon to rejoice; " perhaps the revolution will not hold;" " it will not last;" " the kings of Europe will put it down."   When a sound, healthy child is born, the friends of the family congratulate the parents then; they do not wait till the child has grown up, and got a beard.   Now this is a live child; it is well born in both senses, comes of good parentage, and gives signs of a good constitution.   Let us rejoice at its birth, and not wait to see if it will grow up.   Let us now baptize it in the crystal fountain of our own hope.

In a great revolution, there are always two things to be looked at, namely, the actions, and the ideas which produce the actions. The actions I will say little of; you have all read of them in the newspapers. Some of the actions were bad. It is not true that all at once the French have become angels. There are low and base men who swarm in the lanes and alleys of Paris; for that great city also is like all capitals, girt about with a belt of misery, of vice, and of crime, eating into her painful loins. It was a bad thing to sack the Tuileries; to burn bridges, and chateaux, and railroad stations. Property is under the insurance of mankind, and the human race must pay in public for private depredations. It was a bad thing to kill men; the human race cannot make up that loss; only suffer and be penitent. I am sorry for these bad actions; but I am not surprised at them. You cannot burn down the poor dwelling of a widow in Boston, but some miserable man will steal pot or pan, in the confusion of the fire. How much more should we expect pillage and violence in the earthquake which throws down a king!

I have said enough of the action; but there was one deed too symbolical to be passed by. In the garden of the Tuileries, before the great gate of the palace, there stands a statue of Spartacus, a colossal bronze, his broken chain in the left hand, his Roman sword in the right. Spartacus was a Roman gladiator. He broke his chains; gathered about him other gladiators, fugitive slaves, and assembled an army. He and his comrades fought for freedom; they cut off four consular armies sent against them; at last the hero fell amid a heap of men, slain by his own well-practised hand. When the people took the old and emblematic French throne, and burned it solemnly with emblematic fire, they stripped off some of the crimson trappings of the royal seat, made a tiara thereof, and bound it on the gladiator's brazen head! But red is the color of revolution, the color of blood; the unconscious gladiator was an image too savage for new France. So they hid the Roman sword in his hand, and wreathed it all over with a chaplet of flowers!

Let us say a word of the ideas. Three ideas filled the minds of the nation: the idea of liberty, equality, and fraternity. Three noble words. Liberty meant liberty of all. So, at one word, they set free the slaves, and, if my friend's ciphers are correct, at once three hundred thousand souls rise up from the ground disenthralled, freemen. That is a great act. A population as large as the whole family of our sober sister Connecticut all at once find their chains drop off, and they are free: not beasts, but men. This may not hold. Our Declaration of Independence was not the Confederation of '78 — still less was it the Constitution of '87. The French may be as false as the Americans to their idea of liberty. At any rate, it is a good beginning. Let us rejoice at that.

Equality means that all are equal before the law; equal in rights, however unequal in mights. So all titles of nobility came at once to the ground. The royal family is like the family of our Presidents. The Chamber of Peers is abolished. Universal suffrage is decreed; all men over twenty-one are voters. Men here in America say, " The French are not ready for that." No doubt the king thought so. At any rate, he was not ready for it. But it is not a thing altogether unknown in France. It has been tried several

times before. The French Constitution was accepted
by the whole people in 1800; Napoleon was made
Consul by the whole people; made Emperor by the
whole people. Even in 1815, the " acte additionelle "
to the " Charte " was accepted by the whole people.
To decree universal suffrage was the most natural
thing in the world. Those two ideas, liberty and
equality, have long been American ideas; they were
never American facts. America sought liberty only
for the whites. Our fathers thought not of universal
suffrage.

But France has not only attempted to make our
ideas into facts; she has advanced an idea not hinted
at in the American Declaration; the idea of fraternity.
By this she means human brotherhood. This points
not merely to a political, but to a social revolution.
It is not easy for us to understand how a government
can effect this. Here, all comes from the people, and
the people have to take care of the government, meaning thereby the men in official power; have to furnish
them with ideas, and tell them what application to
make thereof. There all comes from the government.
So the new provisional government of France must
be one that can lead the nation; have ideas in advance
of the nation. Accordingly, it proposes many plans
which with us could never have come from any party
in power. Here, the government is only the servant
of the people. There, it aims to be the father and
teacher thereof; a patriarchal government with Christian thoughts and feelings. But as an eloquent man
is to come after me, whose special aim is to develop
the idea of human brotherhood into social institutions,
I will not dwell on this, save to mention an act of the
provisional authorities. They have abolished the pun-

ishment of death for all political offenses.   You remember the guillotine, the massacres of September, the
drowning in the Loire and the Seine, the dreadful
butchery in the name of the law.

Put this new decree side by side with the old, and
you see why Spartacus, though crowned by a revolution, bears peaceful blossoms in his hand.

But let us hasten on; time would fail me to speak
of the cause or point out the effect of this movement
of the people.   Only a word concerning the objections
made to it.   Some say, " It is only an extempore affair.
Men drunk with new power are telling their fancies,
and trying in their heat to make laws thereof."   It is
not so.   The ideas I have hinted at have been long
known and deeply cherished by the best minds in
France. Last autumn, M. Lamartine, in his own
newspaper, for the deputy for Macon is an editor,
published the programme and confession of his political faith.[2]

Others say, " The whole thing seems rash."   Well,
so it does; so does any good thing seem rash to all
except the man who does it, and such as would do it
if he did not.   What is rash to one is not to another.
It is dangerous for an old man to run, fatal for him
to leap, while his grandson jumps over wall and ditch
without hurt.   The American Revolution was a rash
act; the English Revolution a rash act; the Protestant Reformation was a rash act.   Was it safe to
withstand the Revolution?   Did the king of the French
find it so?   Yet others say, " The leaders are unknown."   " Lamartine, you might as well put any
man in the street at the head of the nation."   But
when the American Revolution began, who, in England, had ever heard of John Hancock, president of

the Congress? To the men who knew him, John Hancock was a country trader, the richest man in a town of ten thousand inhabitants: that did not sound very great at London. Samuel Adams, and John Adams, and Thomas Jefferson, and all the other men, what did the world know of them? Only that they had been christened with Hebrew names. Why, George Washington was only, as Gen. Braddock called him, " A young buckskin." But the world heard of these men afterwards. Let us leave the French statesmen to make to the future what report of themselves they can! Let me tell a story of Dupont de l'Eure, the head of the government at this moment. He was one of the movers of the Revolution of 1830. He dined with the " Citizen King," once, in some council. At the table, he and the king differed; the king affirmed, and Dupont denied. Said the king, " Do you tell me I lie? " Said Dupont, " When the king says yes, and Dupont de l'Eure replies no, France will know which to believe! " The king said, " Yes, we will put the people down;" Dupont said, " No, you shall not put the people down;" and now France knows which to believe.

Again, say others yet, " War may come; royalty may come back, despotism may come back. Other kings will interpose, and put down a republic." Other kings interpose to put down the French! Perhaps they will. They tried it in 1793, but did not like the experiment very well. They will be well off if they do not find it necessary to put down a republic a little nearer at hand; their anti-revolutionary work may begin at home. War followed the American Revolution. It cost money, it cost men. But if we calculate the value of American ideas, they are worth what they cost. Even the French Revolution, with all its carnage, robbery, and butchery, is worth what it cost. But it is possible that war will not come. From a foreign war France has little to fear. There seems little danger that it will come at all. What monarchy will dare fight republican France? Internal trouble may indeed come. It is to be expected that the new republic will make many a misstep. But is it likely that all the old tragedies will be enacted again? Surely not; the burnt child dreads the fire. Besides, the France of '48 is not the France of '89. There is no triple despotism weighing on the nation's neck, a trinity of despotic powers — the throne, the nobility, the church. The king has fled; the nobles have ceased to be; the church seems republican. There is no hatred between class and class, as before. The men of '89 sought freedom for the middle class, not for all classes, neither for the high, nor for the low. Religion pervades the church and the people, as never before. Better ideas prevail. It is not the gospel of Jean Jaques, and the scoffing negations of Voltaire, that are now proclaimed to the people; but the broad maxims of Christian men; the words of human brotherhood. The men of terror knew no weapon but the sword; the provisional government casts the sword from its hands, and will not shed blood for political crimes.

Still, troubles may come; war may come from without, and, worse still, from within; the republic may end. But if it lasts only a day, let us rejoice in that day. Suppose it is only a dream of the nation; it is worth while to dream of liberty, of equality, of fraternity; and to dream that we are awake and trying to make them all into institutions and common life. What is only a dream now, will be a fact at last.

Next Sunday is the election day of France; six millions of voters are to choose nine hundred representatives! Shall not the prayers of all Christian hearts go up with them on that day, a great deep prayer for their success? The other day, the birthday of Washington, the calm, noiseless spirit of death came to release the soul of the patriarch of American statesmen. While his son was slowly sinking in the western sky, the life-star of a new nation was visibly rising there, far off in the east. A pagan might be pardoned for the thought, that the intrepid soul of that old man foresaw the peril, and, slowly quitting its hold of the worn-out body, went thither to kindle anew the flames of liberty he fanned so often here.[3] That is but a pagan thought. This is a Christian thought: The same God who formed the world for man's abode, presides also in the movements of mankind, and directs their voluntary march. See how this earth has been brought to her present firm and settled state. By storm and earthquake continent has been rent from continent; oceans have swept over the mountains, and the scars of ancient war still mark our parent's venerable face. So is it in the growth of human society: it is the child of pain; revolutions have rocked its cradle, war and violence rudely nursed it into hardy life. Good institutions, how painfully, how slowly have they come!

> " Slowly as spreads the green of earth
>   O'er the receding ocean's bed,
>   Dim as the distant stars come forth,
>   Uncertain as a vision, slow,
>   Has been the old world's toiling pace,
>   Ere she can give fair freedom place."

Let us welcome the green spot, when it begins to

spread; let us shout as the sterile sea of barbarism goes back; let us rejoice in the vision of good things to come; let us welcome the distant and rising orb, for it is the Bethlehem star of a great nation, and they who behold it may well say —" Peace on earth, and good-will to men."

VI

THE ANTI-SLAVERY CONVENTION

The design of the abolitionists is this,— to remove and destroy the institution of slavery. To accomplish this well, two things are needed, ideas and actions. Of the ideas first, and then a word of the actions.

What is the idea of the abolitionists? Only this: that all men are created free, endowed with unalienable rights; and in respect of those rights, that all men are equal. This is the idea of Christianity, of human nature. Of course, then, no man has a right to take away another's rights; of course no man may use me for his good, and not my own good also; of course there can be no ownership of man by man; of course no slavery in any form. Such is the idea, and some of the most obvious doctrines that follow from it.

Now, the abolitionists aim to put this idea into the minds of the people, knowing that if it be there, actions will follow fast enough.

It seems a very easy matter to get it there. The idea is nothing new; all the world knows it. Talk with men, Democrats and Whigs, they will say they like freedom in the abstract, they hate slavery in the abstract. But you find that somehow they like slavery in the concrete, and dislike abolitionism when it tries to set free the slave. Slavery is the affair of the whole people; not Congress, but the nation, made slavery; made it national, constitutional. Not Congress, but the voters, must unmake slavery; make it unconstitutional, un-national. They say Congress

176

cannot do it. Well, perhaps it is so; but they that make can break. If the people made slavery, they can unmake it.

You talk with the people; the idea of freedom is there. They tell you they believe the Declaration of Independence — that all men are created equal. But somehow they contrive to believe that negroes now in bondage are an exception to the rule, and so they tell us that slavery must not be meddled with, that we must respect the compromises of the Constitution. So we see that respect for the Constitution overrides respect for the inalienable rights of three millions of negro men.

Now, to move men, it is necessary to know two things — first, what they think, and next, why they think it. Let us look a little at both.

In New England, men over twenty-one years old may be divided into two classes. First, the men that vote, and secondly, the men that choose the governor. The voters in Massachusetts are some hundred and twenty thousand; the men that choose the governor, who tell the people how to vote, whom to vote for, what laws to make, what to forbid, what policy to pursue — they are not very numerous. You may take one hundred men out of Boston, and fifty men from the other large towns in the State — and if you could get them to be silent till next December, and give no counsel on political affairs, the people would not know what to do. The Democrats would not know what to do, nor the Whigs. We are a very democratic people, and suffrage is almost universal; but it is a very few men who tell us how to vote, who make all the most important laws. Do I err in estimating the number at one hundred and fifty? I do not like to exaggerate

— suppose there are six hundred men, three hundred in each party; that six hundred manage the political action of the State, in ordinary times.

I need not stop to ask what the rest of the people think about freedom and slavery. What do the men who control our politics think thereof? I answer, They are not opposed to slavery; to the slavery of three millions of men. They may not like slavery in the abstract, or they may like it, I do not pretend to judge; but slavery in the concrete, at the South, they do like; opposition to that slavery, in the mildest form, or the sternest, they do hate.

That is a serious charge to bring against the prominent rulers of the State. Let me call your attention to a few facts which prove it. Look at the men we send to Congress. There are thirty-one New England men in Congress. By the most liberal construction you can only make out five anti-slavery men in the whole number. Who ever heard of an anti-slavery governor of Massachusetts in this century? Men know what they are about when they select candidates for election. Do the voters always know what they are about when they choose them?

Then these men always are in favor of a pro-slavery President. The President must be a slaveholder. There have been fifteen presidential elections. Men from the free States have filled the chair twelve years, or three terms; men from the slave States forty-four years, or eleven terms. During one term the chair was filled by an amphibious Presidency, by General Harrison, who was nothing but a concrete availability, and John Tyler, who was — John Tyler. They called him an accident; but there are no accidents in politics. A slaveholder presides over the United States forty-eight years out of sixty! Do those men who control the politics of New England not like it? It is no such thing. They love to have it so. We have just seen the Democratic party, or their leaders, nominate General Cass for their candidate — and General Cass is a Northern man; but on that account is he any the less a pro-slavery man? He did oppose the South once, but it was in pressing a war with England. Everybody knows General Cass, and I need say no more about him. But the Northern Whigs have their leaders — are they anti-slavery men? Not a whit more. Next week you will see them nominate, not the great Eastern Whig, though he is no opponent of slavery, only an expounder and defender of the Constitution; not the great Western Whig, the compromiser, though steeped to the lips in slavery; no, they will nominate General Taylor, a man who lives a little further South, and is at this moment dyed a little more scarlet with the sin of slavery.

But go a step further as to the proof. Those men who control the politics of Massachusetts, or New England, or the whole North, they have never opposed the aggressive movements of the slave power. The annexation of Texas, did they oppose that? No, they were glad of it. True, some earnest men came up here in Faneuil Hall, and passed resolutions, which did no good whatever, because it was well known that the real controllers of our politics thought the other way. Then followed the Mexican War. It was a war for slavery, and they knew it; they like it now — that is, if a man's likings can be found out by his doings, not his occasional and exceptional deeds, but his regular and constant actions. They knew that there would be a war against the currency, a war against the

tariff, or a war against Mexico. They chose the latter.
They knew what they were about.

The same thing is shown by the character of the
press. No " respectable " paper is opposed to slavery;
no Whig paper, no Democratic paper. You would as
soon expect a Catholic newspaper to oppose the Pope
and his church, for the slave power is the pope of
America, though not exactly a pious pope. The
churches show the same thing; they also are in the
main pro-slavery, at least not anti-slavery. There are
some forty denominations or sects in New England.
Mr. President, is one of these anti-slavery? Not one!
The land is full of ministers, respectable men, educated men — are they opposed to slavery? I do not
know a single man, eminent in any sect, who is also
eminent in his opposition to slavery. There was one
such man, Dr Channing; but just as he became eminent
in the cause of freedom, he lost power in his own
church, lost caste in his own little sect; and though
men are now glad to make sectarian capital out of
his reputation after he is dead, when he lived, they
cursed him by their gods! Then, too, all the most
prominent men of New England fraternize with
slavery. Massachusetts received such an insult from
South Carolina as no State ever before received from
another State in this Union; an affront which no nation would dare offer another, without grinding its
sword first.[1] And what does Massachusetts do? She
does — nothing. But her foremost man goes off there,
" The schoolmaster that gives no lessons," [2] to accept
the hospitality of the South, to take the chivalry of
South Carolina by the hand; the defender of the Constitution fraternizes with the State which violates the
Constitution, and imprisons his own constituents on
account of the color of their skin.

Put all these things together, and they show that the men who control the politics of Massachusetts, of all New England, do not oppose or dislike slavery.

So much for what they think; and now for the why they think so.

First, there is the general indifference to what is absolutely right. Men think little of it. The Anglo-Saxon race, on both sides of the water, have always felt the instinct of freedom, and often contended stoutly enough for their own rights. But they never cared much for the rights of other men. The slaves are at a distance from us, and so the wrong of this institution is not brought home to men's feelings as if it were our own wrong.

Then the pecuniary interests of the North are supposed to be connected with slavery, so that the North would lose dollars if the South lost slaves. No doubt this is a mistake; still, it is an opinion currently held. The North wants a market for its fabrics, freight for its ships. The South affords it; and, as men think, better than if she had manufactures and ships of her own, both of which she could have, were there no slaves. All this seems to be a mistake. Freedom, I think, can be shown to be the interest of both North and South.

Yet another reason is found in devotion to the interests of a party. Tell a Whig he could make Whig capital out of anti-slavery, he would turn abolitionist in a moment, if he believed you. Tell a Democrat that he can make capital out of abolition, and he also will come over to your side. But the fact is, each party knows it would gain nothing for its political purposes by standing out for the rights of man. The time will come, and sooner too than some men think, when it will be for the interest of a party to favor aboli-

tion, but that time is not yet.   It does seem strange,
that while you can find men who will practise a good
deal of self-denial for their sect or their party, lending, and hoping nothing in return, you so rarely find
a man who will compromise even his popularity for
the sake of mankind.

Then, again, there is the fear of change.   Men who
control our politics seem to have little confidence in
man, little in truth, little in justice, and the eternal
right.   Therefore, while it is never out of season to
do something for the tariff, for the moneyed interests
of men, they think it is never in time to do much for
the great work of elevating mankind itself.   They
have no confidence in the people, and take little pains
to make the people worthy of confidence.   So any
change which gives a more liberal government to a
people, which gives freedom to the slave, they look on
with distrust, if not alarm.   In 1830, when the French
expelled the despotic king who encumbered their throne,
what said Massachusetts, what said New England, in
honor of the deed? Nothing. Your old men?
Nothing. Your young men? Not a word. What
did they care for the freedom of thirty millions of
men? They were looking at their imports and exports.   In 1838, when England set free eight hundred thousand men in a day, what did Massachusetts
say about that? What had New England to say?
Not a word in its favor from these political leaders
of the land.   Nay, they thought the experiment was
dangerous, and ever since that it is with great reluc-
tance you can get them to confess that the scheme
works well.   In 1848, when France again expels her
king, and all the royalty in the kingdom is carted off
in a one horse cab — when the broadest principles of

human government are laid down, and a great nation
sets about the difficult task of moving out of her old
political house and into a new one, without tearing
down the old, without butchering men in the process
of removal,— why, what has Boston to say to that?
What have the political leaders of Massachusetts, of
New England, to say? They have nothing to say for
liberty; they are sorry the experiment was made; they
are afraid the French will not want so much cotton;
they have no confidence in man, and fear every change.

Such are their opinions, to judge by what they do;
such the reasons thereof, judging by what they say.

But how can we change this, and get the idea of
freedom into men's minds? Something can be done
by the gradual elevation of men, by schools and
churches, by the press. The churches and colleges of
New England have not directly aided us in the work
of abolishing slavery. No doubt by their direct action they have retarded that work, and that a good
deal. But indirectly they have done much to hasten
the work. They have helped educate men; helped
make men moral, in a general way; and now this moral
power can be turned to this special business, though
the churches say, " No, you shall not." I see before
me a good and an earnest man,³ who, not opening his
mouth in public against slavery, has yet done a great
service in this way: he has educated the teachers of the
Commonwealth, has taught them to love freedom, to
love justice, to love man and God. That is what I
call sowing the seeds of anti-slavery. The honored
and excellent Secretary of Education,⁴ who has just
gone to stand in the place of a famous man, and I
hope to fill it nobly, has done much in this way. I
wish in his reports on education he had exposed the

wrong which is done here in Boston, by putting all
the colored children in one school, by shutting them
out of the Latin School and the English High School.
I wish he had done that duty, which plainly belongs
to him to do. But without touching that, he has yet
done indirectly a great work towards the abolition of
slavery. He has sown the seeds of education wide
spread over the State. One day these seeds will come
up; come up men, men that will both vote and choose
the governor; men that will love right and justice;
will see the iniquity of American slavery, and sweep
it off the continent, cost what it may cost, spite of all
compromises of the Constitution, and all compromisers.
I look on that as certain. But that is slow work,
this waiting for a general morality to do a special
act. It is going without dinner till the wheat is grown
for your bread.

So we want direct and immediate action upon the
people themselves. The idea must be set directly before them, with all its sanctions displayed, and its obligations made known. This can be done in part by
the pulpit. Dr. Channing shows how much one man
can do, standing on that eminence. You all know
how much he did do. I am sorry that he came so
late, sorry that he did not do more, but thankful for
what he did do. However, you cannot rely on the
pulpit to do much. The pulpit represents the average
goodness and piety; not eminent goodness and piety.
It is unfair to call ordinary men to do extraordinary
works. I do not concur in all the hard things that
are said about the clergy, perhaps it is because I am
one of them; but I do not expect a great deal from
them. It is hard to call a class of men all at once
to rise above all other classes of men, and teach a

degree of virtue which they do not understand. But you may call them to be true to their own consciences.

So the pulpit is not to be relied on for much aid. If all the ministers of New England were abolitionists, with the same zeal that they are Protestants, Universalists, Methodists, Calvinists, or Unitarians, no doubt the whole State would soon be an anti-slavery State, and the day of emancipation would be wonderfully hastened. But that we are not to look for.

Much can be done by lecturers, who shall go to the people and address them, not as Whigs or Democrats, not as sectarians, but as men, and in the name of man and God present the actual condition of the slaves, and show the duty of the North and South, of the nation, in regard to this matter. For this business, we want money and men, the two sinews of war; money to pay the men, men to earn the money. They must appeal to the people in their primary capacity, simply as men.

Much also may be done by the press. How much may be done by these two means, and that in a few years, these men [5] can tell; all the North and South can tell. Men of the most diverse modes of thought can work together in this cause. Here on my right is Mr. Phillips, an old-fashioned Calvinist, who believes all the five points of Calvinism. I am rather a new-fashioned Unitarian, and believe only one of the five points, the one Mr. Phillips has proved — the perseverance of the saints; but we get along without any quarrel by the way.

Some men will try political action. The action of the people, of the nation, must be political action. It may be constitutional, it may be unconstitutional. I see not why men need quarrel about that. Let not

him that voteth condemn him that voteth not, nor let
not him that voteth not condemn him that voteth, but
let every man be faithful to his own convictions.

It is said, the abolitionists waste time and wind in
denunciation. It is partly true. I make no doubt
it inspires the slaveholder's heart to see division
amongst his foes. I ought to say his friends, for
such we are. He thinks the day of justice is deferred,
while the ministers thereof contend. I do not believe
a revolution is to be baptized with rose-water. I do
not believe a great work is to be done without great
passions. It is not to be supposed that the Leviathan
of American slavery will allow himself to be drawn out
of the mire in which he has made his nest, and grown
fat and strong, without some violence and floundering.
When we have caught him fairly, he will put his feet
into the mud to hold on by; he will reach out and
catch hold of everything that will hold him. He has
caught hold of Mr. Clay and Mr. Webster. He will
catch hold of General Cass and Mr. Webster. He
will die, though slowly, and die hard. Still it is a
pity that men who essay to pull him out, should waste
their strength in bickerings with one another, or in
needless denunciation of the Leviathan's friends.[6] Call
slaveholding, slaveholding; let us tell all the evils
which arise from it, if we can find language terrible
enough; let us show up the duplicity of the nation,
the folly of our wise men, the littleness of our great
men, the baseness of our honorable men, if need be;
but all that with no unkind feelings towards any one.
Virtue never appears so lovely as when, destroying sin,
she loves the sinner, and seeks to save him. Absence
of love is absence of the strongest power. See how
much Mr. Adams lost of his influence, how much he

wasted of his strength, by the violence with which he pursued persons. I am glad to acknowledge the great services he performed. He wished to have every man stand on the right side of the anti-slavery line; but I believe there were some men whom he would like to have put there with a pitchfork. On the other hand, Dr. Channing never lost a moment by attacking a personal foe; and see what he gained by it! However, I must say this, that no great revolution of opinion and practice was ever brought about before with so little violence, waste of force, and denunciation. Consider the greatness of the work; it is to restore three millions to liberty; a work, in comparison with which the American Revolution was a little thing. Yet consider the violence, the denunciation, the persecution, and the long years of war which that Revolution cost. I do not wonder that abolitionists are sometimes violent; I only deplore it. Remembering the provocation, I wonder they are not more so and more often. The prize is to be run for, " not without dust and heat."

Working in this way, we are sure to succeed. The idea is an eternal truth. It will find its way into the public mind, for there is that sympathy between man and the truth, that he cannot live without it and be blessed. What allies we have on our side! True, the cupidity, the tyranny, the fear, and the atheism of the land are against us. But all the nobleness, all the honor, all the morality, all the religion, are on our side. I was sorry to hear it said that the religion of the land opposed us. It is not true. Religion never opposed any good work. I know what my friend meant, and I wish he had said it, calling things by their right names. It is the irreligion of the land that favors slavery; it is the idolatry of gold; it is our atheism. Of speculative atheism there is not much; you see how much of the practical!

We are certain of success; the spirit of the age is on our side. See how the old nations shake their tyrants out of the land. See how every steamer brings us good tidings of good things; and do you believe America can keep her slaves? It is idle to think so. So all we want is time. On our side are truth, justice, and the eternal right. Yes, on our side is religion, the religion of Christ; on our side are the hopes of mankind, and the great power of God.

VII

THE FREE SOIL MOVEMENT

The people of the United States have just chosen an officer, who, for the next four years, will have more power than any monarch of Europe; yet three years ago he was scarcely known out of the army in Florida, and even now has appeared only in the character of a successful general. His supporters at the North intend, by means of his election, to change the entire commercial policy of the country, and perhaps, also, its financial policy; they contemplate, or profess to contemplate, a great change. Yet the election has been effected without tumult or noise; not a soldier has drawn his bayonet; scarcely has a constable needed his official rod to keep order withal. In Europe, at the same time, the beginning of a change in the national dynasty or the national policy is only attempted by violence, by soldiers with arms ready for fight, by battle and murder. One day or another, men will be wise enough to see the cause of this difference, and insular statesmen in England, who now sneer at the new government in America, may learn that democracy has at least one quality — that of respecting law and order, and may live to see ours the oldest government in the whole Caucasian race.

Since the election is now over, it is worth while to look a moment at the politics and political parties of the country, that we may gain wisdom for the future, and perhaps hope; at any rate, may see the actual condition of things. Each political party is based on an

idea, which corresponds to a truth, or an interest.
It commonly happens that the idea is represented as
an interest, and the interest as an idea, before either
becomes the foundation of a large party. Now when
a new idea is introduced to any party, or applied to
any institution, if it be only auxiliary to the old doctrines incarnated therein, a regular growth and new
development take place; but when the new idea is
hostile to the old, the development takes place under
the form of a revolution, and that will be greater or
less in proportion to the difference between the new
idea and the old doctrine; in proportion to their relative strength and value. As Aristotle said of seditions,
a revolution comes on slight occasions, but not of
slight causes; the occasion may be obvious and obviously trivial, but the cause obscure and great. The
occasion of the French Revolution of 1848 was afforded by the attempt of the king to prevent a certain
public dinner: he had a legal right to prevent it. The
cause of the Revolution was a little different; but some
men in America and England, at first scarcely looked
beyond the occasion, and taking that for the cause,
thought the Frenchmen fools to make so much ado
about a trifle, and that they had better eat their
soupe maigre at home, and let their victuals stop their
mouths. The occasion of the American Revolution
may be found in the Stamp Act, or the Sugar Act,
the Writs of Assistance, or the Boston Port-Bill; some
men, even now, see no further, and logically conclude
the colonists made a mistake, because for a dozen years
they were far worse off than before the " Rebellion,"
and have never been so lightly taxed since. Such men
do not see the cause of the Revolution, which was not
an unwillingness to pay taxes, but a determination to
govern themselves.

At the present day it is plain that a revolution, neither slow nor silent, is taking place in the political parties of America. The occasion thereof is the nomination of a man for the Presidency, who has no political or civil experience, but who has three qualities that are important in the eyes of the leading men who have supported and pushed him forward: one is, that he is an eminent slaveholder, whose interests and accordingly whose ideas are identical with those of the slaveholders; the next, that he is not hostile to the doctrines of Northern manufacturers respecting a protective tariff; and the third, that he is an eminent and very successful military commander. The last is an accidental quality, and it is not to be supposed that the intelligent and influential men at the North and South who have promoted his election, value him any more on that account, or think that mere military success fits him for his high office, and enables him to settle the complicated difficulties of a modern state. They must know better; but they must have known that many men of little intelligence are so taken with military glory that they will ask for no more in their hero; it was foreseen, also, that honest and intelligent men of all parties would give him their vote because he had never been mixed up with the intrigues of political life. Thus " far-sighted " politicians of the North and South, saw that he might be fairly elected, and then might serve the purpose of the slaveholder, or the manufacturer of the North. The military success of General Taylor, an accidental merit, was only the occasion of his nomination by the Whigs; his substantial merit was found in the fact that he was supposed, or known, to be favorable to the " peculiar institution " of the South, and the protective policy of the manufacturers at the North; this was the cause of his formal nomination by the Whig Convention of Philadelphia, and his real nomination by members of the Whig party at Washington. The men of property at the South wanted an extension of slavery; the men of property at the North, a high protective tariff; and it was thought General Taylor could serve both purposes, and promote the interests of the North and South.

Such is the occasion of the revolution in political parties: the cause is the introduction of a new idea into these parties entirely hostile to some of their former doctrines. In the electioneering contest, the new idea was represented by the words " Free Soil." For present practice it takes a negative form: " No more slave States, no more slave territory," is the motto. But these words and this motto do not adequately represent the idea, only so much thereof as has been needful in the present crisis.

Before now there has been much in the political history of America to provoke the resentment of the North. England has been ruled by various dynasties; the American chair has been chiefly occupied by the Southern House, the dynasty of slaveholders; now and then a member of the Northern House has sat on that seat, but commonly it has been a " Northern man with Southern principles," never a man with mind to see the great idea of America, and will to carry it out in action. Still the spirit of liberty has not died out of the North; the attempt to put an eighth slaveholder in the chair of " the model republic," gave occasion for that spirit to act again.

The new idea is not hostile to the distinctive doctrine of either political party; neither to free trade, nor to protection; so it makes no revolution in respect to them: it is neutral, and leaves both as it found them. It is not hostile to the general theory of the American State, so it makes no revolution there; this idea is assumed as self-evident, in the Declaration of Independence. It is not inimical to the theory of the Constitution of the United States, as set forth in the preamble thereto, where the design of the Constitution is declared to be " To form a more perfect union, establish justice, insure domestic tranquillity, provide for the common defense, promote the general welfare, and secure the blessings of liberty to ourselves and our posterity."

There are clauses in the Constitution which are exceptions to this theory, and hostile to the design mentioned above; to such, this idea will one day prove itself utterly at variance, as it is now plainly hostile to one part of the practice of the American government, and that of both the parties.

We have had several political parties since the Revolution: the Federalists, and anti-federalists,— the latter shading off into Republicans, Democrats, and locofocos; the former tapering into modern Whigs, in which guise some of their fathers would scarcely recognise the family type. We have had a protective party and an anti-protective party; once there was a free-trade party, which no longer appears in politics. There has been a national bank party, which seems to have gone to the realm of things lost on earth. In the rise and fall of these parties, several dramas, tragic and comic, have been performed on the American boards, where " One man in his time plays many parts," and stout representatives of the Hartford Convention find themselves on the same side with

worshippers of the Gerrymander, and shouting the
same cry. It is kindly ordered that memory should
be so short, and brass so common. None of the old
parties is likely to return; the living have buried the
dead. "We are all Federalists," said Mr. Jefferson,
"we are all Democrats," and truly, so far as old
questions are concerned. It is well known that the
present representatives of the old federal party have
abjured the commercial theory of their predecessors;
and the men who were "Jacobins" at the beginning
of the century, curse the new French Revolution by
their gods. At the Presidential election of 1840,
there were but two parties in the field — Democrats
and Whigs. As they both survive, it is well to see
what interests or what ideas they represent.

They differ accidentally in the possession and the
desire of power; in the fact that the former took the
initiative, in annexing Texas, and in making the
Mexican War, while the latter only pretended to oppose either, but zealously and continually co-operated
in both. Then, again, the Democratic party sus-
tains the sub-treasury system, insisting that the
government shall not interfere with banking, shall
keep its own deposits, and give and take only specie
in its business with the people. The Whig party, if
we understand it, has not of late developed any distinctive doctrine on the subject of money and
financial operations, but only complained of the
action of the sub-treasury; yet, as it sustained the
late Bank of the United States, and appropriately
followed as chief mourner at the funeral thereof,
uttering dreadful lamentations and prophecies which
time has not seen fit to accomplish, it still keeps up a
show of differing from the Democrats on this matter.

These are only accidental or historical differences, which do not practically affect the politics of the nation to any great degree.

The substantial difference between the two is this: the Whigs desire a tariff of duties which shall directly and intentionally protect American industry, or, as we understand it, shall directly and intentionally protect manufacturing industry, while the commerical and agricultural interests are to be protected indirectly, not as if they were valuable in themselves, but were a collateral security to the manufacturing interest: a special protection is desired for the great manufactures, which are usually conducted by large capitalists — such as the manufacture of wool, iron, and cotton. On the other hand, the Democrats disclaim all direct protection of any special interest, but, by raising the national revenue from the imports of the nation, actually afford a protection to the articles of domestic origin to the extent of the national revenue, and much more. That is the substantial difference between the two parties — one which has been much insisted on at the late election, especially at the North.

Is this difference of any practical importance at the present moment? There are two methods of raising the revenue of a country: first, by direct taxation, — a direct tax on the person, a direct tax on the property; second, by indirect taxation. To a simple-minded man direct taxation seems the only just and equal mode of collecting the public revenue: thereby, the rich man pays in proportion to his much, the poor to his little. This is so just and obvious, that it is the only method resorted to, in towns of the North, for raising their revenue. But while it requires very little common sense and virtue to appreciate this plan in a town, it seems to require a good deal to endure it in a nation. The four direct taxes levied by the American government since 1787 have been imperfectly collected, and only with great difficulty and long delay. To avoid this difficulty, the government resorts to various indirect modes of taxation, and collects the greater part of its revenue from the imports which reach our shores. In this way a man's national tax is not directly in proportion to his wealth, but directly in proportion to his consumption of imported goods, or directly to that of domestic goods, whose price is enhanced by the duties laid on the foreign article. So it may happen that an Irish laborer, with a dozen children, pays a larger national tax than a millionaire who sees fit to live in a miserly style. Besides, no one knows when he pays or what. At first it seems as if the indirect mode of taxation made the burden light, but in the end it does not always prove so. The remote effect thereof is sometimes remarkable. The tax of one per cent., levied in Massachusetts on articles sold by auction, has produced some results not at all anticipated.

Now since neither party ventures to suggest direct taxation, the actual question between the two is not between free trade and protection, but only between a protective and a revenue tariff. So the real and practical question between them is this: Shall there be a high tariff or a low one? At first sight a man not in favor of free trade might think the present tariff gave sufficient protection to those great manufactures of wool, cotton, and iron, and as much as was reasonable. But the present duty is perhaps scarcely adequate to meet the expenses of the nation, for with new territory new expenses must come; there is a large debt to be discharged, its interest to be paid; large sums will be demanded as pensions for the soldiers. Since these things are so, it is but reasonable to conclude that, under the administration of the Whigs or Democrats, a pretty high tariff of duties will continue for some years to come. So the great and substantial difference between the two parties ceases to be of any great and substantial importance.

In the mean time another party rises up, representing neither of these interests; without developing any peculiar views relative to trade or finance, it proclaims the doctrine that there must be no more slave territory, and no more slave States.[1] This doctrine is of great practical importance, and one in which the free soil party differs substantially from both the other parties. The idea on which the party rests is not new; it does not appear that the men who framed the Constitution, or the people who accepted it, ever contemplated the extension of slavery beyond the limits of the United States at that time; had such a proposition been then made, it would have been indignantly rejected by both. The principle of the Wilmot Proviso boasts the same origin as the Declaration of Independence. The state of feeling at the North occasioned by the Missouri Compromise is well known, but after that there was no political party opposed to slavery. No President has been hostile to it; no Cabinet; no Congress. In 1805, Mr. Pickering, a senator from Massachusetts, brought forward his bill for amending the Constitution, so that slaves should not form part of the basis of representation; but it fell to the ground, not to be lifted up by his successors for years to come. The refusal of John Quincy Adams, while President, to recognise the independence of Hayti, and his efforts to favor the slave power, excited no remark.[2] In 1844, for the first time the anti-slavery votes began seriously to affect the presidential election. At that time the Whigs had nominated Mr. Clay as their candidate, a man of great powers, of popular manners, the friend of Northern industry, but still more the friend of Southern slavery, and more directly identified with that than any man in so high a latitude. The result of the anti-slavery votes is well known. The bitterest reproaches have been heaped on the men who voted against him as the incarnation of the slave power; the annexation of Texas, though accomplished by a Whig Senate, and the Mexican War, though only sixteen members of Congress voted against it, have both been laid to their charge; and some have even affected to wonder that men conscientiously opposed to slavery could not forget their principle for the sake of their party, and put a most decided slaveholder, who had treated not only them but their cause with scorn and contempt, in the highest place of power.

The Whig party renewed its attempt to place a slaveholder in the President's chair, at a time when all Europe was rising to end for ever the tyranny of man. General Taylor was particularly obnoxious to the anti-slavery men. He is a slaveholder, holding one or two hundred men in bondage, and enlarging that number by recent purchases; he employs them in the worst kind of slave labor, the manufacture of sugar; he leaves them to the mercy of overseers, the dregs and refuse of mankind; he has just returned from a war undertaken for the extension of slavery; he is a Southern man with Southern interests, and opinions favorable to slavery, and is uniformly represented by his supporters at the South, as decidedly opposed to the Wilmot Proviso, and in favor of the extension of slavery.

We know this has been denied at the North; but the testimony of the South settles the question. The convention of Democrats in South Carolina, when they also nominated him, said well, " His interests are our interests: . . . we know that on this great, paramount, and leading question of the rights of the South [to extend slavery over the new territory], he is for us and he is with us." Said a newspaper in his own State, " General Taylor is from birth, association, and conviction, identified with the South and her institutions, being one of the most extensive slaveholders in Louisiana, and supported by the slaveholding interest; is opposed to the Wilmot Proviso, and in favor of procuring the privilege to the owners of slaves to remove with them to newly acquired territory."

The Southerners evidently thought the crisis an important one. The following is from the distinguished Whig senator, Mr. Berrien: —

" I consider it the most important Presidential election, especially to Southern men, which has occurred since the foundation of the government.

" We have great and important interests at stake. If we fail to sustain them now, we may be forced too soon to decide whether we will remain in the Union, at the mercy of a band of fanatics or political jugglers, or reluctantly retire from it for the preservation of our domestic institutions, and all our rights as freemen. If we are united, we can sustain them; if we divide on the old party issues, we must be victims.

" With a heart devoted to their interests on this great question, and without respect to party, I implore my fellow-citizens of Georgia, Whig and Democratic, to forget for the time their party divisions: to know each other only as Southern men: to act upon the truism uttered by Mr. Calhoun, that on this vital question — the preservation of our domestic institutions — the Southern man who is furthest from us is nearer to us than any Northern man can be; that General Taylor is identified with us, in feeling and interest, was born in a slaveholding State, educated in a slaveholding State, is himself a slaveholder; that

his slave property constitutes the means of support to himself
and family; that he cannot desert us without sacrificing his
interest, his principle, the habits and feelings of his life; and
that with him, therefore, our institutions are safe. I beseech
them, therefore, from the love which they bear to our noble
State, to rally under the banner of Zachary Taylor, and, with
one united voice, to send him by acclamation to the executive
chair."

All this has been carefully kept from the sight of the
people at the North.

There have always been men in America who were
opposed to the extension and the very existence of
slavery. In 1787, the best and the most celebrated
statesmen were publicly active on the side of freedom.
Some thought slavery a sin, others a mistake, but
nearly all in the Convention thought it an error.
South Carolina and Georgia were the only States
thoroughly devoted to slavery at that time. They
threatened to withdraw from the Union if it were not
sufficiently respected in the new Constitution. If
the other States had said, " You may go, soon as you
like, for hitherto you have been only a curse to us,
and done little but brag," it would have been better for
us all. However, partly for the sake of keeping the
peace, and still more for the purpose of making money
by certain concessions of the South, the North granted
the Southern demands. After the adoption of the Constitution the anti-slavery spirit cooled down; other
matters occupied the public mind. The long disasters
of Europe; the alarm of the English party, who feared
their sons should be " conscripts in the armies of
Napoleon," and the violence of the French party, who
were ready to compromise the dignity of the nation,
and add new elements to the confusion in Europe; the
subsequent conflict with England, and then the efforts

to restore the national character and improve our material condition,— these occupied the thought of the nation, till the Missouri Compromise again disturbed the public mind. But that was soon forgotten; little was said about slavery. In the eighteenth century, it was discussed in the colleges and newspapers, even in the pulpits of the North; but in the first quarter of the nineteenth, little was heard of it. Manufactures got established at the North, and protected by duties; at the South, cotton was cultivated with profit, and a heavy duty protected the slave-grown sugar of Louisiana. The pecuniary interests of North and South became closely connected, and both seemed dependent on the peaceable continuance of slavery. Little was said against it, little thought, and nothing done. Southern masters voluntarily brought their slaves to New England and took them back, no one offering the African the conventional shelter of the law, not to speak of the natural shelter of justice. We well remember the complaint made somewhat later, when a judge decided that a slave, brought here by his master's consent, became, from that moment, free!

But where sin abounded, grace doth much more abound. There rose up one man who would not compromise, nor be silent,— who would be heard.[3] He spoke of the evil, spoke of the sin — for all true reforms are bottomed on religion, and while they seem adverse to many interests, yet represent the idea of the Eternal. He found a few others, a very few, and began the anti-slavery movement. The " platform " of the new party was not an interest, but an idea — that " all men are created equal, and endowed by their Creator with certain unalienable rights." Every truth is also a fact; this was a fact of human consciousness, and a truth of necessity.

The time has not come to write the history of the abolitionists,— other deeds must come before words; but we cannot forbear quoting the testimony of one witness, as to the state of anti-slavery feeling in New England in 1831. It is the late Hon. Harrison Gray Otis, a former mayor of Boston, who speaks in his recent letter.

"The first information received by me, of a disposition to agitate this subject in our State, was from the governors of Virginia and Georgia, severally remonstrating against an incendiary newspaper, published in Boston, and, as they alleged, thrown broadcast among their plantations, inciting to insurrection and its horrid results. It appeared, on inquiry, that no member of the city government [of Boston] had ever heard of the publication. Some time afterwards it was reported to me by the city officers, that they had ferreted out the paper and its editor; that his office was an obscure hole, his only visible auxiliary a negro boy, and his supporters a very few insignificant persons of all colors. This information . . . I communicated to the above-named governors, with an assurance of my belief that the new fanaticism had not made, nor was likely to make, proselytes among the respectable classes of our people."

Such was the state of things in 1831. Anti-slavery had " an obscure hole " for its headquarters; the one agitator, who had filled the two doughty governors of Virginia and Georgia with uncomfortable forebodings, had a " negro boy " for " his only visible auxiliary," and none of the respectable men of Boston had heard of the hole, of the agitator, of the negro boy, or even of the agitation. One thing must be true: either the man and the boy were pretty vigorous, or else there was a great truth in that obscure hole; for, in spite of the governors and the mayors, spite of the many able men in the South and the North, spite, also, of the wealth and respectability of the whole land, it is a plain case that the abolitionists have shaken the nation, and their idea is the idea of the time; and the party which shall warmly welcome that is destined before long to override all the other parties.

One thing must be said of the leaders of the anti-slavery movement. They asked for nothing but justice; not justice for themselves — they were not Socratic enough to ask that,— but only justice for the slave; and to obtain that, they forsook all that human hearts most love.   It is rather a cheap courage that fought at Monterey and Palo Alto, a bravery that can be bought for eight dollars a month; the patriotism which hurrahs for " our side," which makes speeches at Faneuil Hall, nay, which carries torchlights in a procession, is not the very loftiest kind of patriotism; even the man who stands up at the stake, and in one brief hour of agony anticipates the long torment of disease, does not endure the hardest, but only the most obvious kind of martyrdom.   But when a man, for con-science' sake, leaves a calling that would insure him bread and respectability; when he abjures the opinions which give him the esteem of honorable men; when, for the sake of truth and justice, he devotes himself to liberating the most abused and despised class of men, solely because they are men and brothers; when he thus steps forth in front of the world, and encounters poverty and neglect, the scorn, the loathing, and the contempt of mankind — why, there is something not very common in that.   There was once a Man who had not where to lay his head, who was born in " an obscure hole," and had not even a negro boy for his " auxili-ary;" who all his life lived with most obscure persons — eating and drinking with publicans and sinners; who found no favor with mayors or governors, and yet has had some influence on the history of the world.

When intelligent men mock at small beginnings, it is surprising they cannot remember that the greatest institutions have had their times which tried men's souls, and that they who have done all the noblest and best work of mankind sometimes forgot self-interest in looking at a great truth; and though they had not always even a negro boy to help them, or an obscure hole to lay their heads in, yet found the might of the universe was on the side of right, and themselves workers with God!

The abolitionists did not aim to found a political party; they set forth an idea. If they had set up the interest of the Whigs or the Democrats, the manufacturers or the merchants, they might have formed a party and had a high place in it, with money, ease, social rank and a great name in the party — newspapers. Some of them had political talents, ideas more than enough, the power of organizing men, the skill to manage them, and a genius for eloquence. With such talents, it demands not a little manliness to keep out of politics and in the truth.

To found a political party there is no need of a great moral idea: the Whig party has had none such this long time; the Democratic party pretends to none and acts on none; each represents an interest which can be estimated in dollars; neither seems to see that behind questions of political economy there is a question of political morality, and the welfare of the nation depends on the answer we shall give! So long as the abolitionists had nothing but an idea, and but few men had that, there was no inducement for the common run of politicians to join them; they could make nothing by it, so nothing of it. The guardians of education, the trustees of the popular religion, did not like to

invest in such funds. But still the idea went on, spite
of the most entire, the most bitter, the most heartless
and unrelenting opposition ever known in America.
No men were ever hated as the abolitionists; political
parties have joined to despise, and sectarian churches
to curse them. Yet the idea has gone on, till now all
that is most pious in the sects, most patriotic in the
parties, all that is most Christian in modern philanthropy is on its side. It has some representative in almost every family, save here and there one whose God
is mammon alone, where the parents are antediluvian
and the children born old and conservative, with no
faculty but memory to bind them to mankind. It has
its spokesman in the House and the Senate. The tide
rises and swells, and the compact wall of the Whig
party, the tall ramparts of the Democrats, are beginning to " cave in."

As the idea has gained ground, men have begun to
see that an interest is connected with it, and begun
to look after that. One thing the North knows well —
the art of calculation, and of ciphering. So it begins
to ask questions as to the positive and comparative
influence of the slave power on the country. Who
fought the Revolution? Why the North, furnishing
the money and the men, Massachusetts alone sending
fourteen thousand soldiers more than all the present
slave States. Who pays the national taxes? The
North, for the slaves pay but a trifle. Who owns the
greater part of the property, the mills, the shops, the
ships? The North. Who writes the books — the his-
tories, poems, philosophies, works of science, even the
sermons and commentaries on the Bible? Still the
North. Who sends their children to school and college? The North. Who builds the churches, who

founds the Bible societies, education societies, missionary societies, the thousand-and-one institutions for
making men better and better off? Why the North.
In a word, who is it that in seventy years has made
the nation great, rich, and famous for her ideas and
their success all over the world? The answer is still
the North, the North.

Well, says the calculator, but who has the offices of
the nation? The South. Who has filled the Presidential chair forty-eight years out of sixty? Nobody
but slaveholders. Who has held the chief posts of
honor? The South. Who occupy the chief offices in
the army and navy? The South. Who increases the
cost of the post-office and pays so little of its expense? [4]
The South. Who is most blustering and disposed to
quarrel? The South. Who made the Mexican War?
The South. Who sets at nought the Constitution?
The South. Who would bring the greatest peril in
case of war with a strong enemy? Why the South,
the South. But what is the South most noted for
abroad? For her three million slaves; and the North?
for her wealth, freedom, education, religion!

Then the calculator begins to remember past times
— opens the account-books and turns back to old
charges: five slaves count the same as three freemen,
and the three million slaves, which at home are nothing but property, entitle their owners to as many
representatives in Congress as are now sent by all the
one million eight hundred thousand freeman who make
the entire population of Maine, New Hampshire, Vermont, Rhode Island, and Massachusetts, and have
created a vast amount of property, worth more than
all the slave States put together! Then the North
must deliver up the fugitive slaves, and Ohio must

play the traitor, the kidnapper, the bloodhound, for Kentucky! The South wanted to make two slave States out of Florida, and will out of Texas; she makes slavery perpetual in both; she is always bragging as if she made the Revolution, while she only laid the Embargo, and began the late war with England, — but that is going further back than is needful. The South imprisons our colored sailors in her ports, contrary to justice, and even contrary to the Constitution. She drove our commissioners out of South Carolina and Louisiana, when they were sent to look into the matter and legally seek for redress. She affronts the world with a most odious despotism, and tried to make the English return her runaway slaves, making the nation a reproach before the world; she insists on kidnapping men even in Boston; she declares that we shall not abolish slavery in the Capital of the Union; that she will extend it in spite of us from sea to sea. She annexed Texas for a slave-pasture, and then made the Mexican War to enlarge that pasture, but the North must pay for it; she treads the Constitution under her feet, the North under her feet, justice and the unalienable rights of man under her feet.

The North has charged all these items and many more; now they are brought up for settlement, and, if not canceled, will not be forgot till the Muse of History gives up the ghost; some Northern men have the American sentiment, and the American idea, put the man before the dollar, counting man the substance, property the accident. The sentiment and idea of liberty are bottomed on Christianity, as that on human nature; they are quite sure to prevail; the spirit of the nation is on their side — the spirit of the age and the everlasting right.

It is instructive to see how the political parties have hitherto kept clear of anti-slavery. It is " no part of the Whig doctrine;" the Democrats abhor it. Mr. Webster, it is true, once claimed the Wilmot Proviso as his thunder, but he cannot wield it, and so it slips out of his hands, and runs round to the chair of his brother senator from New Hampshire.[5] No leading politician in America has ever been a leader against slavery. Even Mr. Adams only went as he was pushed. True, among the Whigs there are Giddings, Palfrey, Tuck, Mann, Root, and Julian; among the Democrats there is Hale — and a few others; but what are they among so many? The members of the family of Truth are unpopular, they make excellent servants but hard masters, while the members of the family of Interest are all respectable, and are the best company in the world; their livery is attractive; their motto, " The almighty dollar," is a passport everywhere. Now it happens that some of the more advanced members of the family of Truth fight their way into " good society," and make matrimonial alliances with some of the poor relations of the family of Interest. Straightway they become respectable: the church publishes the banns; the marriage is solemnized in the most Christian form; the attorney declares it legal. So the gospel and law are satisfied, Truth and Interest made one, and many persons after this alliance may be seen in the company of Truth who before knew not of her existence.

The Free-soil party has grown out of the anti-slavery movement. It will have no more slave territory, but does not touch slavery in the States, or between them, and says nothing against the compromises of the Constitution; the time has not come for that.

The party has been organized in haste, and is composed, as are all parties, of most discordant materials, some of its members seeming hardly familiar with the idea; some are not yet emancipated from old prejudices, old methods of action, and old interests; but the greater part seem hostile to slavery in all its forms. The immediate triumph of this new party is not to be looked for, not desirable. In Massachusetts they have gained large numbers in a very short period, and under every disadvantage. What their future history is to be, we will not now attempt to conjecture; but this is plain, that they cannot remain long in their present position; either they will go back, and after due penance, receive political absolution from the church of the Whigs or the Democrats,— and this seems impossible, — or else they must go forward where the idea of justice impels them. One day the motto, " No more slave territory " will give place to this, " No slavery in America." The revolution in ideas is not over till that is done, nor the corresponding revolution in deeds while a single slave remains in America. A man who studies the great movements of mankind feels sure that that day is not far off; that no combination of Northern and Southern interest, no declamation, no violence, no love of money, no party zeal, no fraud and no lies, no compromise, can long put off the time. Bad passions will ere long league with the holiest love of right, and that wickedness may be put down with the strong hand which might easily be ended at little cost and without any violence, even of speech. One day the Democratic party of the North will remember the grievances which they have suffered from the South, and, if they embrace the idea of freedom, no constitutional scruple will long hold them from destroying

VIII—14

the " peculiar institution." What slavery is in the
middle of the nineteenth century is quite plain; what
it will be at the beginning of the twentieth it is not
difficult to foresee. The slave power has gained a
great victory: one more such will cost its life. South
Carolina did not forget her usual craft in voting for
a Northern man that was devoted to slavery.

Let us now speak briefly of the conduct of the
election. It has been attended, at least in New England, with more intellectual action than any election
that I remember, and with less violence, denunciation,
and vulgar appeals to low passions and sordid interest.
Massachusetts has shown herself worthy of her best
days; the Free-soil vote may be looked on with pride
by men who conscientiously cast their ballot the other
way. Men of ability and integrity have been active
on both sides, and able speeches have been made, while
the vulgarity that marked the " Harrison campaign "
has not been repeated.

In this contest the Democratic party made a good
confession, and " owned up " to the full extent of
their conduct. They stated the question at issue,
fairly, clearly, and entirely; the point could not be mistaken. The Baltimore Convention dealt honestly in
declaring the political opinions of the party; the opinions of their candidate on the great party questions,
and the subject of slavery, were made known with
exemplary clearness and fidelity. The party did not
fight in the dark; they had no dislike to holding slaves,
and they pretended none. In all parts of the land
they went before the people with the same doctrines
and the same arguments; everywhere they " repudiated " the Wilmot Proviso. This gave them an advantage over a party with a different policy. They

had a platform of doctrines; they knew what it was; the party stood on the platform; the candidate stood on it.

The Whig party have conducted differently; they did not publish their confession of faith. We know what was the Whig platform in 1840 and in 1844. But what is it in 1848? Particular men may publish their opinions, but the doctrines of the party are " not communicated to the public." For once in the history of America there was a Whig convention which passed no " resolutions;" it was the Convention at Phila- delphia. But on one point, of the greatest importance too, it expressed the opinions of the Whigs: it re- jected the Wilmot Proviso, and Mr. Webster's thunder, which had fallen harmless and without lightning from his hands, was " kicked out of the meeting! " As the party had no platform, so their candidate had no political opinions. " What! " says one, " choose a President who does not declare his opinions,— then it must be because they are perfectly well known! " Not at all: General Taylor is raw in politics, and has not taken his first " drill! " " Then he must be a man of such great political and moral ability, that his will may take the place of reason! " Not at all: he is known only as a successful soldier, and his reputation is scarcely three years old. Mr. Webster declared his nomination " not fit to be made," and nobody has any authentic statement of his political opinions; perhaps not even General Taylor himself.

In the electioneering campaign there has been a cer- tain duplicity in the supporters of General Taylor: at the North it was maintained that he was not opposed to the Wilmot Proviso, while at the South quite uni- formly the opposite was maintained. This duplicity

had the appearance of dishonesty. In New England
the Whigs did not meet the facts and arguments of
the free soil party; in the beginning of the campaign
the attempt was made, but was afterwards comparatively abandoned; the matter of slavery was left out
of the case, and the old question of the subtreasury
and the tariff was brought up again, and a stranger
would have thought, from some Whig newspapers, that
that was the only question of any importance. Few
men were prepared to see a man of the ability and
experience of Mr. Webster in his electioneering speeches
pass wholly over the subject of slavery. The nation
is presently to decide whether slavery is to extend over
the new territory or not; even in a commercial and
financial point of view, this is far more important
than the question of banks and tariffs; but when its
importance is estimated by its relation to freedom,
right, human welfare in general,— we beg the pardon
of American politicians for speaking of such things,
— one is amazed to find the Whig party of the opinion that it is more important to restore the tariff of
1842 than to prohibit slavery in a country as large
as the thirteen States which fought the Revolution!
It might have been expected of little, ephemeral men,
— minute politicians, who are the pest of the State,—
but when at such a crisis a great man rises,[6] amid a
sea of upturned faces, to instruct the lesser men, and
forgets right, forgets freedom, forgets man, and forgets God, talking only of the tariff and of banks,
why a stranger is amazed, till he remembers the peculiar relation of the great man to the moneyed men,
— that he is their attorney, retained, paid, and pensioned to do the work of men whose interest it is to
keep the question of slavery out of sight. If General

Cavaignac had received a pension from the manufacturers of Lyons and of Lisle, to the amount of half a million of francs, should we be surprised if he forgot the needy millions of the land? Nay, only if he did not forget them![7]

It was a little hardy to ask the anti-slavery men to vote for General Taylor; it was like asking the members of a temperance society to choose an eminent distiller for president of their association. Still, we know that honest anti-slavery men did honestly vote for him. We know nothing to impeach the political integrity of General Taylor; the simple fact that he is a slaveholder, seems reason enough why he should not be President of a nation who believe that " all men are created equal, and endowed by their Creator with certain unalienable rights." Men will be astonished in the next century to learn that the " model republic," had such an affection for slaveholders. Here is a remarkable document, which we think should be preserved:

DEED OF SALE.

" JOHN HAGARD, SR., TO ZACHARIAH TAYLOR.

" *Received for Record*, 18*th Feb.*, 1843.

" *This Indenture*, made this twenty-first day of April, eighteen hundred and forty-two, between John Hagard, Sr., of the City of New Orleans, State of Louisiana, of one part, and Zachariah Taylor, of the other part, *Witnesseth*, that the said John Hagard, Sr., for and in consideration of the sum of *Ninety-Five Thousand Dollars* to him in hand paid, and secured to be paid, as hereafter stated by the said Zachariah Taylor, at and before the sealing and delivering of these Presents, has this day bargained, sold, and delivered, conveyed, and confirmed, and by these Presents does bargain, sell, deliver, and confirm unto the said Zachariah Taylor, his heirs and assigns, for ever, all that plantation and tract of land: . . . .

" ALSO, all the following Slaves — Nelson, Milley, Peldea,

Mason, Willis, Rachel, Caroline, Lucinda, Ramdall, Wirman, Carson, Little Ann, Winna, Jane, Tom, Sally, Gracia, Big Jane, Louisa, Maria, Charles, Barnard, Mira, Sally, Carson, Paul, Sansford, Mansfield, Harry Oden, Harry Horley, Carter, Henrietta, Ben, Charlotte, Wood, Dick, Harrietta, Clarissa, Ben, Anthony, Jacob, Hamby, Jim, Gabriel, Emeline, Armstead, George, Wilson, Cherry, Peggy, Walker, Jane, Wallace, Bartlett, Martha, Letitia, Barbara, Matilda, Lucy, John, Sarah, Bigg Ann, Allen, Tom, George, John, Dick, Fielding, Nelson, or Isom, Winna, Shellod, Lidney, Little Cherry, Puck, Sam, Hannah, or Anna, Mary, Ellen, Henrietta, and two small children:— Also, all the Horses, Mules, Cattle, Hogs, Farming Utensils, and Tools, now on said Plantation — together with all and singular the hereditaments, appurtenances, privileges, and advantages unto the said Land and Slaves belonging or appertaining. *To have and to hold* the said Plantation and tract of Land and Slaves, and other property above described, unto the said Zachariah Taylor, his heirs and assigns, for ever, and to his and to their only proper use, benefits, and behoof, for ever. And the said John Hagard, Sr., for himself, his heirs, executors, and administrators, does covenant, promise and agree to and with said Zachariah Taylor, his heirs and assigns, that the aforesaid Plantation and tract of Land and Slaves, and other property, with the appurtenances, unto the said Zachariah Taylor, his heirs and assigns, against the claim or claims of all persons whomsoever claiming or to claim the same, or any part or parcel thereof, shall and will warrant, and by these Presents for ever defend.

"*In Testimony Whereof,* the said John Hagard, Sr., has hereunto set his hand and seal, the day and year first above written."

If this document had been discovered among some Egyptian papyri, with the date 1848 before Christ, it would have been remarkable as a sign of the times. In a republic, nearly four thousand years later, it has a meaning which some future historian will appreciate.

The Free-soil party have been plain and explicit as the Democrats; they published their creed in the celebrated Buffalo platform. The questions of subtreasury and tariff are set aside; " No more slave territory " is the watchword. In part they represent an

interest, for slavery is an injury to the North in many
ways, and to a certain extent puts the North into the
hands of the South; but chiefly an idea. Nobody
thought they would elect their candidate, whosoever
he might be; they could only arrest public attention
and call men to the great questions at issue, and so,
perhaps, prevent the evil which the South was bent on
accomplishing. This they have done, and done well.
The result has been highly gratifying. It was pleasant and encouraging to see men ready to sacrifice their
old party attachments and their private interests, of-
tentimes, for the sake of a moral principle. I do not
mean to say that there was no moral principle in the
other parties — I know better. But it seems to me
that the Free-soilers committed a great error in select-
ing Mr. Van Buren as their candidate. True, he is
a man of ability, who has held the highest offices and
acquitted himself honorably in all; but he had been
the " Northern man with the Southern principles;" had
shown a degree of subserviency to the South, which
was remarkable, if not singular or strange: his promise, made and repeated in the most solemn manner, to
veto any act of Congress, abolishing slavery in the
Capital, was an insult to the country, and a disgrace
to himself. He had a general reputation for insta-
bility and want of political firmness. It is true, he
had opposed the annexation of Texas, and lost his
nomination in 1844 by that act; but it is also true
that he advised his party to vote for Mr. Polk, who
was notoriously in favor of annexation.[8] His nomination, I must confess, was unfortunate; the Buffalo
Convention seems to have looked at his availability
more than his fitness, and in their contest for a principle, began by making a compromise of that very

principle itself. It was thought he could " carry "
the State of New York; and so a man who was not
a fair representative of the idea, was set up. It was
a bad beginning. It is better to be defeated a thousand times, rather than seem to succeed by a compromise of the principle contended for. Still, enough
has been done to show the nation that the dollar is
not almighty; that the South is not always to insult
the North and rule the land, annexing, plundering,
and making slaves when she will; that the North has
men who will not abandon the great sentiment of freedom, which is the boast of the nation and the age.

General Taylor is elected by a large popular vote;
some voted for him on account of his splendid military
success; some because he is a slaveholder, and true to
the interests of the slave-power; some because he is a
" good Whig," and wants a high tariff of duties. But
we think there are men who gave him their support
because he has never been concerned in the intrigues
of a party, is indebted to none for past favors, is
pledged to none, bribed by none, and intimidated by
none; because he seems to be an honest man, with a
certain rustic intelligence; a plain blunt man, that loves
his country and mankind. We hope this was a large
class. If he is such a man, he will enter upon his
office under favorable auspices, and with the best wishes
of all good men.

But what shall the Free-soil party do next? They
cannot go back,— conscience waves behind them her
glittering wings and bids them on; they cannot stand
still, for as yet their measures and their watchword
do not fully represent their idea. They must go forward, as the early abolitionists went, with this for
their motto: " No slavery in America." " He that

would lead men, must walk but one step before them,"
says somebody. Well, but he must think many steps
before them, or they will presently tread him under
their feet. The present success of the idea is doubtful; the interests of the South will demand the extension of slavery;[9] the interests of the party now
coming into power, will demand their peculiar boon.
So another compromise is to be feared, and the extension of slavery yet further west. But the ultimate
triumph of the genius of freedom is certain. In
Europe, it shakes the earth with mighty tread; thrones
fall before its conquering feet. While in the eastern
continent, kings, armies, emperors, are impotent before
that power, shall a hundred thousand slaveholders stay
it here with a bit of parchment?

VIII

REPLY TO WEBSTER

Mr. President and Fellow Citizens: It is an important occasion which has brought us together. A great crisis has occurred in the affairs of the United States. There is a great question now before the people. In any European country west of Russia and east of Spain, it would produce a revolution, and be settled with gunpowder. It narrowly concerns the material welfare of the nation. The decision that is made will help millions of human beings into life, or will hinder and prevent millions from being born. It will help or hinder the advance of the nation in wealth for a long time to come. It is a question which involves the honor of the people. Your honor and my honor are concerned in this matter, which is presently to be passed upon by the people of the United States. More than all this, it concerns the morality of the people. We are presently to do a right deed, or to inflict a great wrong on others and on ourselves, and thereby entail an evil upon this continent which will blight and curse it for many an age.

It is a great question, comprising many smaller ones: — Shall we extend and foster slavery, or shall we extend and foster freedom? slavery, with its consequences, material, political, intellectual, moral; or freedom, with the consequences thereof?

A question so important seldom comes to be decided before any generation of men. This age is full of great questions, but this of freedom is the chief. It

is the same question which in other forms comes up in
Europe. This is presently to be decided here in the
United States by the servants of the people, I mean,
by the Congress- of the nation; in the name of the
people; for the people, if justly decided; against them,
if unjustly. If it were to be left to-morrow to the
naked votes of the majority, I should have no fear.
But the public servants of the people may decide
otherwise. The political parties, as such, are not to
pass judgment. It is not a question between Whigs
and Democrats; old party distinctions, once so sacred
and rigidly observed, here vanish out of sight. The
party of slavery or the party of freedom is to swallow
up all the other parties. Questions about tariffs and
banks can hardly get a hearing. On the approach of
a battle, men do not talk of the weather.

Four great men in the Senate of the United States
have given us their decision; the four most eminent in
the party politics of the nation — two great Whigs,
two great Democrats.[1] The Shibboleth of their party
is forgotten by each; there is a strange unanimity in
their decision. The Herod of free trade and the Pilate
of protection are "made friends," when freedom is to
be crucified. All four decide adverse to freedom; in
favor of slavery; against the people. Their decisions
are such as you might look for in the politicians of
Austria and Russia. Many smaller ones have spoken
on this side or on that. Last of all, but greatest,
the most illustrious of the four, so far as great gifts
of the understanding are concerned, a son of New
England, long known, and often and deservedly honored, has given his decision. We waited long for his
words; we held our peace in his silence; we listened
for his counsel. Here it is; adverse to freedom be-

yond the fears of his friends, and the hopes even of
his foes. He has done wrong things before, cowardly
things more than once; but this, the wrongest and most
cowardly of them all: we did not look for it. No
great man in America has had his faults or his fail-
ings so leniently dealt with; private scandal we will
not credit, public shame we have tried to excuse, or,
if inexcusable, to forget. We have all of us been
proud to go forward and honor his noble deeds, his
noble efforts, even his noble words. I wish we could
take a mantle big and black enough, and go backward
and cover up the shame of the great man who has fallen
in the midst of us, and hide him till his honor and
his conscience shall return. But no, it cannot be; his
deed is done in the face of the world, and nothing
can hide it.

We have come together to-night in Faneuil Hall, to
talk the matter over, in our New England way; to
look each other in the face; to say a few words of
warning, a few of counsel, perhaps something which
may serve for guidance. We are not met here to-
night to " calculate the value of the Union," but to
calculate the worth of freedom and the rights of man;
to calculate the value of the Wilmot Proviso. Let
us be cool and careful, not violent, not rash; true and
firm, not hasty or timid.[2]

Important matters have brought our fathers here
many times before now. Before the Revolution, they
came here to talk about the Molasses Act, or the Sugar
Act, or the Stamp Act, the Boston Port Bill, and the
long list of grievances which stirred up their manly
stomachs to the Revolution; afterwards, they met to
consult about the Embargo, and the seizure of the
Chesapeake, and many other matters. Not long ago,

only five years since, we came here to protest against the annexation of Texas. But before the Revolution or after it, meetings have seldom been called in Faneuil Hall on such solemn occasions as this. Not only is there a great public wrong contemplated, as in the annexation of Texas, but the character and conduct of a great public servant of the people come up to be looked after. This present conduct of Mr. Webster is a thing to be solemnly considered. A similar thing once happened before. In 1807, a senator from Massachusetts was disposed to accept a measure the President had advised, because he had " recommended " it " on his high responsibility." " I would *not consider*," said the senator, " I would *not deliberate*, I would *act*." [3] He did so; and with little deliberation, with small counsel, as men thought at the time, he voted for the Embargo, and the Embargo came. This was a measure which doomed eight hundred thousand tons of shipping to rot at the wharf. It touched the pockets of New England and all the North. It affected the daily meals of millions of men. There was indignation, deep and loud indignation; but it was political in its nature and personal in its form; the obnoxious measure was purely political, not obviously immoral and unjust. But, long as John Quincy Adams lived, much as he did in his latter years for mankind, he never wholly wiped off the stain which his conduct then brought upon him. Yet it may be that he was honest in his vote; it may have been an error of judgment, and nothing more; nay, there are men who think it was no error at all, but a piece of political wisdom.

A senator of Massachusetts has now committed a fault far greater than was ever charged upon Mr.

Adams by his most inveterate political foes. It does not directly affect the shipping of New England and the North: I wish it did. It does not immediately concern our daily bread; if it were so, the contemplated wrong would receive a speedy adjustment. But it concerns the liberty of millions of men yet unborn.

Let us look at the matter carefully.

Here is a profile of our national action on the subject now before the people.

In 1774, we agreed to import no more slaves after that year, and never finally repealed this act of agreement.

In 1776, we declared that all men are created equal, and endowed by their Creator with certain unalienable rights, among which are life, liberty, and the pursuit of happiness.

In 1778, we formed the Confederacy, with no provision for the surrender of fugitive slaves.

In 1787, we shut out slavery from the Northwest Territory for ever, by the celebrated proviso of Mr. Jefferson.[4]

In 1788, the Constitution was formed, with its compromises and guarantees.

In 1808, the importation of slaves was forbidden. But,

In 1803, we annexed Louisiana, and slavery along with it.

In 1819, we annexed Florida, with more slavery.

In 1820, we legally established slavery in the territory west of the Mississippi, south of 36 deg. 30 min.

In 1845, we annexed Texas, with three hundred and twenty-five thousand five hundred and twenty square miles, as a slave State.

In 1848, we acquired, by conquest and by treaty,

the vast territory of California and New Mexico, containing five hundred and twenty-six thousand and seventy-eight square miles. Of this two hundred and four thousand three hundred and eighty-three square miles are south of the slave line — south of 36 deg. 30 min. Here is territory enough to make more than thirty slave States of the size of Massachusetts.

At the present day, it is proposed to have some further action on the matter of slavery. Connected with this subject, four great questions come up to be decided : —

1. Shall four new slave States at any time be made out of Texas? This is not a question which is to be decided at present, yet it is one of great present importance, and furnishes an excellent test of the moral character and political conduct of politicians at this moment. The other questions are of immediate and pressing concern. Here they are:

2. Shall slavery be prohibited in California?

3. Shall slavery be prohibited in New Mexico?

4. What laws shall be passed relative to fugitive slaves?

Mr. Webster, in this speech, defines his position in regard to each of these four questions.

I. In regard to the new States to be made hereafter out of Texas, he gives us his opinion, in language well studied, and even with an excess of caution. Let us look at it, and the resolution which annexed Texas. That declares that " new States . . . not exceeding four in number, in addition to said State of Texas . . . may hereafter, by the consent of said State, be formed out of the territory thereof, which shall be entitled to admission under the provisions of the Federal Constitution. And such

States . . . shall be admitted with or without slavery, as the people of each State asking admission may desire."

I will not stop to consider the constitutionality of the joint resolution which annexed Texas. Mr. Webster's opinion on that subject is well known. But the resolution does two things: 1. It confers a power, the power to make four new States on certain conditions; a qualified power, restricted by the terms of the act. 2nd. It imposes an obligation, namely, the obligation to leave it to the people of the new State to keep slaves or not, when the State is admitted. The words *may be*, etc., indicate the conferring of a power: the words *shall be*, etc., the imposing of an obligation. But as the power is a qualified power, so is the obligation a qualified obligation; the *shall be* is dependent on the *may be*, as much as the *may be* on the *shall*. Admitting in argument what Mr. Webster has denied, that Congress had the constitutional right to annex Texas by joint resolution, and also that the resolution of one Congress binds the future Congress, it is plain Congress may admit new States from Texas, on those conditions, or refuse to admit them. This is plain, by any fair construction of the language. The resolution does not say, they *shall* be formed, only " *may* be formed," and " shall be entitled to admission, under the provisions of the Federal Constitution "— not in spite of those provisions. The provisions of the Constitution, in relation to the formation and admission of new States, are well known, and sufficiently clear. Congress is no more bound to admit a new slave State formed out of Texas, than out of Kentucky. But Mr. Webster seems to say that Congress is bound to make four new States out of Texas, when there is suf-

ficient population to warrant the measure, and a desire for it in the States themselves, and to admit them
with a Constitution allowing slavery. He says, " Its
guaranty is, that new States shall be made out of it,
. . . and that such States . . . may come in
as slave States," etc. Quite the contrary. It is only
said that they " *may be* formed," and admitted " under the provisions of the Constitution." The *shall be*
does not relate to the fact of admission.

Then he says, there is " a solemn pledge," " that if
she shall be divided into States, those States may come
in as slave States." But there is no " solemn pledge "
that they *shall come* in at all. I make a " solemn
pledge " to John Doe, that if ever I give him any land,
it shall be a thousand acres in the meadows on Connecticut River; but it does not follow from this that I am
bound to give John Doe any land at all. This solemn
pledge is worth nothing, if Congress says to new
States, You shall not come in with your slave Constitution. To make this " stipulation with Texas "
binding, it ought to have provided that " new
States . . . shall be formed out of the territory
thereof . . . such States shall be entitled to admission, in spite of the provisions of the Constitution."
Even then it would be of no value; for as there can be
no moral obligation to do an immoral deed, so there
can be no constitutional obligation to do an unconstitutional deed. So much for the first question. You
see that Mr. Webster proposes to do what we never
stipulated to do, what is not " so nominated in the
bond." He wrests the resolution against freedom, and
for the furtherance of the slave power.

II. and III. Mr. Webster has given his answer to
the second and third questions, which may be con-

sidered as a single question, Shall slavery be legally forbidden by Congress in California and New Mexico? Mr. Webster is opposed to the prohibition by Congress. Here are his words: "Now, as to California and New Mexico, I hold slavery to be excluded from those territories by a law even superior to that which admits and sanctions it in Texas. I mean the law of nature, of physical geography, the law of the formation of the earth." . . . "I will say further, that if a resolution or a law were now before us to provide a territorial government for New Mexico, I would not vote to put any prohibition into it whatever. The use of such a prohibition would be idle, as it respects any effect it would have upon the territory: and I would not take pains to re-affirm an ordinance of nature, nor to re-enact the will of God." "The gentlemen who belong to the Southern States would think it a taunt, an indignity; they would think it an act taking away from them what they regard as a proper equality of privilege" . . . "a plain theoretic wrong," "more or less derogatory to their character and their rights."

"African slavery," he tells us, "cannot exist there." It could once exist in Massachusetts and New Hampshire. Very little of this territory lies north of Mason and Dixon's line, the northern limit of Maryland; none above the parallel of forty-two degrees; none of it extends fifty miles above the northern limit of Virginia; two hundred and four thousand three hundred and fifty-three square miles of it lie south of the line of the Missouri Compromise, south of 36° 30′. Almost all of it is in the latitude of Virginia and the Carolinas. If slavery can exist on the west coast of the Atlantic, I see not why it cannot

on the east of the Pacific, and all the way between.
There is no reason why it cannot. It will, unless we
forbid it by positive laws, laws which no man can misunderstand. Why, in 1787, it was thought necessary
to forbid slavery in the Northwest Territory, which
extends from the Ohio River to the forty-ninth
parallel of north latitude.

Not exclude slavery from California and New
Mexico, because it can never exist there! Why, it was
there once, and Mexico abolished it by positive law.
Abolished, did I say! We are not so sure of that; I
mean, not sure that the Senate of the United States
is sure of it. Not a month before Mr. Webster made
this very speech, on the 13th and 14th of last February, Mr. Davis, the senator from Mississippi, maintained that slavery is not abolished in California and
New Mexico. He denies that the acts abolishing
slavery in Mexico were made by competent powers;
denies that they have the force of law. But even if
they have, he tells us, " Suppose it be conceded that
by law it was abolished — could that law be perpetual?
Could it extend to the territory after it became the
property of the United States? Did we admit territory from Mexico, subject to the Constitution and laws
of Mexico? Did we pay fifteen million dollars for
jurisdiction over California and New Mexico, that it
might be held subordinate to the laws of Mexico? "
The Commissioners of Mexico, he tells us, did not think
that " we were to be bound by the edicts and statutes
of Mexico." They pressed this point in the negotia-
tion, " the continuation of their law for the exclusion of slavery;" and Mr. Trist told them he could
not make a treaty on that condition; if they would
offer him the land " covered a foot thick with pure

gold, upon the single condition that slavery should be excluded therefrom, I could not entertain the offer for a moment." Does not Mr. Webster know this? He knows it too well.

But Mr. Davis goes further. He does not think slavery is excluded by legislation stronger than a joint resolution. This is his language: "I believe it is essential, on account of the climate, productions, soil, and the peculiar character of cultivation, that we shall, during its first settlement, have that slavery [African slavery] in a part, at least, of California and New Mexico." Now on questions of "A law of nature and physical geography," the senator from Mississippi is as good authority as the senator from Massachusetts, and a good deal nearer to the facts of the case.

In the House of Representatives, Mr. Clingman, of North Carolina, amongst others, wants New Mexico for slave soil. Pass the Wilmot Proviso over this territory, and the question is settled, disposed of for ever. Omit to pass it, and slavery will go there, and you may get it out if you can. Once there, it will be said that the " Compromises of the Constitution " are on its side, and we have no jurisdiction over the slavery which we have established there.

Hear what Mr. Foote said of a similar matter on the 26th of June, 1848, in his place in the Senate: " Gentlemen have said this is not a practical question, that slaves will never be taken to Oregon. With all deference to their opinion, I differ with them totally. I believe, if permitted, slaves would be carried there, and that slavery would continue, at least, as long as in Maryland or Virginia. [' The whole of Oregon ' is north of forty-two degrees.] The Pacific coast is totally different in temperature from the Atlantic. It

is far milder. . . . Green peas are eaten in the
Oregon city at Christmas. Where is the corresponding climate to be found on this side the continent?
Where we sit — near the thirty-ninth? No, sir; but
to the south of us." " The latitude of Georgia gives,
on the Pacific, a tropical climate." " The prohibition of slavery in the laws of Oregon was adopted for
the express purpose of excluding slaves." " A few
had been brought in; further importations were expected; and it was with a view to put a stop to them,
that the prohibitory act was passed."

Now, Mr. Foote of Mississippi —" Hangman
Foote," as he has been called — understands the laws of
the formation of the earth as well as the distinguished
senator from Massachusetts. Why, the inhabitants of
that part of the Northwest Territory, which now
forms the States of Indiana and Illinois, repeatedly
asked Congress to allow them to introduce slaves north
of the Ohio; and but for the Ordinance of '87, that
territory would now be covered with the mildew of
slavery!

But I have not yet adduced all the testimony of Mr.
Foote. Last year, on the 23rd of February, 1849, he
declared: " No one acquainted with the vast mineral
resources of California and New Mexico, and who is
aware of the peculiar adaptedness of slave labor to the
development of mineral treasures, can doubt for a moment that were slaves introduced into California and
New Mexico, being employed in the mining operations there in progress, their labor would result in the
acquisition of pecuniary profits not heretofore realized
by the most successful cotton or sugar planter of this
country." Does not Mr. Webster know this? Perhaps he did not hear Mr. Foote's speech last year;

perhaps he has a short memory, and has forgotten it.
Then let us remind the nation of what its senator forgets. Not know this — forget it? .Who will credit
such a statement? Mr. Webster is not an obscure
clergyman, busy with far different things, but the foremost politician of the United States.

But why do I mention the speeches of Mr. Foote, a
year ago? Here is something hardly dry from the
printing-press. Here is an advertisement from the
" Mississippian " of March 7th, 1850, the very day
of that speech. The " Mississippian " is published at
the city of Jackson, in Mississippi.

" CALIFORNIA,

" THE SOUTHERN SLAVE COLONY.

" Citizens of the slave States, desirous of emigrating to California with their slave property, are requested to send their
names, number of slaves, and period of contemplated departure,
to the address of ' SOUTHERN SLAVE COLONY, Jackson,
Miss. . . .

" It is the desire of the friends of this enterprise to settle in
the richest mining and agricultural portions of California, and
to have the uninterrupted enjoyment of slave property. It is
estimated that, by the 1st of May next, the members of this
Slave Colony will amount to about five thousand, and the slaves
to about ten thousand. The mode of effecting organization, &c.,
will be privately transmitted to actual members.

" Jackson (Miss.), Feb. 24, 1850.   " dtf."

What does Mr. Webster say in view of all this?
" If a proposition were now here for a government
for New Mexico, and it was moved to insert a provision for the prohibition of slavery, I would not vote for
it." Why not vote for it? There is a specious pretense, which is publicly proclaimed, but there is a real
reason for it which is not mentioned!

In the face of all these facts, Mr. Webster says that these men would wish " to protect the everlasting snows of Canada from the pest of slavery by the same overspreading wing of an act of Congress." Exactly so. If we ever annex Labrador — if we " re-annex " Greenland, and Kamtchatka, I would extend the Wilmot Proviso, there, and exclude slavery for ever and for ever.

But Mr. Webster would not " re-affirm an ordinance of nature," nor " re-enact the will of God." I would. I would re-affirm nothing else, enact nothing else. What is justice but the " ordinance of nature? " What is right but " the will of God? " When you make a law, " Thou shalt not kill," what do you but " re-enact the will of God? " When you make laws for the security of the " unalienable rights " of man and protect for every man the right to life, liberty, and the pursuit of happiness, are you not re-affirming an ordinance of nature? Not re-enact the will of God? Why, I would enact nothing else. The will of God is a theological term; it means truth and justice, in common speech. What is the theological opposite to " The will of God? " It is " The will of the devil." One of the two you must enact — either the will of God, or of the devil. The two are the only theological categories for such matters. *Aut Deus aut diabolus.* There is no other alternative, " Choose you which you will serve."

So much for the second and third questions. Let us now come to the last thing to be considered. What laws shall be enacted relative to fugitive slaves? Let us look at Mr. Webster's opinion on this point.

The Constitution provides — you all know that too well — that every person " held to service or labor in one State, . . . escaping into another, shall be delivered up." By whom shall he be delivered up? There are only three parties to whom this phrase can possibly apply. They are,

1. Individual men and women: or,
2. The local authorities of the States concerned; or,
3. The Federal Government itself.

It has sometimes been contended that the Constitution imposes an obligation on you, and me, and every other man, to deliver up fugitive slaves. But there are no laws or decisions that favor that construction. Mr. Webster takes the next scheme and says, " I always thought that the Constitution addressed itself to the legislatures of the States, or to the States themselves." " It seems to me that the import of the passage is, that the State itself . . . shall cause him [the fugitive] to be delivered up. That is my judgment." But the Supreme Court, some years ago, decided otherwise, that " the business of seeing that these fugitives are delivered up resides in the power of Congress and the national judicature." So the matter stands now. But it is proposed to make more stringent laws relative to the return of fugitive slaves. So continues Mr. Webster —" My friend at the head of the judiciary committee has a bill on the subject now before the Senate, with some amendments to it, which I propose to support, with all its provisions, to the fullest extent."

Everybody knows the act of Congress of 1793, relative to the surrender of fugitive slaves, and the decision of the Supreme Court in the " Prigg Case," 1842. But everybody does not know the bill of Mr. Webster's " friend at the head of the judiciary committee." There is a bill providing " for the more

effectual execution of the third clause of the second
section of the fourth article of the Constitution of the
United States." It is as follows: —

" *Be it enacted by the Senate and House of Representatives
of the United States of America, in Congress assembled,* That
when a person held to service or labor, in any State or territory
of the United States, under the laws of such State or territory,
shall escape into any other of the said States or territories, the
person to whom such service or labor may be due, his or her
agent, or attorney, is hereby empowered to seize or arrest such
fugitive from service or labor, and to take him or her before
any Judge of the Circuit or District Courts of the United
States, or before any commissioner or clerk of such courts, or
marshal thereof, or before any postmaster of the United States,
or collector of the customs of the United States, residing or
being within such State wherein such seizure or arrest shall be
made; and, upon proof to the satisfaction of such judge, commissioner, clerk, postmaster, or collector, as the case may be,
either by oral testimony or affidavit taken before and certified
by any person authorized to administer an oath under the laws
of the United States, or of any State, that the person so seized
or arrested, under the laws of the State or territory, from which
he or she fled, owes service or labor to the person claiming him
or her, it shall be the duty of such judge, commissioner, clerk,
marshal, postmaster, or collector, to give a certificate thereof to
such claimant, his or her agent or attorney, which certificate
shall be a sufficient warrant for taking and removing such fugitive from service or labor to the State or territory from which
he or she fled.

" Sec. 2. *And be it further enacted,* That when a person held
to service or labor, as mentioned in the first section of this act,
shall escape from such service or labor, therein-mentioned, the
person to whom such service or labor may be due, his or her
agent or attorney, may apply to any one of the officers of the
United States named in said section, other than a marshal of
the United States, for a warrant to seize and arrest such fugitive; and upon affidavit being made before such officer (each
of whom, for the purposes of this act, is hereby authorized
to administer an oath or affirmation), by such claimant, his or
her agent, that such person does, under the laws of the State
or territory from which he or she fled, owe service or labor to
such claimant, it shall be and is hereby made the duty of such
officer, to and before whom such application and affidavits are
made to issue his warrant to any marshal of any of the courts

of the United States, to seize and arrest such alleged fugitive, and to bring him or her forthwith, or on a day to be named in such warrant, before the officer issuing such warrant, or either of the other officers mentioned in said first section, except the marshal to whom the said warrant is directed, which said warrant or authority, the said marshal is hereby authorized and directed in all things to obey.

"Sec. 3. *And be it further enacted,* That upon affidavit made as aforesaid, by the claimant of such fugitive, his agent or attorney, after such certificate has been issued, that he has reason to apprehend that such fugitive shall be rescued by force from his or their possession, before he can be taken beyond the limits of the State in which the arrest is made, it shall be the duty of the officer in making the arrest, to retain such fugitive in his custody, and to remove him to the State whence he fled, and there to deliver him to said claimant, his agent or attorney. And to this end, the officer aforesaid is hereby authorized and required to employ so many persons as he may deem necessary to overcome such force, and to retain them in his service, so long as circumstances may require. The said officer and his assistants, while so employed, to receive the same compensation, and to be allowed the same expenses as are now allowed by law, for transportation of criminals, to be certified by the judge of the district within which the arrest is made, and paid out of the treasury of the United States: *Provided,* That before such charges are incurred, the claimant, his agent, or attorney, shall secure to said officer payment of the same, and in case no actual force be opposed, then they shall be paid by such claimant, his agent or attorney.

"Sec. 4. *And be it further enacted,* When a warrant shall have been issued by any of the officers under the second section of this act, and there shall be no marshal or deputy marshal within ten miles of the place where such warrant is issued, it shall be the duty of the officer issuing the same, at the request of the claimant, his agent, or attorney, to appoint some fit and discreet person, who shall be willing to act as marshal, for the purpose of executing said warrant; and such persons so appointed shall, to the extent of executing such warrant, and detaining and transporting the fugitive named therein, have all the power and the authority, and he, with his assistants, entitled to the same compensation and expenses, provided in this act, in cases where the services are performed by the marshals of the courts.

"Sec. 5. *And be it further enacted,* That any person who shall knowingly and wilfully obstruct or hinder such claimant, his

agent, or attorney, or any person or persons assisting him, her,
or them, in so serving or arresting such fugitive from service
or labor, or shall rescue such fugitive from such claimant, his
agent, or attorney, when so arrested, pursuant to the authority
herein given or declared, or shall aid, abet, or assist such person
so owing service or labor, to escape from such claimant, his
agent, or attorney, shall harbor or conceal such person, after
notice that he or she was a fugitive from labor, as aforesaid,
shall, for either of the said offenses, forfeit and pay the sum
of one thousand dollars, which penalty may be recovered by,
and for the benefit of, such claimant, by action of debt in any
court proper to try the same, saving, moreover, to the person
claiming such labor or service, his right of action for, on account of, the said injuries, or either of them.

"Sec. 6. *And be it further enacted,* That when such person is
seized and arrested, under and by virtue of the said warrant, by
such marshal, and is brought before either of the officers aforesaid, other than said marshal, it shall be the duty of such officer
to proceed in the case of such person, in the same way that he
is directed and authorized to do, when such person is seized
and arrested by the person claiming him, or by his or her agent,
or attorney, and is brought before such officer or attorney,
under the provisions of the first section of this act."

This is the bill known as " Mason's Bill," introduced by Mr. Butler, of South Carolina, on the 16th
of January last. This is the bill which Mr. Webster
proposes to support, " with all its provisions to the
fullest extent." It is a bill of abominations, but there
are " some amendments to it," which modify the bill
a little. Look at them. Here they are. The first
provides in addition to the fine of one thousand dollars
for aiding and abetting the escape of a fugitive, for
harboring and concealing him, that the offender " shall
also be imprisoned twelve months." The second
amendment is as follows —" And in no trial or hearing
under this act shall the testimony of such fugitive be
admitted in evidence."

These are Mr. Mason's amendments, offered on the
23rd of last January. This is the bill, " with some

amendments," which Mr. Webster says, " I propose to support, with all its provisions, to the fullest extent." Mr. Seward's bill was also before the Senate — a bill granting the fugitive slave a trial by jury in the State where he is found, to determine whether or not he is a slave. Mr. Webster says not a word about this bill. He does not propose to support it.

Suppose the bill of Mr. Webster's friend shall pass Congress, what will the action of it be? A slave-hunter comes here to Boston, he seizes any dark-looking man that is unknown and friendless, he has him before the postmaster, the collector of customs, or some clerk or marshal of some United States' court, and makes oath that the dark man is his slave. The slave-hunter is allowed his oath. The fugitive is not allowed his testimony. The man born free as you and I, on the false oath of a slave-hunter, or the purchased affidavit of some one, is surrendered to a southern State, to bondage life-long and irremediable. Will you say, the postmaster, the collector, the clerks and marshals in Boston would not act in such matters? They have no option; it is their official business to do so. But they would not decide against the unalienable rights of men — the right to life, liberty, and the pursuit of happiness. That may be, or may not be. The slave-hunter may have his " fugitive " before the collector of Boston, or the postmaster of Truro, if he sees fit. If they, remembering their Old Testament, refuse to " betray him that wandereth," the slave-hunter may bring on his officer with him from Georgia or Florida; he may bring the custom-house officer from Mobile or Wilmington, some little petty postmaster from a town you never heard of in South Carolina or Texas, and have any dark man in Boston up before that " magis-

trate," and on his decision have the fugitive carried off
to Louisiana or Arkansas, to bondage for ever. The
bill provides that the trial may be had before any such
officer, " residing or being " in the State where the
fugitive is found!

There were three fugitives at my house the other
night. Ellen Craft was one of them. You all know
Ellen Craft is a slave: she, with her husband, fled from
Georgia to Philadelphia, and is here before us now.
She is not so dark as Mr. Webster himself, if any of
you think freedom is to be dealt out in proportion to
the whiteness of the skin. If Mason's bill passes, I
might have some miserable postmaster from Texas or
the District of Columbia, some purchased agent of
Messrs. Bruin and Hill, the great slave-dealers of the
Capital, have him here in Boston, take Ellen Craft
before the caitiff, and on his decision hurry her off to
bondage as cheerless, as hopeless, and as irremediable
as the grave!

Let me interest you in a scene which might happen.
Suppose a poor fugitive, wrongfully held as a slave —
let it be Ellen Craft — has escaped from Savannah in
some northern ship. No one knows of her presence
on board; she has lain with the cargo in the hold of
the vessel. Harder things have happened. Men have
journeyed hundreds of miles bent double in a box half
the size of a coffin, journeying towards freedom.
Suppose the ship comes up to Long Wharf, at the
foot of State Street. Bulk is broken to remove the
cargo; the woman escapes, emaciated with hunger,
feeble from long confinement in a ship's hold, sick
with the tossing of the heedless sea, and still further
etiolated and blanched with the mingling emotions of
hope and fear. She escapes to land. But her pur-

suer, more remorseless than the sea, has been here be-
forehand; laid his case before the official he has
brought with him, or purchased here, and claims his
slave. She runs for her life, fear adding wings.
Imagine the scene — the flight, the hot pursuit through
State Street, Merchants' Row — your magistrates in
hot pursuit. To make the irony of nature still more
complete, let us suppose this shall take place on some
of the memorable days in the history of America — on
the 19th of April, when our fathers first laid down
their lives " in the sacred cause of God and their
country;" on the 17th of June, the 22nd of December,
or on any of the sacramental days in the long sad history of our struggle for our own freedom! Suppose
the weary fugitive takes refuge in Faneuil Hall, and
here, in the old Cradle of Liberty, in the midst of its
associations, under that eye of Samuel Adams, the
blood-hounds seize their prey! Imagine Mr. Webster
and Mr. Winthrop looking on, cheering the slave-
hunter, intercepting the fugitive fleeing for her life.
Would not that be a pretty spectacle? [5]

Propose to support that bill to the fullest extent,
with all its provisions! Ridiculous talk! Does Mr.
Webster suppose that such a law could be executed in
Boston? That the people of Massachusetts will ever
return a single fugitive slave, under such an act as
that? Then he knows his constituents very little, and
proves that he needs " instruction."

" Slavery is a moral and religious blessing," says
somebody in the present Congress. But it seems some
thirty thousand slaves have been blind to the benefits —
moral and religious benefits — which it confers, and
have fled to the free States. Mr. Clingman estimates
the value of all the fugitive slaves in the North at

$15,000,000. Delaware loses $100,000 in a year in this way; her riches taking to themselves not wings, but legs. Maryland lost $100,000 in six months. I fear Mr. Mason's bill and Mr. Webster's speech will not do much to protect that sort of " property " from this kind of loss. Such action is prevented " by a law even superior to that which admits and sanctions it in Texas."

Such are Mr. Webster's opinions on these four great questions. Now, there are two ways of accounting for this speech, or, at least, two ways of looking at it. One is, to regard it as the work of a statesman seeking to avert some great evil from the whole nation. This is the way Mr. Webster would have us look at it, I suppose. His friends tell us it is a statesmanlike speech — very statesmanlike. He himself says, *Vera pro gratis* — true words in preference to words merely pleasing. *Etsi meum ingenium non moneret necessitas cogit* — Albeit my own humor should not prompt the counsel, necessity compels it. The necessity so cogent is the attempt to dissolve the Union, in case the Wilmot Proviso should be extended over the new territory. Does any man seriously believe that Mr. Webster really fears a dissolution of this Union undertaken and accomplished on this plea, and by the Southern States? I will not insult the foremost understanding of this continent by supposing he deems it possible. No, we cannot take this view of his conduct.[6]

The other way is to regard it as the work of a politician, seeking something beside the permanent good of a great nation. The lease of the Presidency is to be disposed of for the next four years by a sort of auction. It is in the hands of certain political brokers, who " operate " in Presidential and other political stock. The majority of those brokers are slavehold-

ers or pro-slavery men; they must be conciliated, or
they will " not understand the nod " of the candidate —
I mean of the man who bids for the lease. All the
illustrious men in the national politics have an eye on
the transaction, but sometimes the bid has been taken
for persons whose chance at the sale seemed very poor.
General Cass made his bid some time ago. I think his
offer is recorded in the famous " Nicholson letter." He
was a Northern man, and bid non-intervention — the
unconstitutionality of any intervention with slavery in
the new territory. Mr. Clay made his bid, for old
Kentucky " never tires," the same old bid that he has
often made — a compromise. Mr. Calhoun did as he
has always done. I will not say he made any bid at
all; he was too sick for that, too sick for any thought
of the Presidency. Perhaps at this moment the angel
of death is dealing with that famed and remarkable
man. Nay, he may already have gone where " The
servant is free from his master, and the weary are at
rest;" have gone home to his God, who is the Father
of the great politician and the feeblest-minded slave.
If it be so, let us follow him only with pity for his
errors, and the prayer that his soul may be at rest.
He has fought manfully in an unmanly cause. He
seemed sincerely in the wrong, and spite of the badness
of the cause to which he devoted his best energies, you
cannot but respect the man.

Last of all, Mr. Webster makes his bid for the lease
of " that bad eminence," the Presidency. He bids
higher than the others, of course, as coming later; bids
Non-intervention, Four new slave States in Texas,
Mason's Bill for Capturing Fugitive Slaves and Denunciation of all the Anti-slavery movements of the
North, public and private. That is what he bids, look-

ing to the Southern side of the board of political brokers. Then he nods Northward, and says, The Wilmot Proviso is my "thunder;" then timidly glances to the South and adds, But I will never use it.

I think this is the only reasonable way in which we can estimate this speech — as a bid for the Presidency. I will not insult that mighty intellect by supposing that he, in his private heart, regards it in any other light. Mr. Calhoun might well be content with that, and say, "Organize the territories on the principle of that gentleman, and give us a free scope and sufficient time to get in — we ask nothing but that, and we never will ask it."

Such are the four great questions before us; such Mr. Webster's answers thereunto; such the two ways of looking at his speech. He decides in advance against freedom in Texas, against freedom in California, against freedom in New Mexico, against freedom in the United States, by his gratuitous offer of support to Mr. Mason's bill. His great eloquence, his great understanding, his great name, give weight to all his words. Pains are industriously taken to make it appear that his opinions are the opinions of Boston. Is it so? [Cries of No, No.] That was rather a feeble cry. Perhaps it is the opinion of the prevailing party in Boston. [No, No.] But I put it to you. Is it the opinion of Massachusetts? [Loud cries of No, No, No.] Well, so I say, No; it is not the opinion of Massachusetts.

Before now, servants of the people and leaders of the people have proved false to their employers, and betrayed their trust. Amongst all political men who have been weighed in the balance, and found wanting, with whom shall I compare him? Not with John
VIII—16

Quincy Adams, who, in 1807, voted for the Embargo.
It may have been the mistake of an honest intention,
though I confess I cannot think so yet. At any rate,
laying an Embargo, which he probably thought would
last but a few months, was a small thing compared
with the refusal to restrict slavery, willingness to enact laws to the disadvantage of mankind, and the
voluntary support of Mason's iniquitous bill. Besides, Mr. Adams lived a long life; if he erred, or if
he sinned in this matter, he afterwards fought most
valiantly for the rights of man.

Shall I compare Mr. Webster with Thomas Wentworth, the great Earl of Strafford, a man " whose
doubtful character and memorable end have made him
the most conspicuous character of a reign so fertile
in recollections "? He, like Webster, was a man of
large powers, and once devoted them to noble uses.
Did Wentworth defend the " Petition of Right? " So
did Webster many times defend the great cause of
liberty. But it was written of Strafford, that " in his
self-interested and ambitious mind," patriotism was
" the seed sown among thorns ! " " If we reflect upon
this man's cold-blooded apostasy on the first lure to
his ambition, and on his splendid abilities, which
enhanced the guilt of that desertion, we must feel
some indignation at those who have palliated all his
iniquities, and embalmed his memory with the attributes
of patriot heroism. Great he surely was, since that
epithet can never be denied without paradox to so
much comprehension of mind, such ardor and energy,
such courage and eloquence, those commanding qualities of soul, which, impressed upon his dark and stern
countenance, struck his contemporaries with mingled
awe and hate. . . . But it may be reckoned a

sufficient ground for distrusting any one's attachment
to the English Constitution, that he reveres the name
of Strafford." His measures for stifling liberty in
England, which he and his contemporaries signifi-
cantly called " Thorough," in the reign of Charles
I., were not more atrocious than the measures which
Daniel Webster proposes himself, or proposes to support " to the fullest extent." But Strafford paid the
forfeit — tasting the sharp and bitter edge of the
remorseless axe. Let his awful shade pass by. I
mourn at the parallel between him and the mighty
son of our own New England. Would God it were
not thus.

For a sadder parallel, I shall turn off from the sour
features of that great British politician, and find another man in our own fair land. This name carries us
back to " the times that tried men's souls," when also
there were souls that could not stand the rack. It
calls me back to " The famous year of '80;" to the
little American army in the highlands of New York;
to the time when the torch of American liberty which
now sends its blaze far up to heaven, at the same time
lighting the northern lakes and the Mexique Bay,
tinging with welcome radiance the eastern and the
western sea, was a feeble flame flickering about a thin
and hungry wick, and one hand was raised to quench
in darkness, and put out for ever, that feeble and uncertain flame. Gentlemen, I hate to speak thus. I
honor the majestic talents of this great man. I hate
to couple his name with that other, which few
Americans care to pronounce. But I know no deed
in American history, done by a son of New England,
to which I can compare this, but the act of Benedict
Arnold!

Shame that I should say this of any man; but his own motto shall be mine — *vera pro gratis* — and I am not responsible for what he has made the truth; certainly, *meum ingenium non moneret, necessitas cogit!*

I would speak with all possible tenderness of any man, of every man; of such an one, so honored, and so able, with respect I feel for superior powers. I would often question my sense of justice, before I dared to pronounce an adverse conclusion. But the wrong is palpable, the injustice is open as the day. I must remember, here are twenty millions, whose material welfare his counsel defeats: whose honor his counsel stains; whose political, intellectual, moral growth he is using all his mighty powers to hinder and keep back. "*Vera pro gratis. Necessitas cogit. Vellem, equidem, vobis placere, sed multo malo vos salvos esse, qualicunque erga me animo futuri estis.*"

Let me take a word of warning and of counsel from the same author; yes, from the same imaginary speech of Quintus Capitolinus, whence Mr. Webster has drawn his motto: — *Ante portas est bellum: si inde non pellitur, jam intra mœnia erit, et arcem et Capitolium scandet, et in domos vestras vos persequetur.* The war [against the extension of slavery, not against the Volscians, in this case] is before your very doors: if not driven thence, it will be within your walls [namely, it will be in California and New Mexico]; it will ascend the citadel and the Capitol [to wit, it will be in the House of Representatives and the Senate]; and it will follow you into your very homes [that is, the curse of slavery will corrupt the morals of the nation].

Sedemus desides domi, mulierum ritu inter nos altercantes; præsenti pace læti, nec cernentes ex otio illo

brevi multiplex bellum rediturum. We [the famous
senators of the United States] sit idle at home, wrang-
ling amongst ourselves like women [to see who shall
get the lease of the Presidency], glad of the present
truce [meaning that which is brought about by a
compromise], not perceiving that for this brief ces-
sátion of trouble, a manifold war will follow [that is,
" horrid internecine war " which will come here as it
has been elsewhere, if justice be too long delayed]!

It is a great question before us, concerning the existence of millions of men. To many men in politics,
it is merely a question of party rivalry; a question
of in and out, and nothing more. To many men in
cities, it is a question of commerce, like the establishment of a bank, or the building of one railroad more
or less. But to serious men, who love man and love
their God, this is a question of morals, a question
of religion, to be settled with no regard to party
rivalry, none to fleeting interests of to-day, but to be
settled under the awful eye of conscience, and by the
just law of God.

Shall we shut up slavery or extend it? It is for us
to answer. Will you deal with the question now, or
leave it to your children, when the evil is ten times
greater? In 1749, there was not a slave in Georgia;
now, two hundred and eighty thousand. In 1750, in
all the United States, but two hundred thousand; now,
three millions. In 1950, let Mr. Webster's counsels
be followed, there will be thirty millions. Thirty
millions! Will it then be easier for your children to
set limits to this crime against human nature, than
now for you? Our fathers made a political, and a
commercial, and a moral error — shall we repeat it?
They did a wrong; shall we extend and multiply the

wrong? Was it an error in our fathers; not barely a wrong — was it a sin? No, not in them; they knew it not. But what in them to establish was only an error, in us to extend or to foster is a sin!

Perpetuate slavery, we cannot do it. Nothing will save it. It is girt about by a ring of fire which daily grows narrower, and sends terrible sparkles into the very center of the shameful thing. "Joint resolutions" cannot save it; annexations cannot save it — not if we re-annex all the West Indies; delinquent representatives cannot save it; uninstructed senators refusing instructions, cannot save it — no, not with all their logic, all their eloquence, which smites as an earthquake smites the sea. No, slavery cannot be saved; by no compromise, no non-intervention, no Mason's Bill in the Senate. It cannot be saved in this age of the world until you nullify every ordinance of nature, until you repeal the will of God, and dissolve the union He has made between righteousness and the welfare of the people. Then, when you displace God from the throne of the world, and instead of His eternal justice, re-enact the will of the devil, then you may keep slavery; keep it for ever, keep it in peace. Not till then.

The question is, not if slavery is to cease, and soon to cease, but shall it end as it ended in Massachusetts, in New Hampshire, in Pennsylvania, in New York; or shall it end as in St. Domingo? Follow the counsel of Mr. Webster — it will end in fire and blood. God forgive us for our cowardice, if we let it come to this, that three millions or thirty millions of degraded human beings, degraded by us, must wade through slaughter to their unalienable rights.

Mr. Webster has spoken noble words — at Plymouth,

standing on the altar-stone of New England; at
Bunker Hill, the spot so early reddened with the blood
of our fathers. But at this hour, when we looked for
great counsel, when we forgot the paltry things which
he has often done and said, " Now he will rouse his
noble soul, and be the man his early speeches once
bespoke," who dared to fear that Olympian head would
bow so low, so deeply kiss the ground? Try it morally, try it intellectually, try it by the statesman's
test, world-wide justice; nay, try it by the politician's
basest test, the personal expediency of to-day — it is
a speech " not fit to be made," and when made, not
fit to be confirmed.

" We see dimly in the distance what is small and what is great,
    Slow of faith how weak an arm may turn the iron helm of
        fate;
    But the soul is still oracular; amid the market's din,
    List the ominous stern whisper from the Delphic cave within —
    ' They enslave their children's children, who make compromise
        with sin.' "

IX

THE SLAVE POWER

MR. PRESIDENT,— If we look hastily at the present aspect of American affairs, there is much to discourage a man who believes in the progress of his race. In this republic, with the Declaration of Independence for its political creed, neither of the great political parties is hostile to the existence of slavery. That institution has the continual support of both the Whig and Democratic parties. There are now four eminent men in the Senate of the United States, all of them friends of slavery. Two of these are from the North, both natives of New England; but they surpass their Southern rivals in the zeal with which they defend that institution, and in the concessions which they demand of the friends of justice at the North. These four men are all competitors for the Presidency. Not one of them is the friend of freedom; he that is apparently least its foe, is Mr. Benton, the senator from Missouri. Mr. Clay, of Kentucky, is less effectually the advocate of slavery than Mr. Webster, of Massachusetts. Mr. Webster himself has said, " There is no North," and, to prove it experimentally, stands there as one mighty instance of his own rule.

In the Senate of the United States, only Seward and Chase and Hale can be relied on as hostile to slavery. In the House, there are Root and Giddings, and Wilmot and Mann, and a few others. " But what are these among so many? "

See " how it strikes a stranger." Here is an extract

from the letter of a distinguished and learned man,[1] sent out here by the king of Sweden to examine our public schools: "I have just returned from Washington, where I have been witnessing the singular spectacle of this free and enlightened nation being buried in sorrow, on account of the death of that great advocate of slavery, Mr. Calhoun. Mr. Webster's speech seems to have made a very strong impression upon the people of the South, as I have heard it repeated almost as a lesson of the catechism by every person I have met within the slave territory. It seems now to be an established belief, that slavery is not a *malum necessarium*, still less an evil difficult to get rid of, but desirable soon to get rid of. No, far from that; it seems to be considered as quite a natural, most happy, and essentially Christian institution!" [2]

Not satisfied with keeping an institution which the more Christian religion of the Mohammedan Bey of Tunis has rejected as a "sin against God," we seek to extend it, to perpetuate it, even on soil which the half-civilized Mexicans made clear from its pollutions. The great organs of the party politics of the land are in favor of the extension; the great political men of the land seek to extend it; the leading men in the large mercantile towns of the North — in Boston, New York, and Philadelphia — are also in favor of extending slavery. All this is plain.

But, sir, as I come up here to this Convention year after year, I find some signs of encouragement. Even in the present state of things, the star of hope appears, and we may safely and reasonably say, "Now is our salvation nearer than when we first believed" in anti-slavery. Let us look a little at the condition of America at this moment, to see what there is to help or what to hinder us.

First, I will speak of the present crisis in our affairs; then of the political parties amongst us; then of the manner in which this crisis is met; next of the foes of freedom; and last, of its friends. I will speak with all coolness, and try to speak short. By the middle of the anniversary week, men get a little heated; I am sure I shall be cool, and I think I may also be dull.

There must be unity of action in a nation, as well as in a man, or there cannot be harmony and welfare. As a man " cannot serve two masters " antagonistic and diametrically opposed to one another, as God and Mammon, no more can a nation serve two opposite principles at the same time.

Now, there are two opposite and conflicting principles recognized in the political action of America: at this moment, they contend for the mastery, each striving to destroy the other.

There is what I call the American idea. I so name it because it seems to me to lie at the basis of all our truly original, distinctive, and American institutions. It is itself a complex idea, composed of three subordinate and more simple ideas, namely: The idea that all men have unalienable rights; that in respect thereof, all men are created equal; and that government is to be established and sustained for the purpose of giving every man an opportunity for the enjoyment and development of all these unalienable rights. This idea demands, as the proximate organization thereof, a democracy, that is, a government of all the people, by all the people, for all the people; of course, a government after the principles of eternal justice, the unchanging law of God; for shortness' sake I will call it the idea of freedom.

That is one idea; and the other is, that one man has

a right to hold another man in thraldom, not for the slave's good, but for the master's convenience; not on account of any wrong the slave has done or intended, but solely for the benefit of the master. This idea is not peculiarly American. For shortness' sake, I will call this the idea of slavery. It demands for its proximate organization, an aristocracy, that is, a government of all the people by a part of the people — the masters; for a part of the people — the masters; against a part of the people — the slaves; a government contrary to the principles of eternal justice, contrary to the unchanging law of God. These two ideas are hostile, irreconcilably hostile, and can no more be compromised and made to coalesce in the life of this nation, than the worship of the real God and the worship of the imaginary devil can be combined and made to coalesce in the life of a single man. An attempt has been made to reconcile and unite the two. The slavery clauses of the Constitution of the United States is one monument of this attempt; the results of this attempt — you see what they are, not order, but confusion.

We cannot have any settled and lasting harmony until one or the other of these ideas is cast out of the councils of the nation: so there must be war between them before there can be peace. Hitherto, the nation has not been clearly aware of the existence of these two adverse principles; or, if aware of their existence, has thought of their irreconcilable diversity. At the present time, this fact is brought home to our consciousness with great clearness. On the one hand, the friends of freedom set forth the idea of freedom, clearly and distinctly, demanding liberty for each man. This has been done as never before. Even in the

Senate of the United States it has been done, and re
peatedly during the present session of Congress. On
the other hand, the enemies of freedom set forth the
idea of slavery as this has not been done in other
countries for a long time. Slavery has not been so
lauded in any legislative body for many a year, as in
the American Senate in 1850. Some of the discussions
remind one of the spirit which prevailed in the Roman
Senate, A. D. 62, when about four hundred slaves were
crucified, because their master, Pedanius Secundus, a
man of consular dignity, was found murdered in his
bed. I mean to say, the same disregard of the welfare
of the slaves, the same willingness to sacrifice them —
if not their lives, which are not now at peril, at least
their welfare, to the convenience of their masters.
Anybody can read the story in Tacitus,[3] and it is
worth reading, and instructive, too, at these times.

Here are some of the statements relative to slavery
made in the thirty-first Congress of the United States.
Hearken to the testimony of the Hon. Mr. Badger, of
North Carolina:

"It is clear that this institution [slavery] not only was not
disapproved of, but was expressly recognized, approved, and
its continuance sanctioned by the divine lawgiver of the Jews."

"Whether an evil or not, it is not a sin; it is not a violation
of the divine law.

"What treatment did it receive from the founder of the gospel dispensation? It was approved, first negatively, because, in
the whole New Testament, there is not to be found one single
word, either spoken by the Saviour, or by any of the evangelists
or apostles, in which that institution is either directly or indirectly condemned; and also affirmatively." This he endeavors
to show, by quoting the passages from St. Paul, usually quoted
for that purpose. "Nothing would be easier than for St. Paul
to have said —' Slaves, be obedient to your heathen masters; but
I say to you, feeling masters, emancipate your slaves; the law
of Christ is against that relation, and you are bound, therefore,
to set them at liberty.' No such word is spoken."

Thus far goes the Hon. Senator Badger, of North Carolina.

Mr. Brown, of Mississippi, goes further yet. He knows what some men think of slavery, and tells them, " Very well, think so; but keep your thoughts to yourselves." He is not content with bidding the " freest and most enlightened nation in the world," be silent on this matter: he is not content, with Mr. Badger, to declare that if an evil, it is not a sin, and to find it upheld in the Old Testament, and allowed in the New Testament; he tells us that he regards slavery " as a great moral, social, political, and religious blessing — a blessing to the slave, and a blessing to the master."

Thus, the issue is fairly made between the two principles. The contradiction is plain. The battle between the two is open, and in sight of the world.

But this is not the first time there has been a quarrel between the idea of slavery and the idea of freedom in America. The quarrel has lasted, with an occasional truce, for more than sixty years. In six battles, slavery has been victorious over freedom.

1. In the adoption of the Constitution supporting slavery.

2. In the acquisition of Louisiana as slave territory.

3. In the acquisition of Florida as slave territory.

4. In making the Missouri Compromise.

5. In the annexation of Texas as a slave State.

6. In the Mexican War — a war mean and wicked, even amongst wars.

Since the Revolution, there have been three instances of great national importance, in which freedom has overcome slavery; there have been three victories:

1. In prohibiting slavery from the Northwest Territory, before the adoption of the Constitution.

2. In prohibiting the slave-trade in 1808. I mean, in prohibiting the African slave-trade; the American slave-trade is still carried on in the Capital of the United States.

3. The prohibition of slavery in Oregon may be regarded as a third victory, though not apparently of so much consequence as the others.

Now comes another battle, and it remains to be decided whether the idea of slavery or the idea of freedom is to prevail in the territory we have conquered and stolen from Mexico. The present strife is to settle that question. Now, as before, it is a battle between freedom and slavery; one on which the material and spiritual welfare of millions of men depends; but now the difference between freedom and slavery is more clearly seen than in 1787; the consequences of each are better understood, and the sin of slavery is felt and acknowledged by a class of persons who had few representatives sixty years ago. It is a much greater triumph for slavery to prevail now, and carry its institutions into New Mexico in 1850, than it was to pass the pro-slavery provisions of the Constitution in 1787. It will be a greater sin now to extend slavery, than it was to establish it in 1620, when slaves were first brought to Virginia.

Ever since the adoption of the Constitution, protected by that shield, mastering the energies of the nation, and fighting with that weapon, slavery has been continually aggressive. The slave-driver has coveted new soil; has claimed it; has had his claim allowed. Louisiana, Florida, Texas, California, and New Mexico are the results of Southern aggression. Now the slave-driver reaches out his hand towards Cuba, trying to clutch that emerald gem set in the tropic sea. How easy it was to surrender to Great Britain portions of the Oregon Territory in a high northern latitude! Had it been south of 36° 30′, it would not have been so easy to settle the Oregon question by a compromise. So when we make a compromise there, " the reciprocity must be all on one side."

Let us next look at the position of the political parties with respect to the present crisis. There are now four political parties in the land.

1. There is the Government party, represented by the President, and portions of his Cabinet, if not the whole of it. This party does not attempt to meet the question which comes up, but to dodge and avoid it. Shall freedom or slavery prevail in the new territory is the question. The Government has no opinion; it will leave the matter to be settled by the people of the territory. This party wishes California to come into the Union without slavery for it is her own desire so to come; and does not wish a territorial government to be formed by Congress in New Mexico, but to leave the people there to form a State, excluding or establishing slavery as they see fit. The motto of this party is inaction, not intervention. King James I. once proposed a question to the judges of England. They declined to answer it, and the king said, " If ye give no counsel, then why be ye counsellors? " The people of the United States might ask the Government, " If ye give us no leading, then why be ye leaders? " This party is not hostile to slavery; not opposed to its extension.

2. Then there is the Whig party. This party has one distinctive idea; the idea of a tariff for protection; whether for the protection of American labor, or merely American capital, I will not now stop to inquire. The

Whig party is no more opposed to slavery, or its extension, than the Government party itself.

However, there are two divisions of the Whigs, the Whig party South, and the Whig party North. The two agree in their ideas of protection, and their pro-slavery character. But the Whig party South advocates slavery and protection; the Whig party North, protection and slavery.

In the North there are many Whigs who are opposed to slavery, especially to the extension of slavery; there are also many other persons, not of the Whig party, opposed to the extension of slavery; therefore in the late electioneering campaign, to secure the votes of these persons, it was necessary for the Whig party North to make profession of anti-slavery. This was done accordingly, in a general form, and in special an attempt was made to show that the Whig party was opposed to the extension of slavery.

Hear what Senator Chase says on this point. I read from his speech in the Senate, on March 26, 1850: —

"On the Whig side it was urged that the candidate of the Philadelphia Convention was, if not positively favorable to the Proviso, at least pledged to leave the matter to Congress free from executive influence, and ready to prove it when enacted by that body."

General Cass had written the celebrated "Nicholson letter," in which he declared that Congress had no constitutional power to enact the Proviso. But so anxious were the Democrats of the North to assume an anti-slavery aspect,— continues Mr. Chase,— that

"Notwithstanding this letter, many of his friends in the free States persisted in asserting that he would not, if elected, veto the Proviso; many also insisted that he regarded slavery as excluded from the territories by the Mexican laws still in force; while others maintained that he regarded slavery as an institution of positive law, and Congress as constitutionally incompetent to enact such law, and that therefore it was impossible for slavery to get into the territories, whether Mexican law was in force or not."

This, says Mr. Chase, was the Whig argument: —

"Prohibition is essential to the certain exclusion of slavery from the territories. If the Democratic candidate shall be elected, prohibition is impossible, for the veto will be used: if the Whig candidate shall be elected, prohibition is certain, provided you elect a Congress who will carry out your will. Vote, therefore, for the Whigs."

Such was the general argument of the Whig party. Let us see what it was in Massachusetts in special. Here I have documentary evidence. This is the statement of the Whig Convention at Worcester in 1848, published shortly before the election; —

"We understand the Whig party to be committed in favor of the principles contained in the Ordinance of 1787, the prohibition of slavery in territory now free, and of its abolition wherever it can be constitutionally effected."

They professed to aim at the same thing which the Free-soil party aimed at, only the work must be done by the old Whig organization. Free-soil cloth must be manufactured, but it must be woven in the old Whig mill, with the old Whig machinery, and by the Whig weavers. See what the Convention says of the Democratic party: —

"We understand the Democratic party to be pledged to decline any legislation upon the subject of slavery, with a view either to its prohibition or restriction in places where it does not exist, or to its abolition in any of the territories of the United States."

VIII—17

There is no ambiguity in that language. Men can talk very plain when they will. Still there were some that doubted; so the great and famous men of the party came out to convince the doubters that the Whigs were the men to save the country from the disgrace of slavery.

Here let me introduce the testimony of Mr. Choate. This which follows is from his speech at Salem. He tells us the great work is, "The passage of a law to-day that California and New Mexico shall remain for ever free. That is . . . an object of great and transcendent importance: . . . we should go up to the very limits of the Constitution itself . . . to defeat the always detested and for-ever-to-be detested object of the dark ambition of that candidate of the Baltimore Convention, who has consented to pledge himself in advance, that he will veto the future law of freedom!" "Is there a Whig upon this floor who doubts that the strength of the Whig party next March will extend freedom to California and New Mexico, if by the Constitution they are entitled to freedom at all? Is there a member of Congress that would not vote for freedom?" [*Sancta simplicitas! Ora pro nobis!*] "Is there a single Whig constituency, in any free State in this country, that would return any man that would not vote for freedom? Do you believe that Daniel Webster himself could be returned, if there was the least doubt upon this question?"

That is plain speech. But, to pass from the special to the particular, hear Mr. Webster himself. What follows is from his famous speech at Marshfield, September, 1848.

"General Cass (he says) will have the Senate; and with the patronage of the Government, with the interest that he, as a Northern man, can bring to bear, co-operating with every interest that the South can bring to bear, we cry *safety* before we are out of the woods, if we feel that there is no danger as to these new territories!" "In my judgment, the interests of the country and the feelings of a vast majority of the people require that a President of these United States shall be elected, who will neither use his official influence to promote, nor who feels any disposition in his heart to promote, the further extension of slavery in this country, and the further influence of it in the public councils."

Speaking of the Free-soil party and the Buffalo platform he says —" I hold myself to be as good a Free-soil man as any of the Buffalo convention." Of the platform, he says —" I can stand upon it pretty well." " I beg to know who is to inspire into my breast a more resolute and fixed determination to resist, unyieldingly, the encroachments and advances of the slave power in this country, than has inspired it, ever since the day that I first opened my mouth in the councils of the country."

If such language as this would not " deceive the very elect," what was more to the point, it was quite enough to deceive the electors. But now this language is forgotten; forgotten in general by the Whig party North; forgotten in special by those who seemed to be the exponents of the Whig party in Massachusetts; forgotten at any rate by the nine hundred and eighty-seven men who signed the letter to Mr. Webster; and in particular it is forgotten by Mr. Webster himself, who now says that it would disgrace his own understanding to vote for the extension of the Wilmot Proviso over the new territory!

There were some men in New England who did not believe the statements of the Whig party North in

1848, because they knew the men that uttered the
sentiments of the Whig party South. The leaders
put their thumbs in the eyes of the people, and then
said, " Do you see any dough in our faces? " " No! "
said the people, " not a speck." " Then vote our
ticket, and never say we are not hostile to slavery so
long as you live."

At the South, the Whig party used language somewhat different. Here is a sample from the New Orleans Bee: —

" General Taylor is from birth, association, and conviction,
identified with the South and her institutions; being one of the
most extensive slaveholders in Louisiana — and supported by
the slaveholding interest, as opposed to the Wilmot Proviso,
and in favor of securing the privilege to the owners of slaves
to remove with them to newly acquired territory."

3. Then there is the Democratic party. The distinctive idea of the Democrats is represented by the
word anti-protection, or revenue tariff. This party, as
such, is still less opposed to slavery than the Whigs;
however, there are connected with it, at the North,
many men who oppose the extension of slavery. This
party is divided into two divisions, the Democratic
party South, and the Democratic party North. They
agree in their idea of anti-protection and slavery, differing only in the emphasis which they give to the two
words. The Democrats of the South say slavery and
anti-protection; the Democrats North, anti-protection
and slavery. Thus you see, that while there is a
specific difference between Democrats and Whigs, there
is also a generic agreement in the matter of slavery.
According to the doctrine of elective affinities, both
drop what they have a feeble affinity for, and hold
on with what their stronger affinity demands. The

Whigs and Democrats of the South are united in
their attachment to slavery, not only mechanically, but
by a sort of chemical union.

Mr. Cass's " Nicholson letter " is well known. He
says, Congress has no constitutional right to restrict
slavery in the territories. Here is the difference between him and General Taylor. General Taylor does
not interfere at all in the matter. If Congress puts
slavery in, he says, Very well! If Congress puts
slavery out, he says the same, Very well! But if
Congress puts slavery out, General Cass would say,
No. You shall not put it out. One has the policy
of King Log, the other that of King Serpent. So
far as that goes Log is the better king.

So much for the Democratic party.

4. The Free-soil party opposes slavery so far as it
is possible to do, and yet comply with the Constitution
of the United States. Its idea is declared by its
words,— No more slave territory. It does not profess to be an anti-slavery party in general, only an
anti-slavery party subject to the Constitution. In
the present crisis in the Congress of the United States,
it seems to me the men who represent this idea, though
not always professing allegiance to the party, have yet
done the nation good and substantial service. I refer
more particularly to Messrs. Chase, Seward, and Hale
in the Senate, to Messrs. Root, Giddings, and Mann
in the House. Those gentlemen swear to keep the
Constitution; in what sense and with what limitations
I know not. It is for them to settle that matter with
their own consciences. I do know this, that these men
have spoken very noble words against slavery; heroic
words in behalf of freedom. It is not to be supposed
that the Free-soil party, as such, has attained the same

convictions as to the sin of slavery, which the anti-
slavery party has long arrived at. Still they may be
as faithful to their convictions as any of the men
about this platform. If they have less light to walk
by, they have less to be accountable for. For my own
part, spite of their shortcomings, and of some things
which to me seem wrong in the late elections in New
England, I cannot help thinking they have done good
as individuals, and as a party; it seems to me they
have done good both ways. I will honor all manly
opposition to slavery, whether it come up to my mark,
or does not come near it. I will ask every man to
be true to his conscience, and his reason, not to mine.

In speaking of the parties, I ought not to omit to
say a word or two respecting some of the most prominent men, and their position in reference to this slavery
question. It is a little curious, that of all the candidates for the Presidency, Mr. Benton, of Missouri,
should be the least inclined to support the pretensions
of the slave power. But so it is.

Of Mr. Cass, nothing more need be said at present;
his position is defined and well known. But a word
must be said of Mr. Clay. He comes forward, as
usual, with a compromise. Here it is, in the famous
" Omnibus Bill." In one point it is not so good as
the government scheme. General Taylor, as the organ
of the party, recommends the admission of California,
as an independent measure. He does not huddle and
lump it together with any other matters; and in this
respect, his scheme is more favorable to freedom than
the other; for Mr. Clay couples the admission of California with other things. But in two points Mr.
Clay's bill has the superiority over the General's
scheme.

1. It limits the western and northern boundaries of Texas, and so reduces the territory of that State, where slavery is now established by law. Yet, as I understand it, he takes off from New Mexico about seventy thousand square miles, enough to make eight or ten States like Massachusetts, and delivers it over to Texas to be slave soil; as Mr. Webster says, out of the power of Congress to redeem from that scourge.

2. It does not maintain that Congress has no power to exclude slavery in admitting a new State; whereas, if I understand the President in his message, he considers such an act " An invasion of their rights." [4]

Let us pass by Mr. Clay, and come to the other aspirant for the Presidency.

At the Philadelphia Convention, Mr. Webster, at the most, could only get one half the votes of New England; several of these not given in earnest, but only as a compliment to the great man from the North. Now, finding his Presidential wares not likely to be bought by New England, he takes them to a wider market; with what success we shall one day see.

Something has already been said in the newspapers and elsewhere, about Mr. Webster's speech. No speech ever delivered in America has excited such deep and righteous indignation. I know there are influential men in Boston, and in all large towns, who must always have somebody to sustain and applaud. They some time since applauded Mr. Webster, for reasons very well known, and now continue their applause of him. His late speech pleases them; its worst parts please them most. All that is as was to be expected; men like what they must like. But, in the country, among the sober men of Massachusetts and New England, who prize right above the political expediency of to-day,

I think Mr. Webster's speech is read with indignation. I believe no one political act in America, since the treachery of Benedict Arnold, has excited so much moral indignation, as the conduct of Daniel Webster.

But I pass by his speech, to speak of other things connected with that famous man. One of the most influential pro-slavery newspapers of Boston calls the gentlemen who signed the letter to him, the "retainers" of Mr. Webster. The word is well chosen and quite descriptive. This word is used in a common, feudal, and a legal sense. In the common sense, it means one who has complete possession of the thing retained; in the feudal sense, it means a dependent or vassal, who is bound to support his liege lord; in the legal sense, it means the person who hires an attorney to do his business; and the sum given to secure his services, or prevent him from acting for the opposite party, is called a retaining fee. I take it the word "retainers" is used in the legal sense; certainly it is not in the feudal sense, for these gentlemen do not owe allegiance to Mr. Webster. Nor is it in its common sense, for events have shown that they have not a "complete possession" of Mr. Webster.

Now a word about this letter to him. Mr. Webster's retainers — nine hundred and eighty-seven in number — tell him, "You have pointed out to a whole people the path of duty, have convinced the understanding, and touched the conscience of a nation." "We desire, therefore, to express to you our entire concurrence in the sentiments of your speech, and our heartfelt thanks for the inestimable aid it has afforded towards the preservation and perpetuation of the Union."

They express their entire concurrence in the sentiments of his speech. In the speech, as published in the edition "revised and corrected by himself," Mr. Webster declares his intention to support the famous Fugitive Slave Bill, and the amendments thereto, "with all its provisions, to the fullest extent." When the retainers express their "entire concurrence in the sentiments of the speech," they express their entire concurrence in that intention. There is no ambiguity in the language; they make a universal affirmation — (*affirmatio de omni*). Now Mr. Webster comes out, by two agents, and recants this declaration. Let me do him no injustice. He shall be heard by his next friend, who wishes to amend the record, a correspondent of the Boston Courier, of May 6th: —

"The speech now reads thus:—'My friend at the head of the Judiciary Committee has a bill on the subject now before the Senate, with some amendments to it, which I propose to support, with all its provisions, to the fullest extent.' Change the position of the word which, and the sentence would read thus:—'My friend at the head of the Judiciary Committee has a bill on the subject now before the Senate, which, with some amendments to it, I propose to support, with all its provisions, to the fullest extent.'"

"Call you that backing your friends?" Really, it is too bad, after his retainers have expressed their "entire concurrence in the sentiments of the speech," for him to back out, to deny that he entertained one of the sentiments already approved of and concurred in! Can it be possible, we ask, that Mr. Webster can resort to this device to defend himself, leaving his retainers in the lurch? It does not look like him to do such a thing. But the correspondent of the Courier goes on as follows: —

"We are authorized to state, first — that Mr. Webster did not revise this portion of his speech with any view to examine its exact accuracy of phrase; and second — that Mr. Webster at the time of the delivery of the speech had in his desk three emendatory sections, . . . and one of which provides expressly for the right of trial by jury."

But who is the person " authorized to state " such a thing? Professor Stuart informs the public that it " comes from the hand of a man who might claim a near place to Mr. Webster, in respect to talent, integrity, and patriotism."

Still, this recantation is so unlike Mr. Webster that one would almost doubt the testimony of so great an unknown as is the writer in the Courier. But Mr. Stuart removes all doubt, and says —" I merely add that Mr. Webster himself has personally assured me that his speech was in accordance with the correction here made, and that he has now in his desk the amendments to which the corrector refers." So the retainers must bear the honor, or the shame, whichsoever it may be, of volunteering the advocacy of that remarkable bill.

When Paul was persecuted for righteousness' sake, how easily might " the offense of the cross " have been made to cease, by a mere transposition! Had he pursued that plan, he need not have been let down from the wall in a basket: he might have had a dinner given him by forty scribes, at the first hotel in Jerusalem, and a doctor of the law to defend him in a pamphlet.

But, alas! in Mr. Webster's case, admitting the transposition is real, the transubstantiation is not thereby effected; the transfer of the *which* does not alter the character of the sentence of the requisite degree. The bill, which he volunteers to advocate, contains provisions to this effect: That the owner of a fugitive slave may seize his fugitive, and, on the warrant of any " judge, commissioner, clerk, marshal,

post-master, or collector," " residing or being " within
the State where the seizure is made, the fugitive,
without any trial by jury, shall be delivered up to
his master, and carried out of the State.   Now, this
is the bill which Mr. Webster proposes " to support,
with all its provisions, to the fullest extent."   Let
him transfer his *which*, it does not transubstantiate
his statement so that he can consistently introduce a
section which " provides expressly for the right of
trial by jury."   This attempt to evade the plain
meaning of a plain statement is too small a thing for
a great man.

I make no doubt that Mr. Webster had in his desk,
at the time alleged, a bill designed to secure the trial
by jury to fugitive slaves, prepared as it is set forth.
But how do you think it came there, and for what
purpose?   Last February Mr. Webster was intending
to make a very different speech; and then, I make no
doubt, it was that this bill was prepared, with the design of introducing it!   But I see no reason for
supposing that when he made his celebrated speech,
he intended to introduce it as an amendment to Mr.
Mason's or Butler's bill.   It is said that he will present it to the Senate.   Let us wait and see.[5]

But, since the speech at Washington, Mr. Webster
has said things at Boston almost as bad.   Here they
are; extracts from his speech at the Revere House.
I quote from the report in the " Daily Advertiser."
" Neither you nor I shall see the legislation of the
country proceed in the old harmonious way, until the
discussions in Congress and out of Congress upon the
subject, to which you have alluded [the subject of
slavery], shall be, in some way, suppressed.   Take
that truth home with you — and take it as truth."

A very pretty truth that is to take home with us, that
" discussion " must be " suppressed! "

Again, he says : —

> " Sir, the question is, whether Massachusetts will stand to the
> truth against temptation [that is the question]! whether she
> will be just against temptation! whether she will defend herself
> against her own prejudices! She has conquered everything
> else in her time; she has conquered this ocean which washes her
> shore; she has conquered her own sterile soil; she has conquered
> her stern and inflexible climate; she has fought her way to the
> universal respect of the world; she has conquered every one's
> prejudices but her own. The question is, whether she will con-
> quer her own prejudices!"

The trumpet gives no uncertain sound; but before
we prepare ourselves for battle, let us see who is the
foe. What are the " prejudices " Massachusetts is
to conquer? The prejudice in favor of the American
idea; the prejudice in favor of what our fathers
called self-evident truths; that all men " are endowed
with certain unalienable rights;" that " all men are
created equal," and that " to secure these rights,
governments are instituted amongst men." These
are the prejudices Massachusetts is called on to conquer. There are some men who will do this " with
alacrity;" but will Massachusetts conquer her prejudices in favor of the " unalienable rights of man "?
I think, Mr. President, she will first have to forget
two hundred years of history. She must efface
Lexington and Bunker Hill from her memory, and
tear the old rock of Plymouth out from her bosom.
These are prejudices which Massachusetts will not
conquer till the ocean ceases to wash her shore, and
granite to harden her hills. Massachusetts has conquered a good many things, as Mr. Webster tells us.
I think there are several other things we shall try our

hand upon, before we conquer our prejudice in favor of the unalienable rights of man.

There is one pleasant thing about this position of Mr. Webster. He is alarmed at the fire which has been kindled in his rear. He finds "considerable differences of opinion prevail . . . on the subject of that speech," and is "grateful to receive. . . . opinions so decidedly concurring with" his own,— so he tells the citizens of Newburyport. He feels obliged to do something to escape the obloquy which naturally comes upon him. So he revises his speech; now supplying an omission, now altering a little; authorizes another great man to transpose his relative pronoun and anchor it fast to another antecedent; appeals to amendments in the senatorial desk, designed to secure a jury trial for fugitive slaves; derides his opponents, and compares them with the patriots of ancient times. Here is his letter to the citizens of Newburyport — a very remarkable document. It contains some surprising legal doctrines, which I leave others to pass upon. But in it he explains the Fugitive Slave Law of 1793, which does not "provide for the trial of any question whatever by jury, in the State in which the arrest is made." "At that time," nobody regarded any of the provisions of that bill as "repugnant to religion, liberty, the Constitution, or humanity;" and he has "no more objections to the provisions of this law, than was seen to them" by the framers of the law itself. If he sees therein nothing "repugnant to religion, liberty, the Constitution, or humanity," then why transpose that relative pronoun, and have an amendment "which provides expressly for the right of trial by jury?"

" In order to allay excitement," he answers, " and remove objections." " There are many difficulties, however, attending any
such provision [of a jury trial]; and a main one, and perhaps
the only insuperable one, has been created by the States themselves, by making it a penal offense in their own officers, to render any aid in apprehending or securing such fugitives, and
absolutely refusing the use of their jails for keeping them in
custody, till a jury could be impanelled, witnesses summoned,
and a regular trial be had."

Think of that! It is Massachusetts, Pennsylvania,
Ohio, and New York, which prohibit the fugitive from
getting a trial for his freedom, before a jury of twelve
good men and true! But Mr. Webster goes on: " It
is not too much to say that to these State laws is to
be attributed the actual and practical denial of trial
by jury in these cases." Generally, the cause is
thought to precede the effect, but here is a case in
which, according to Mr. Webster, the effect has got
the start of the cause by more than fifty years. The
Fugitive Slave Law of Congress which allowed the
master to capture the runaway, was passed in 1793;
but the State laws he refers to, to which " is to be attributed the actual and practical denial of trial by
jury in these cases," were not passed till after 1840.
" To what base uses may we come at last!" Mr.
Webster would never have made such a defense of his
pro-slavery conduct, had he not been afraid of the
fire in his rear, and thought his retainers not able to
put it out. He seems to think this fire is set in the
name of religion: so, to help us " conquer our prejudices," he cautions us against the use of religion,
and quotes from the private letter of " one of the
most distinguished men in England," dated as late as
the 29th of January —" Religion is an excellent thing
in every matter except in politics: there it seems to

make men mad." In this respect, it seems religion
is inferior to money, for the Proverbs tell us that
money " answereth all things;" religion, it seems,
" answereth all things," except politics. Poor Mr.
Webster! If religion is not good in politics, I suppose irreligion is good there; and, really, it is often
enough introduced there. So, if religion " seems to
make men mad " in politics, I suppose irreligion makes
them sober in politics. But Mr. Webster, fresh from
his transposition of his own relative, explains this:
His friend ascribes the evils not to " true and genuine
religion," but to " that fantastic notion of religion."
So, making the transposition, it would read thus:
" That fantastical notion of religion," " is an excellent
thing in any matter except politics." Alas! Mr.
Webster does not expound his friend's letter, nor his
own language, so well as he used to expound the Constitution. But he says: " The religion in the New
Testament is as sure a guide to duty in politics, as in
any other concern of life." So, in the name of " conscience and the Constitution," Professor Stuart comes
forward to defend Mr. Webster, " by the religion of
the New Testament; that religion which is founded on
the teachings of Jesus and his apostles." How are
the mighty fallen!

Mr. Webster makes a " great speech," lending his
mighty influence to the support and extension of
slavery, with all its attendant consequences, which
paralyze the hand of industry, enfeeble the thinking
mind, and brutify the conscience which should discern
between right and wrong; nine hundred and eighty-
seven of his retainers in Boston thank him for remind-
ing them of their duty. But still the fire in his rear
is so hot that he must come on to Boston, talk about

having discussion suppressed, and ask Massachusetts to conquer her prejudices. That is not enough. He must go up to Andover and get a minister to defend him, in the name of " conscience and the Constitution," supporting slavery out of the Old Testament and New Testament. " To what mean uses may we not descend ! "

There is a " short and easy method " with Professor Stuart, and all other men who defend slavery out of the Bible. If the Bible defends slavery, it is not so much the better for slavery, but so much the worse for the Bible. If Mr. Stuart and Mr. Webster do not see that, there are plenty of obscurer men that do. Of all the attacks ever made on the Bible, by " deists " and " infidels," none would do so much to bring it into disrepute, as to show that it sanctioned American slavery.

It is rather a remarkable fact that an orthodox minister should be on Mr. Webster's paper, endorsing for the Christianity of slavery.

Let me say a word respecting the position of the representative from Boston. I speak only of his position, not of his personal character. Let him, and all men, have the benefit of the distinction between their personal character and official conduct. Mr. Winthrop is a consistent Whig; a representative of the idea of the Whig party North, protection and slavery. When he first went into Congress, it was distinctly understood that he was not going to meddle with the matter of slavery; the tariff was the thing. All this was consistent. It is to be supposed that a Northern Whig will put the mills of the North before the black men of the South: and " Property before persons," might safely be writ on the banner of the Whig party, North or South.

Mr. Winthrop seems a little uneasy in his position. Some time ago he complained of a " nest of vipers " in Boston, who had broken their own teeth in gnawing a file; meaning the " vipers " in the Free-soil party, I suppose, whose teeth, however, have a little edge still left on them. He finds it necessary to define his position, and show that he has kept up his communication with the base line of operations from which he started. This circumstance is a little suspicious.

Unlike Mr. Webster, Mr. Winthrop seems to think religion is a good thing in politics, for in his speech of May 7th, he says —" I acknowledge my allegiance to the whole Constitution of the United States. . . . And whenever I perceive a plain conflict of jurisdiction and authority between the Constitution of my country and the laws of my God, my course is clear. I shall resign my office, whatever it may be, and renounce all connection with public service of any sort." That is fair and manly. He will not hold a position under the Constitution of the United States which is inconsistent with the Constitution of the Universe. But he says: —" There are provisions in the Constitution [of the United States, he means, not of the universe], which involve us in painful obligations, and from which some of us would rejoice to be relieved; and this [the restoration of fugitive slaves] is one of them. But there is none, none, in my judgment, which involves any conscientious or religious difficulty." So he has no " conscientious or religious " objection to return a fugitive slave. He thinks the Constitution of the United States " avoids the idea that there can be property in man," but recognizes that " there may be property in the service or labor of man." But when it is property in the service of man without value

VIII—18

received by the servant, and a claim which continues
to attach to a man and his children for ever, it looks
very like the idea of property in man.   At any rate,
there is only a distinction in the words, no difference
in the things.   To claim the sum of the accidents, all
and several of a thing, is practically to claim the thing.

Mr. Winthrop once voted for the Wilmot Proviso,
in its application to the Oregon Territory.   Some
persons have honored him for it, and even contended
that he also was a Free-soiler.   He wipes off that
calumny by declaring that he attached that proviso
to the Oregon bill for the purpose of defeating the
bill itself.   " This proviso was one of the means upon
which I mainly relied for the purpose."   " There can
be little doubt," he says, " that this clause had its influence in arresting the bill in the other end of the
Capitol," where it was " finally lost."   That is his
apology for appearing to desire to prevent the extension of slavery.   It is worth while to remember this.

Unlike Mr. Webster, he thinks slavery may go into
New Mexico.   " We may hesitate to admit that nature
has everywhere [in the new territory] settled the
question against slavery."   Still he would not now
pass the proviso to exclude slavery.   It " would
. . . unite the South as one man, and if it did
not actually rend the Union asunder, would create an
alienation and irritation in that quarter of the country,
which would render the Union hardly worth preserving."   " Is there not ample reason for an abatement
of the Northern tone, for a forbearance of Northern
urgency upon this subject, without the imputation of
tergiversation and treachery ? "

Here I am reminded of a remarkable sentence in
Mr. Webster's speech at Marshfield, in relation to the

Northern men who helped to annex Texas. Here it
is : —

"For my part, I think that 'dough-faces' is an epithet not
sufficiently reproachful. Now, I think such persons are dough-
faces, dough-heads, and dough-souls, that they are all dough;
that the coarsest potter may mould them at pleasure to vessels
of honor or dishonor, but most readily to vessels of dishonor."

The representative from Boston, in the year 1850,
has small objection to the extension of slave soil.
Hearken to his words : —

"I can never put the question of extending slave soil on the
same footing with one of directly increasing slavery and mul-
tiplying slaves. If a positive issue could ever again be made
up for our decision, whether human beings, few or many, of
whatever race, complexion, or condition, should be freshly sub-
jected to a system of hereditary bondage, and be changed from
freemen into slaves, I can conceive that no bonds of union, no
ties of interest, no cords of sympathy, no consideration of
past glory, present welfare, or future grandeur, should be suffered to interfere, for an instant, with our resolute and un-
ceasing resistance to a measure so iniquitous and abominable.
There would be a clear, unquestionable moral element in such
an issue, which would admit of no compromise, no concession,
no forbearance whatever. . . . A million of swords would
leap from their scabbards to assert it, and the Union itself
would be shivered like a Prince Rupert's drop in the shock.
"But, Sir, the question whether the institution of slavery, as
it already exists, shall be permitted to extend itself over a
hundred or a hundred thousand more square miles than it now
occupies, is a different question. . . . It is not, in my
judgment, such an issue that conscientious and religious men
may not be free to acquiesce in whatever decision may be
arrived at by the constituted authorities of the country. . . .
It is not with a view of cooping up slavery . . . within limits
too narrow for its natural growth; . . . it is not for the
purpose of girding it round with lines of fire, till its sting,
like that of the scorpion, shall be turned upon itself, . . .
that I have ever advocated the principles of the Ordinance of
1787." [6]

Mr. Mann, I think, is still called a Whig, but no

member of the Free-soil party has more readily or more
ably stood up against the extensions of slavery. His
noble words stand in marvelous contrast to the discourse of the representative from Boston. Mr. Mann
represents the country, and not the "metropolis."
His speech last February, and his recent letter to his
constituents, are too well known, and too justly prized,
to require any commendation here. But I cannot fail
to make a remark on a passage in the letter. He says,
if we allow Mr. Clay's compromise to be accepted:
"Were it not for the horrible consequences which it
would involve, a roar of laughter, like a *feu de joie*,
would run down the the course of the ages." He
afterwards says:—" Should the South succeed in their
present attempt upon the territories, they will im-
patiently await the retirement of General Taylor from
the executive chair to add the 'State of Cuba'
. . . to this noble triumph." One is a little inclined to start such a laugh himself at the idea of the
South waiting for that event before they undertake
that plan!

Mr. Mann says: "If no moral or religious obligation existed against holding slaves, would not many
of those opulent and respectable gentlemen who signed
the letter of thanks to Mr. Webster, and hundreds of
others, indeed, instead of applying to intelligence
offices for domestics, go at once to the auction room,
and buy a man or a woman with as little hesitancy
or compunction as they now send to Brighton for
beeves?" This remark has drawn on him some censures not at all merited. There are men enough in
Boston, who have no objection to slavery. I know
such men, who would have been glad if slavery had been
continued here. Are Boston merchants unwilling to

take mortgages on plantations and negroes? Do
Northern men not acquire negroes by marrying wealthy
women at the South, and keep the negroes as slaves?
If the truth could be known, I think it would appear
that Dr. Palfrey had lost more reputation in Boston
than he gained, by emancipating the human beings
which fell to his lot. But here is a story which I take
from the "Boston Republican." It is worth preserving as a monument of the morals of Boston in
1850, and may be worth preserving at the end of the
century : —

"A year or two since, a bright-looking mulatto youth, about
twenty years of age, and whose complexion was not much, if
any, darker than that of the great 'Expounder of the Constitution,' entered the counting-room, on some errand for his
master, a Kentuckian, who was making a visit here. A merchant on one of our principal wharves, who came in and
spoke to him, remarked to the writer that he once owned this
"boy" and his mother, and sold them for several hundred
dollars. Upon my expressing astonishment to him that he could
thus deal in human flesh, he remarked that 'when you are
among the Romans, you must do as the Romans do.' I know
of others of my Northern acquaintances, and good Whigs, too,
who have owned slaves at the South, and who, if public opinion
warranted it, would be as likely, I presume, to buy and sell them
at the North."

I have yet to learn that the controlling men of this
city have any considerable aversion to domestic slavery.

Mr. Mann's zeal in behalf of freedom, and against
the extension of slavery, has drawn upon him the indignation of Mr. Webster, who is grieved to see him so
ignorant of American law. But Mr. Mann is able to
do his own fighting.

So much for the political parties and their relation
to the matters at issue at this moment. Still, there is
some reason to hope that the attempt to extend slavery,

made in the face of the world, and supported by such talent, will yet fail; that it will bring only shame on the men who aim to extend and perpetuate so foul a blight. The fact that Mr. Webster's retainers must come to the rescue of their attorney; that himself must write letters to defend himself, and must even obtain the services of a clergyman to help him — this shows the fear that is felt from the anti-slavery spirit of the North. Depend upon it, a politician is pretty far gone when he sends for the minister, and he thinks his credit failing when he gets a clergyman on his paper to indorse for the Christian character of American slavery.

Here I ought to speak of the party not politicians, who contend against slavery not only beyond the limits of the Constitution, but within those limits; who are opposed not only to the extension, but to the continuance of slavery; who declare that they will keep no compromises which conflict with the eternal laws of God,—of the anti-slavery party. Mr. President, if I were speaking to Whigs, to Democrats, or to Freesoil men, perhaps, I might say what I think of this party, of their conduct, and their motives; but, Sir, I pass it by with the single remark that I think the future will find this party where they have always been found. I have before now attempted to point out the faults of this party, and before these men; that work I will not now attempt a second time, and this is not the audience before which I choose to chant its praises.

There are several forces which oppose the anti-slavery movement at this day. Here are some of the most important.

The demagogues of the parties are all, or nearly all, against it. By demagogue I mean the man who undertakes to lead the people for his own advantage, to the harm and loss of the people themselves. All of this class of men, or most of them, now support slavery — not, as I suppose, because they have any special friendship for it, but because they think it will serve their turn. Some noble men in politics are still friends of the slave.

The demagogues of the churches must come next. I am not inclined to attribute so much original power to the churches as some men do. I look on them as indications of public opinion, and not sources thereof — not the wind, but only the vane which shows which way it blows. Once the clergy were the masters of the people, and the authors of public opinion to a great degree; now they are chiefly the servants of the people, and follow public opinion, and but seldom aspire to lead it, except in matters of their own craft, such as the technicalities of a sect, or the form of a ritual. They may lead public opinion in regard to the " posture in prayer," to the " form of baptism," and the like. In important matters which concern the welfare of the nation, the clergy have none or very little weight. Still, as representatives of public opinion, we really find most of the clergy of all denominations, arrayed against the cause of eternal justice. I pass over this matter briefly, because it is hardly necessary for me to give any opinion on the subject. But I am glad to add, that in all denominations here in New England, and perhaps in all the North, there are noble men who apply the principles of justice to this question of the nation, and bear a manly testimony in the midst of bad examples. Some of the theological newspapers have shown a hostility to slavery and an attachment to the cause of liberty which few men expected; which were quite unknown in those quarters before. To do full justice to men in the sects who speak against this great and popular sin of the nation, we ought to remember that it is harder for a minister than for almost any other man to become a reformer. It is very plain that it is not thought to belong to the calling of a minister, especially in a large town, to oppose the actual and popular sins of his time. So when I see a minister yielding to the public opinion which favors unrighteousness, and passing by, in silence and on the other side, causes which need and deserve his labors and his prayers, I remember what he is hired for, and paid for,— to represent the popular form of religion; if that be idolatry, to represent that. But when I see a minister oppose a real sin which is popular, I cannot but feel a great admiration for the man. We have lately seen some examples of this.

Yet, on the other side, there are some very sad examples of the opposite. Here comes forward a man of high standing in the New England churches, a man who has done real service in promoting a liberal study of matters connected with religion, and defends slavery out of what he deems the "infallible Word of God,"—the Old Testament and the New Testament. Well, if Christianity supports American slavery, so much the worse for Christianity, that is all. Perhaps I ought not to say, *if* Christianity supports slavery. We all know it does not, never did, and never can. But if Paul was an apologist for slavery, so much the worse for Paul. If Calvinism or Catholicism supports slavery, so much the worse for them, not so much the better for slavery! I can easily understand the conduct of the leaders of the New York mob: considering the character of the men, their ignorance and general position, I can easily suppose they may have thought they were doing right in disturbing the meetings there. Considering the apathy of the public author- ities, and the attempt, openly made by some men,— unluckily of influence in that city,— to excite others to violence, I have a good deal of charity for Rynders and his gang. But it is not so easy to excuse the conspicuous ecclesiastical defenders of slavery. They cannot plead their ignorance. Let them alone, to make the best defense they can.

The Toryism of America is also against us. I call that man a Tory, who prefers the accidents of man to the substance of manhood. I mean one who prefers the possessions and property of mankind to man him- self, to reason and to justice. Of this Toryism we have much in America, much in New England, much in Boston. In this town, I cannot but think the pre- vailing influence is still a Tory influence. It is this which is the support of the demagogues of the State and the Church.

Toryism exists in all lands. In some, there is a good deal of excuse to be made for it. I can under- stand the Toryism of the Duke of Medina Sidonia, and of such men. If a man has been born to great wealth and power, derived from ancestors for many centuries held in admiration and in awe; if he has been bred to account himself a superior being, and to be treated accordingly, I can easily understand the Toryism of such a man, and find some excuse for it. I can understand the Tory literature of other na- tions. The Toryism of the " London Quarterly," of " Blackwood," is easily accounted for, and forgiven.

It is, besides, sometimes adorned with wit, and often set off by much learning. It is respectable Toryism. But the Toryism of men who only know they had a grandfather by inference, not by positive testimony; who inherited nothing but their bare limbs; who began their career as tradesmen or mechanics,— mechanics in divinity or law as well as in trade,— and get their bread by any of the useful and honorable callings of life — that such men, getting rich, or lifting their heads out of the obscurity they were once in, should become Tories, in a land, too, where institutions are founded on the idea of freedom and equity and natural justice — that is another thing. The Toryism of American journals, with little scholarship, with no wit, and wisdom in homœopathic doses; the Toryism of a man who started from nothing, the architect of his own fortune; the Toryism of a Republican, of a Yankee, the Toryism of a snob,— it is Toryism reduced to its lowest denomination, made vulgar and contemptible; it is the little end of the tail of Toryism. Let us loathe the unclean thing in the depth of our soul, but let us pity the poor Tory; for he, also, in common with the negro slave, is " a man and a brother."

Then the spirit of trade is often against us. Mr. Mann, in his letter, speaks of the opposition made to Wilberforce by the " Guinea merchants " of Liverpool, in his attempts to put an end to the slave-trade. The Corporation of Liverpool spent over ten thousand pounds in defense of a traffic, " the worst the sun ever shone upon." This would seem to be a reflection upon some of the merchants of Boston. It seems, from a statement in the " Atlas," that Mr. Mann did not intend his remarks to apply to Boston, but to New York and Philadelphia, where mass meetings of merchants

had been held, to sustain Mr. Clay's compromise resolutions.   Although Mr. Mann did not apply his remarks to Boston, I fear they will apply here as well
as to our sister cities.   I have yet to learn that the
letter of Mr. Webster's retainers was any less well
adapted to continue and extend slavery, than the
resolutions passed at New York and Philadelphia.   I
wish the insinuations of Mr. Mann did not apply here.

One of the signers of the letter to Mr. Webster
incautiously betrayed, I think, the open secret of the
retainers when he said —" I don't care a damn how
many slave States they annex!" This is a secret,
because not avowed; openly, because generally known,
or at least believed, to be the sentiment of a strong
party in Massachusetts. I am glad to have it also
expressed; now the issue is joined, and we do not fight
in the dark.

It has long been suspected that some inhabitants of
Boston were engaged in the slave-trade.   Not long
since, the Brig " Lucy Anne," of Boston, was captured
on the coast of Africa, with five hundred and forty-
seven slaves on board. This vessel was built at
Thomaston in 1839; repaired at Boston in 1848, and
now hails from this port. She was commanded by
one " Captain Otis," and is owned by one " Salem
Charles." This, I suppose, is a fictitious name, for
certainly it would not be respectable in Boston to extend slavery in this way. Even Mr. Winthrop is opposed to that, and thinks " a million swords would
leap from their scabbards to oppose it." But it may
be that there are men in Boston who do not think
it any worse to steal men who are born free, and have
grown up free in Africa, and make slaves of them,
than to steal such as are born free in America, before

they are grown up.   If we have the Old Testament decidedly sustaining slavery, and the New Testament never forbidding it; if, as we are often told, neither Jesus nor his early followers ever said a word against slavery; if scarcely a Christian minister in Boston ever preaches against this national sin; if the representative from Boston has no religious scruples against returning a fugitive slave, or extending slavery over a " hundred or a hundred thousand square miles " of new territory; if the great senator from Massachusetts refuses to vote for the Wilmot Proviso, or re-affirm an ordinance of nature, and re-enact the will of God; if he calls on us to return fugitive slaves " with alacrity," and demands of Massachusetts that she shall conquer her prejudices; if nine hundred and eighty-seven men in this vicinity, of lawful age, are thankful to him for enlightening them as to their duty, and a professor of theology comes forward to sanction American slavery in the name of religion — why, I think Mr. " Salem Charles," with his " Captain Otis," may not be the worst man in the world, after all!   Let us pity him also, as " a man and a brother."

Such is the crisis in our affairs; such the special issue in the general question between freedom and slavery; such the position of parties and of great men in relation to this question; such the foes to freedom in America.

On our side, there are great and powerful allies. The American idea is with us; the spirit of the majority of men in the North, when they are not blindfolded and muzzled by the demagogues of State and Church. The religion of the land, also, is on our side; the irreligion, the idolatry, the infidelity thereof, all of that is opposed to us.   Religion is love of God and love of man: surely, all of that, under any form, Catholic or Quaker, is in favor of the unalienable rights of man. We know that we are right; we are sure to prevail. But in times present and future, as in times past we need heroism, self-denial, a continual watchfulness, and an industry which never tires.

Let us not be deceived about the real question at issue. It is not merely whether we shall return fugitive slaves without trial by jury. We will not return them with trial by jury, neither " with alacrity," nor " with the solemnity of judicial proceedings!" It is not merely whether slavery shall be extended or not.

By and by there will be a political party with a wider basis than the Free-soil party, who will declare that the nation itself must put an end to slavery in the nation; and if the Constitution of the United States will not allow it, there is another Constitution that will. Then the title, " Defender and Expounder of the Constitution of the United States," will give way to this,—" Defender and Expounder of the Constitution of the Universe," and we shall re-affirm the ordinance of nature, and re-enact the will of God. You may not live to see it, Mr. President, nor I live to see it; but it is written on the iron leaf that it must come; come, too, before long. Then the speech of Mr. Webster, and the defense thereof by Mr. Stuart, the letter of the retainers and the letters of the retained, will be a curiosity; the conduct of the Whigs and Democrats an amazement, and the peculiar institution a proverb amongst all the nations of the earth. In the turmoil of party politics, and of personal controversy, let us not forget continually to move the previous question, whether freedom or slavery is to prevail in America. There is no attribute of God which is not on our side; because, in this matter, we are on the side of God.

Mr. President: I began by congratulating you on the favorable signs of the times. One of the most favorable is the determination of the South to use the powers of government to extend slavery. At this day, we exhibit a fact worse than Christendom has elsewhere to disclose; the fact that one-sixth part of our population are mere property; not men, but things. England has a proletary population, the lowest in Europe; we have three million of proletaries lower than the " pauper laborers " of England, which the Whig protectionists hold up to us in terror. The South wishes to increase the number of slaves, to spread this blot, this blight and baneful scourge of civilization, over new territory. Hot-headed men of the South declare that, unless it is done, they will divide the Union; famous men of the North " cave in," and verify their own statements about " dough-faces " and " dough-souls." All this is preaching anti-slavery to the thinking men of the North; to the sober men of all parties, who prefer conscience to cotton. The present session of Congress has done much to overturn slavery. " Whom the gods destroy they first make mad."

X

THE FUNCTION OF CONSCIENCE

Herein do I exercise myself to have always a conscience void of offence toward God and toward men.— Acts xxiv. 16.

There are some things which are true, independent of all human opinions. Such things we call facts. Thus it is true that one and one are equal to two, that the earth moves round the sun, that all men have certain natural unalienable rights, rights which a man can alienate only for himself, and not for another. No man made these things true; no man can make them false. If all the men in Jerusalem and ever so many more, if all the men in the world, were to pass a unanimous vote that one and one were not equal to two, that the earth did not move round the sun, that all men had not natural and unalienable rights, the opinion would not alter the fact, nor make truth false and falsehood true.

So there are likewise some things which are right, independent of all human opinions. Thus it is right to love a man and not to hate him, to do him justice and not injustice, to allow him the natural rights which he has not alienated. No man made these things right; no man can make them wrong. If all the men in Jerusalem and ever so many more, if all the men in the world, were to pass a unanimous vote that it was right to hate a man and not love him, right to do him injustice and not justice, right to deprive him of his natural rights not alienated by himself, the opinion would not alter the fact, nor make right wrong and wrong right.

287

There are certain constant and general facts which occur in the material world, the world of external perception, which represent what are called the laws of matter, in virtue of which things take place so and not otherwise. These laws are the same everywhere and always; they never change. They are not made by men, but only discovered by men, are inherent in the constitution of matter, and seem designed to secure the welfare of the material world. These natural laws of matter, inherent in its constitution, are never violated, nor can be, for material nature is passive, or at least contains no element or will that is adverse to the will of God, the ultimate Cause of these laws as of matter itself. The observance of these laws is a constant fact of the universe; "the most ancient heavens thereby are fresh and strong." These laws represent the infinity of God in the world of matter, His infinite power, wisdom, justice, love, and holiness.

So there are likewise certain constant and general facts which occur in what may be called the spiritual world, the world of internal consciousness. They represent the laws of spirit — that is, of the human spirit — in virtue of which things are designed to take place so and not otherwise. These laws are the same everywhere and always; they never change. They are not made by men, but only discovered by men. They are inherent in the constitution of man, and as you cannot conceive of a particle of matter without extension, impenetrability, figure, and so on, no more can you conceive of man without these laws inhering in him. They seem designed to secure the welfare of the spiritual world. They represent the infinity of God in the world of man, His infinite power, wisdom,

justice, love, and holiness. But while matter is sta-
tionary, bound by necessity, and man is progressive
and partially free, to the extent of a certain tether,
so it is plain that there may be a will in the world of
man adverse to the will of God, and thus the laws of
man's spirit may be violated to a certain extent. The
laws of matter depend for their execution only on the
infinite will of God, and so cannot be violated. The
laws of man depend for their execution also on the
finite will of man, and so may be broken.[1]

Let us select a portion of these laws of the human
spirit; such as relate to a man's conduct in dealing
with his fellowmen, a portion of what are commonly
called moral laws, and examine them. They partake
of the general characteristics mentioned above; they
are universal and unchangeable, are only discovered
and not made by man, are inherent in man, designed
to secure his welfare, and represent the infinity of
God. These laws are absolutely right; to obey them
is to be and do absolutely right. So being and doing, a man answers the moral purpose of his existence,
and attains moral manhood. If I and all men keep
all the laws of man's spirit, I have peace in my own
heart, peace with my brother, peace with my God; I
have my delight in myself, in my brother, in my God,
they theirs and God His in me.

What is absolutely right is commonly called justice.
It is the point in morals common to me and all mankind, common to me and God, to mankind and God;
the point where all duties unite — to myself, my brethren, and my God; the point where all interests meet
and balance — my interests, those of mankind, and the
interests of God. When justice is done, all is harmony
and peaceful progress in the world of man; but when
VIII—19

justice is not done, the reverse follows, discord and
confusion; for injustice is not the point where all
duties and all interests meet and balance, not the point
of morals common to mankind and me, or to us and
God.

We may observe and study the constant facts of
the material world, thus learn the laws they represent,
and so get at a theory of the world which is founded
on the facts thereof. Such a theory is true; it represents the thought of God, the infinity of God. Then
for every point of theory we have a point of fact.
Instead of pursuing this course we may neglect these
constant facts, with the laws they represent, and forge
a theory which shall not rest on these facts. Such a
theory will be false and will represent the imperfection
of men, and not the facts of the universe and the
infinity of God.

In like manner we may study the constant facts of
the spiritual world, and, in special, of man's moral
nature, and thereby obtain a rule to regulate our conduct. If this rule is founded on the constant facts of
man's moral nature, then it will be absolutely right,
and represent justice, the thought of God, the infinity
of God, and for every point of moral theory we shall
have a moral fact. Instead of pursuing that course,
we may forge a rule for our conduct, and so get a
theory which shall not rest on those facts. Such a
rule will be wrong, representing only the imperfection
of men.

In striving to learn the laws of the universe, the
wisest men often go astray, propound theories which
do not rest upon facts, and lay down human rules for
the conduct of the universe, which do not agree with its
nature. But the universe is not responsible for that;

material nature takes no notice thereof.   The opinion
of an astronomer, of the American academy, does not
alter a law of the material universe, or a fact therein.
The philosophers once thought that the sun went round
the earth, and framed laws on that assumption; but
that did not make it a fact; the sun did not go out
of his way to verify the theory, but kept to the law
of God, and swung the earth round him once a year,
say the philosophers what they might say, leaving them
to learn the fact and thereby correct their theory.

In the same way, before men attain the knowledge
of the absolute right, they often make theories which
do not rest upon the fact of man's moral nature, and
enact human rules for the conduct of men which do
not agree with the moral nature of man.   These are
rules which men make and do not find made.   They
are not a part of man's moral nature, writ therein,
and so obligatory thereon, no more than the false
rules for the conduct of matter are writ therein and
so obligatory thereon.   You and I are no more morally
bound to keep such rules of conduct, because King
Pharaoh or King People say we shall, than the sun
is materially bound to go round the earth every day,
because Hipparchus and Ptolemy say it does.   The
opinion or command of a king, or a people, can no
more change a fact and alter a law of man's nature,
than the opinion of a philosopher can do this in
material nature.

We learn the laws of matter slowly, by observation,
experiment, and induction, and only get an outside
knowledge thereof, as objects of thought.   In the
same way we might study the facts of man's moral
nature, and arrive at rules of conduct, and get a merely
outside acquaintance with the moral law as something

wholly external. The law might appear curious, useful, even beautiful, moral gravitation as wonderful as material attraction. But no sense of duty would attach us to it. In addition to the purely intellectual powers, we have a faculty whose special function it is to discover the rules for a man's moral conduct. This is conscience, called also by many names. As the mind has for its object absolute truth, so conscience has for its object absolute justice. Conscience enables us not merely to learn the right by experiment and induction, but intuitively, and in advance of experiment; so, in addition to the experimental way, whereby we learn justice from the facts of human history, we have a transcendental way, and learn it from the facts of human nature, from immediate consciousness.

It is the function of conscience to discover to men the moral law of God. It will not do this with infallible certainty, for, at its best estate, neither conscience nor any other faculty of man is absolutely perfect, so as never to mistake. Absolute perfection belongs only to the faculties of God. But conscience, like each other faculty, is relatively perfect,— is adequate to the purpose God meant it for. It is often immature in the young, who have not had time for the growth and ripening of the faculty, and in the old, who have checked and hindered its development. Here it is feeble from neglect, there from abuse. It may give an imperfect answer to the question, What is absolutely right?

Now, though the conscience of a man lacks the absolute perfection of that of God, in all that relates to my dealing with men, it is still the last standard of appeal. I will hear what my friends have to say, what public opinion has to offer, what the best men can advise me to, then I am to ask my own conscience, and follow its decision; not that of my next friend, the public, or the best of men. I will not say that my conscience will always disclose to me the absolute right, according to the conscience of God, but it will disclose the relatively right, what is my conviction of right to-day, with all the light I can get on the matter; and as all I can know of the absolute right is my conviction thereof, so I must be true to that conviction. Then I am faithful to my own conscience, and faithful to my God. If I do the best thing I can know to-day, and to-morrow find a better one and do that, I am not to be blamed, nor to be called a sinner against God, because not so just to-day as I shall be to-morrow. I am to do God's will soon as I know it, not before, and to take all possible pains to find it out; but am not to blame for acting childish when a child, nor to be ashamed of it when grown up to be a man. Such is the function of conscience.

Having determined what is absolutely right, by the conscience of God, or at least relatively right, according to my conscience to-day, then it becomes my duty to keep it. I owe it to God to obey His law, or what I deem His law; that is my duty. It may be uncomfortable to keep it, unpopular, contrary to my present desires, to my passions, to my immediate interests; it may conflict with my plans in life; that makes no difference. I owe entire allegiance to my God. It is a duty to keep His law, a personal duty, my duty as a man. I owe it to myself, for I am to keep the integrity of my own consciousness; I owe it to my brother, and to my God. Nothing can absolve me from this duty, neither the fact that it is uncomfortable or unpopular, nor that it conflicts with my desires, my passions, my immediate interests, and my plans in life. Such is the place of conscience amongst other faculties of my nature.

I believe all this is perfectly plain, but now see what it leads to. In the complicated relations of human life, various rules for the moral conduct of men have been devised, some of them in the form of statute laws, some in the form of customs; and in virtue of these rules, certain artificial demands are made of men, which have no foundation in the moral nature of man; these demands are thought to represent duties. We have the same word to describe what I ought to do as subject to the law of God, and what is demanded of me by custom, or the statute. We call each a duty. Hence comes no small confusion: the conventional and official obligation is thought to rest on the same foundation as the natural and personal duty. As the natural duty is at first sight a little vague, and not written out in the law-book, or defined by custom, while the conventional obligation is well understood, men think that in case of any collision between the two, the natural duty must give way to the official obligation.

For clearness' sake, the natural and personal obligation to keep the law of God as my conscience declares it, I will call Duty; the conventional and official obligation to comply with some custom, keep some statute, or serve some special interest, I will call Business. Here then are two things — my natural and personal duty, my conventional and official business. Which of the two shall give way to the other,— personal duty or official business? Let it be remembered that I am a man first of all, and all else that I am is but a modification of my manhood, which makes me a clergyman, a fisherman, or a statesman; but the clergy, the fish, and the state, are not to strip me of my manhood. They are valuable in so far as they serve my manhood, not as it serves them. My official business as clergyman, fisherman, or statesman, is always beneath my personal duty as man. In case of any conflict between the two, the natural duty ought to prevail and carry the day before the official business; for the natural duty represents the permanent law of God, the absolute right, justice, the balance-point of all interests; while the official business represents only the transient conventions of men, some partial interest; and besides, the man who owes the personal duty is immortal, while the officer who performs the official business is but for a time. At death, the man is to be tried by the justice of God, for the deeds done, and character attained, for his natural duty, but he does not enter the next life as a clergyman, with his surplice and prayer-book, or a fisherman, with his angles and net, nor yet as a statesman, with his franking privilege, and title of honorable and member of Congress. The officer dies, of a vote or a fever. The man lives for ever. From the relation between a man and his occupation, it is plain, in general, that all conventional and official business is to be overruled by natural personal duty. This is the great circle, drawn by God, and discovered by conscience, which girdles my sphere, including all the smaller circles, and itself included by none of them. The law of God has eminent domain everywhere, over the private passions of Oliver and Charles, the special interests of Carthage and of Rome, over all customs, all official business, all precedents, all human statutes, all treaties between Judas and Pilate, or England and France, over all the conventional affairs of one man or of mankind. My

own conscience is to declare that law for me, yours
for you, and is before all private passions, or public
interests, the decision of majorities, and a world full of
precedents. You may resign your office, and escape
its obligations, forsake your country, and owe it no
allegiance, but you cannot move out of the dominions of
God, nor escape where conscience has not eminent domain.

See some examples of a conflict between the personal
duty and the official business. A man may be a clergyman, and it may be his official business to expound and
defend the creed which is set up for him by his employers, his bishop, his association, or his parish, to
defend and hold it good against all comers; it may be,
also, in a certain solemn sort, to please the audience,
who come to be soothed, caressed, and comforted,— to
represent the average of religion in his society, and
so to bless popular virtues and ban unpopular vices,
but never to shake off or even jostle with one of his
fingers the load of sin, beloved and popular, which
crushes his hearers down till they are bowed together
and can in nowise lift themselves up; unpopular excellence he is to call fanaticism, if not infidelity. But
his natural duty as a man, standing in this position,
overrides his official business, and commands him to
tell men of the false things in their creed, of great
truths not in it; commands him to inform his audience
with new virtue, to represent all of religion he can
attain, to undo the heavy burdens of popular sin,
private or national, and let the men oppressed therewith
go free. Excellence, popular or odious, he is to com-
mend by its own name, to stimulate men to all nobleness
of character and life, whether it please or offend.
This is his duty, however uncomfortable, unpopular,

against his desires, and conflicting with his immediate interests and plans of life. Which shall he do? His official business, and pimp and pander to the public lust, with base compliance serving the popular idols, which here are money and respectability, or shall he serve his God? That is the question. If the man considers himself substantially a man, and accidentally a clergyman, he will perform his natural duty; if he counts the priesthood his substance, and manhood an accident of that, he will do only his official business.

I may be a merchant, and my official business may be to buy, and sell, and get gain; I may see that the traffic in ardent spirits is the readiest way to accomplish this. So it becomes my official business to make rum, sell rum, and by all means to induce men to drink it. But presently I see that the common use of it makes the thriving unthrifty, the rich less wealthy, the poor miserable, the sound sick, and the sane mad; that it brings hundreds to the jail, thousands to the alms-house, and millions to poverty and shame, producing an amount of suffering, wretchedness, and sin, beyond the power of man to picture or conceive. Then my natural duty as man is very clear, very imperative. Shall I sacrifice my manhood to money? — the integrity of my consciousness to my gains by rum-selling? That is the question. And my answer will depend on the fact, whether I am more a man or more a rum-seller. Suppose I compromise the matter, and draw a line somewhere between my natural duty as man, and my official business as rum-seller, and for every three cents that I make by iniquity, give one cent to the American Tract Society, or the Board for Foreign Missions, or the Unitarian Association, or the excellent Society for Propagating the Gospel among the Indians and Others in North America. That does not help the matter; business is not satisfied, though I draw the line never so near to money; nor conscience, unless the line comes up to my duty.

I am a citizen, and the State says, " You must obey all the statutes made by the proper authorities; that is your official business! " Suppose there is a statute adverse to the natural law of God, and the convictions of my own conscience, and I plead that fact in abatement of my obligation to keep the statute, the State says, " Obey it none the less, or we will hang you. Religion is an excellent thing in every matter except politics; there it seems to make men mad." Shall I keep the commandment of men, or the law of my God?

A statute was once enacted by King Pharaoh for the destruction of the Israelites in Egypt; it was made the official business of all citizens to aid in their destruction: " Pharaoh charged all his people saying, Every son that is born ye shall cast into the river, and every daughter ye shall save alive." It was the official business of every Egyptian who found a Hebrew boy to throw him into the Nile,— if he refused, he offended against the peace and dignity of the kingdom of Egypt, and the form of law in such case made and provided. But if he obeyed, he murdered a man. Which should he obey, the Lord Pharaoh, or the Lord God? That was the question. I make no doubt that the priests of Osiris, Orus, Apis, Isis, and the judges, and the justices of the peace and quorum, and the members of Congress of that time, said, " Keep the king's commandment, O ye that worship the crocodile and fear the cat, or ye shall not sleep in a whole skin any longer! " So said everything that loveth and maketh a lie.

King Charles II. made a statute some one hundred
and ninety years ago, to punish with death the rem-
nant of the nine-and-fifty judges who had brought his
father's head to the block, teaching kings that "they
also had a joint in their necks." He called on all
his subjects to aid in the capture of these judges.
It was made their official business as citizens to do
so; a reward was offered for the apprehension of some
of them "alive or dead," punishment hung over
the head of any who should harbor or conceal them.
Three of these regicides, who had adjudged a king for
his felony, came to New England. Many Americans
knew where they were, and thought the condemnation
of Charles I. was the best thing these judges ever did.
With that conviction ought they to have delivered up
these fugitives, or afforded them shelter? In time of
peril, when officers of the English government were on
the lookout for some of these men, a clergyman in
the town where one of them was concealed, preached,
it is said, on the text "Bewray not him that wandereth," an occasional sermon, and put the duty of a man
far before the business of a citizen. When Sir Edmund Andros was at New Haven looking after one of
the judges, and attended public worship in the same
meeting-house with the fugitive, the congregation sang
an awful hymn in his very ears.[2]

Would the men of Connecticut have done right, be-
wraying him that wandered, and exposing the outcast,
to give up the man who had defended the liberties
of the world and the rights of mankind against a
tyrant,— give him up because a wanton king, and his
loose men and loose women, made such a commandment? One of the regicides dwelt in peace eight-and-
twenty years in New England, a monument of the
virtue of the people.

Of old time the Roman statute commanded the Christians to sacrifice to Jupiter; they deemed it the highest sin to do so, but it was their official business as Roman citizens. Some of them were true to their natural duty as men, and took the same cross Jesus had borne before them; Peter and John had said at their outset to the authorities —" Whether it be right in the sight of God to hearken unto you more than unto God, judge ye." The Emperor once made it the official business of every citizen to deliver up the Christians. But God made it no man's duty. Nay, it was each man's duty to help them. In such cases what shall a man do? You know what we think of men who comply basely, and save their life with the loss of their soul. You know how the Christian world honors the saints and martyrs who laid down their lives for the sake of truth and right; a handful of their dust, which was quieted of its trouble by the headsman's axe seventeen hundred years ago, and is now gathered from the catacombs of Saint Agnes at Rome — why it is enough to consecrate half of the Catholic churches in New England. As I have stood among their graves, have handled the instruments with which they tasted of bitter death, and crumbled their bones in my hands,— I keep their relics still with reverent awe,— I have thought there was a little difference between their religion, and the pale decency that haunts the churches of our time, and is afraid lest it lose its dividends, or its respectability, or hurt its usefulness, which is in no danger.

Do I speak of martyrs for conscience' sake? To-day is St. Maurice's day, consecrated to him and the " Thebæan legion." Maurice appears to have been a military tribune in the Christian legion, levied in the

Thebais, a part of Egypt. In the latter part of the third century this legion was at Octodurum, near the little village of Martigni, in Valais, a Swiss Canton, under the command of Maximian, the associate emperor, just then named Herculeus, going to fight the Bagaudæ. The legion was ordered to sacrifice to the gods after the heathen fashion. The soldiers refused; every tenth man was hewn down by Maximian's command. They would not submit, and so the whole legion, as the Catholic story tells us, perished there on the 22nd of September, fifteen hundred and fifty-three years ago this day. Perhaps the account is not true; it is probable that the number of martyrs is much exaggerated, for six hundred soldiers would not stand still and be slaughtered without striking a blow. But the fact that the Catholic church sets apart one day in the calendar to honor this alleged heroism, shows the value men put on fidelity to conscience in such cases.

Last winter a bill for the capture of fugitive slaves was introduced into the Senate of the United States of America; the senator who so ably represented the opinions and wishes of the controlling men of this city, proposed to support that bill, " with all its provisions to the fullest extent;" that bill, with various alterations, some for the better, others for the worse, has become a law — it received the vote of the representative from Boston, who was not sent there, I hope, for the purpose of voting for it. That statute allows the slaveholder, or his agent, to come here, and by summary process seize a fugitive slave, and, without the formality of a trial by jury, to carry him back to eternal bondage. The statute makes it the official business of certain magistrates to aid in enslaving a man; it empowers them to call out force enough to overcome any resistance which may be offered, to summon the bystanders to aid in that work. It provides a punishment for any one who shall aid and abet, directly or indirectly, and harbor, or conceal the man who is seeking to maintain his natural and unalienable right to life, liberty, and the pursuit of happiness. He may be fined a thousand dollars, imprisoned six months, and be liable to a civil action for a thousand dollars more!

This statute is not to be laid to the charge of the slaveholders of the South alone; its most effective supporters are Northern men; Boston is more to be blamed for it than Charleston or Savannah, for nearly a thousand persons of this city and neighborhood, most of them men of influence through money if by no other means, addressed a letter of thanks to the distinguished man who had volunteered to support that infamous bill, telling him that he had " convinced the understanding and touched the conscience of the nation." A man falls low when he consents to be a slave, and is spurned for his lack of manhood; to consent to be a catcher of fugitive slaves is to fall lower yet; but to consent to be the defender of a slave-catcher — it is seldom that human nature is base enough for that. But such examples are found in this city! This is now the law of the land. It is the official business of judges, commissioners, and marshals, as magistrates, to execute the statute and deliver a fugitive up to slavery; it is your official business and mine, as citizens, when legally summoned, to aid in capturing the man. Does the command make it any man's duty? The natural duty to keep the law of God overrides the obligation to observe any human statute, and continually commands us to love a man and not

hate him, to do him justice, and not injustice, to allow
him his natural rights not alienated by himself; yes,
to defend him in them, not only by all means legal,
but by all means moral.

Let us look a little at our duty under this statute.
It a man falls into the water and is in danger of
drowning, it is the natural duty of the bystanders to
aid in pulling him out, even at the risk of wetting
their garments. We should think a man a coward who
could swim, and would not save a drowning girl for
fear of spoiling his coat. He would be indictable
at common law. If a troop of wolves or tigers were
about to seize a man, and devour him, and you and
I could help him, it would be our duty to do so, even
to peril our own limbs and life for the purpose. If
a man undertakes to murder or steal a man, it is the
duty of the bystanders to help their brother, who is
in peril, against wrong from the two-legged man, as
much as against the four-legged beast. But suppose
the invader who seizes the man is an officer of the
United States, has a commission in his pocket, a warrant for his deed in his hand, and seizes as a slave a
man who has done nothing to alienate his natural
rights — does that give him any more natural right
to enslave a man than he had before? Can any piece
of parchment make right wrong, and wrong right?

The fugitive has been a slave before? Does the
wrong you committed yesterday, give you a natural
right to commit wrong afresh and continually? Because you enslaved this man's father, have you a natural right to enslave his child? The same right you
would have to murder a man because you butchered
his father first. The right to murder is as much
transmissible by inheritance as the right to enslave!

It is plain to me that it is the natural duty of citizens to rescue every fugitive slave from the hands of the marshal who essays to return him to bondage; to do it peaceably if they can, forcibly if they must, but by all means to do it. Will you stand by and see your countrymen, your fellow-citizens of Boston, sent off to slavery by some commissioner? Shall I see my own parishioners taken from under my eyes and carried back to bondage, by a man whose constitutional business it is to work wickedness by statute? Shall I never lift an arm to protect him? When I consent to that, you may call me a hireling shepherd, an infidel, a wolf in sheep's clothing, even a defender of slave-catching if you will; and I will confess I was a poor dumb dog, barking always at the moon, but silent as the moon when the murderer came near.

I am not a man who loves violence. I respect the sacredness of human life. But this I say, solemnly, that I will do all in my power to rescue any fugitive slave from the hands of any officer who attempts to return him to bondage. I will resist him as gently as I know how, but with such strength as I can command; I will ring the bells, and alarm the town; I will serve as head, as foot, or as hand to any body of serious and earnest men, who will go with me, with no weapons but their hands, in this work. I will do it as readily as I would lift a man out of the water, or pluck him from the teeth of a wolf, or snatch him from the hands of a murderer. What is a fine of a thousand dollars, and jailing for six months, to the liberty of a man? My money perish with me, if it stand between me and the eternal law of God! I trust there are manly men enough in this house to secure the freedom of every fugitive slave in Boston, without breaking a limb or rending a garment.

One thing more I think is very plain, that the fugitive has the same natural right to defend himself against the slave-catcher, or his constitutional tool, that he has against a murderer or a wolf. The man who attacks me to reduce me to slavery, in that moment of attack alienates his right to life, and if I were the fugitive, and could escape in no other way, I would kill him with as little compunction as I would drive a mosquito from my face. It is high time this was said. What grasshoppers we are before the statute of men! what Goliaths against the law of God! What capitalist heeds your statute of usury when he can get illegal interest? How many banks are content with six per cent. when money is scarce? Did you never hear of a merchant evading the duties of the custom-house? When a man's liberty is concerned, we must keep the law, must we? betray the wanderer, and expose the outcast?

In the same manner the natural duty of a man overrides all the special obligations which a man takes on himself as a magistrate by his official oath. Our theory of office is this: The man is sunk in the magistrate; he is *un homme couvert;* his individual manhood is covered up and extinguished by his official cap; he is no longer a man, but a mere president, general, governor, representative, sheriff, juror, or constable; he is absolved from all allegiance to God's law of the universe when it conflicts with man's law of the land; his official business as a magistrate supersedes his natural duty as a man. In virtue of this theory, President Polk, and his coadjutors in Congress and out of it, with malice aforethought, and intent to rob and to kill, did officially invade Mexico, and therein " slay, kill, and murder " some thousands of men, as

VIII—20

well Americans as Mexicans. This is thought right because he did it officially. But the fact that he and they were magistrates, doing official business, did not make the killing any the less a wrong than if he and they had been private men, with General Lopez and not General Taylor to head or back them. The official killing of a man who has not alienated his right to life, is just as much violation of the law of God, and the natural duty of man, as the unofficial killing of such a person. Because you and I and some other foolish people put a man in a high office and get him to take an oath, does that, all at once, invest him with a natural right to kill anybody he sees fit; to kill an innocent Mexican? All his natural rights he had before, and it would be difficult to ascertain where the people could find the right to authorize him to do a wrong. A man does not escape from the jurisdiction of natural law and the dominion of God by enlisting in the army, or by taking the oath of the President; for justice, the law paramount of the universe, extends over armies and nations.

A little while ago a murderer was hanged in Boston, by the sheriff of Suffolk county, at the command of the Governor and Council of Massachusetts, by the aid of certain persons called grand and petit jurors, all of them acting in their official capacity, and doing the official business they had sworn to do. If it be a wrong thing to hang a man, or to take his life except in self-defense, and while in imminent peril, then it is not any less a wrong because men do it in their official character, in compliance with their oath. I am speaking of absolute wrong, not merely what is wrong relatively to the man's own judgment, for I doubt not that all those officers were entirely con-

scientious in what they did, and therefore no blame
rests on them. But if a man believes it wrong to take
human life deliberately, except in the cases named, then
I do not see how, with a good conscience, he can be
partaker in the death of any man, notwithstanding his
official oath.

Let me suppose a case which may happen here, and
before long. A woman flies from South Carolina to
Massachusetts to escape from bondage. Mr. Greatheart aids her in her escape, harbors and conceals her,
and is brought to trial for it. The punishment is a
fine of one thousand dollars and imprisonment for six
months. I am drawn to serve as a juror, and pass
upon this offense. I may refuse to serve, and be
punished for that, leaving men with no scruples to
take my place, or I may take the juror's oath to give
a verdict according to the law and the testimony.
The law is plain, let us suppose, and the testimony
conclusive. Greatheart himself confesses that he did
the deed alleged, saving one ready to perish. The
judge charges, that if the jurors are satisfied of that
fact, then they must return that he is guilty. This
is a nice matter. Here are two questions. The one,
put to me in my official capacity as juror, is this:
"Did Greatheart aid the woman?" The other,
put to me in my natural character as man, is this:
"Will you help punish Greatheart with fine and imprisonment for helping a woman obtain her unalienable rights?" I am to answer both. If I have extinguished my manhood by my juror's oath, then I
shall do my official business and find Greatheart guilty,
and I shall seem to be a true man; but if I value my
manhood, I shall answer after my natural duty to
love a man and not hate him, to do him justice, not in-

justice, to allow him the natural rights he has not alienated, and shall say " Not guilty." Then foolish men, blinded by the dust of courts, may call me forsworn and a liar; but I think human nature will justify the verdict.

In cases of this kind, when justice is on one side and the court on the other, it seems to me a conscientious man must either refuse to serve as a juror, or else return a verdict at variance with the facts and what courts declare to be his official business as juror; but the eyes of some men have been so long blinded by what the court declares is the law, and by its notion of the juror's function, that they will help inflict such a punishment on their brother, and the judge decree the sentence, in a case where the arrest, the verdict, and the sentence are the only wrong in which the prisoner is concerned. It seems to me it is time this matter should be understood, and that it should be known that no official oath can take a man out of the jurisdiction of God's natural law of the universe.

A case may be brought before a commissioner or judge of the United States, to determine whether Daniel is a slave, and therefore to be surrendered up. His official business, sanctioned by his oath, enforced by the law of the land, demands the surrender; his natural duty, sanctioned by his conscience, enforced by absolute justice, forbids the surrender. What shall he do? There is no serving of God and Mammon both. He may abandon his commission and refuse to remain thus halting between two opposites. But if he keeps his office, I see not how he can renounce his nature and send back a fugitive slave, and do as great a wrong as to make a freeman a slave!

Suppose the Constitution had been altered, and

Congress had made a law, making it the business of the United States' commissioners to enslave and sell at public outcry all the red-haired men in the nation, and forbid us to aid and abet their escape, to harbor and conceal them, under the same penalties just now mentioned; do you think any commissioner would be justified before God by his oath in kidnapping the red-haired men, or any person in punishing such as harbored or concealed them, such as forcibly took the victims out of the hand of officials who would work mischief by statute? Will the color of a hair make right wrong, and wrong right?

Suppose a man has sworn to keep the Constitution of the United States, and the Constitution is found to be wrong in certain particulars: then his oath is not morally binding, for before his oath, by his very existence, he is morally bound to keep the law of God as fast as he learns it. No oath can absolve him from his natural allegiance to God. Yet I see not how a man can knowingly, and with a good conscience, swear to keep what he deems wrong to keep, and will not keep, and does not intend to keep.

It seems to me very strange that men so misunderstand the rights of conscience and their obligations to obey their country. Not long ago, an eminent man taunted one of his opponents, telling him he had better adhere to the " higher law." The newspapers echoed the sneer, as if there were no law higher than the Constitution. Latterly, the Democratic party, even more completely than the Whig party, seems to have forgotten that there is any law higher than the Constitution, any rights above vested rights.[3]

An eminent theologian of New England, who has hitherto done good and great service in his profession,

grinding off the barb of Calvinism, wrote a book in
defense of slave-catching, on "Conscience and the
Constitution," a book which not only sins against the
sense of the righteous in being wicked, but against the
worldliness of the world in being weak,— and he puts
the official business of keeping "a compact" far before the natural duty of keeping a conscience void of
offense, and serving God. But suppose forty thieves
assemble on Fire Island, and make a compact to rob
every vessel wrecked on their coast, and reduce the
survivors to bondage. Suppose I am born amongst
that brotherhood of pirates, am I morally bound to
keep that compact, or to perform any function which
grows out of it? Nay, I am morally bound to violate
the compact, to keep the pirates from their plunder
and their prey. Instead of forty thieves on Fire
Island, suppose twenty millions of men in the United
States make a compact to enslave every sixth man —
the dark men — am I morally bound to heed that compact, or to perform any function which grows out of
it? Nay, I am morally bound to violate the compact,
in every way that is just and wise. The very men
who make such a compact are morally discharged from
it as soon as they see it is wrong. The forty Jews
who bound themselves by wicked oath to kill Paul
before they broke their fast,— were they morally
bound to keep their word? Nay, morally bound to
break it.

I will tell you a portion of the story of a fugitive
slave whom I have known. I will call his name Joseph,
though he was in worse than Egyptian bondage. He
was "owned" by a notorious gambler, and once ran
away, but was retaken. His master proceeded to
punish him for that crime, took him to a chamber,

locked the door, and lighted a fire; he then beat the
slave severely. After that he put the branding-iron
in the fire, took a knife,— I am not telling what
took place in Algiers, but in Alabama,— and proceeded to cut off the ears of his victim! The owner's
wife, alarmed at the shrieks of the sufferer, beat down
the door with a sledge-hammer, and prevented that
catastrophe. Afterwards, two slaves of this gambler,
for stealing their master's sheep, were beaten so that
they died of the stripes. The " minister " came to
the funeral, told the others that those were wicked
slaves, who deserved their fate; that they would never
" rise " in the general resurrection, and were not fit
to be buried! Accordingly their bodies were thrown
into a hole and left there. Joseph ran away again;
he came to Boston; was sheltered by a man whose
charity never fails; he has been in my house, and often
has worshipped here with us. Shall I take that man
and deliver him up? — do it " with alacrity "? Shall
I suffer that gambler to carry his prey from this city?
Will you allow it — though all the laws and constitutions of men give the commandment? God do so unto us if we suffer it. [4]

This we need continually to remember: that nothing
in the world without is so sacred as the eternal law of
God; of the world within nothing is more venerable
than our own conscience, the permanent, everlasting
oracle of God. The Urim and Thummin were but
Jewish or Egyptian toys on the breastplate of the
Hebrew priest; the Delphic oracle was only a subtle
cheat; but this is the true Shekinah and presence of
God in your heart: as this

> ——" pronounces lastly on each deed,
> Of so much fame in heaven expect your meed."

If I am consciously and continually false to this,
it is of no avail that I seem loyal to all besides; I make
the light that is in me darkness, and how great is that
darkness! The center of my manhood is gone, and
I am rotten at my heart. Men may respect me, honor
me, but I am not respectable, I am a base, dishonorable
man, and like a tree, broad-branched, and leafed with
green, but all its heart gnawed out by secret worms;
at some slight touch one day, my rotten trunk will
fall with horrid squelch, bringing my leafy honors
to dishonored dust, and men will wonder that bark
could hide such rottenness and ruin.

But if I am true to this legate of God, holding His
court within my soul, then my power to discover the
just and right will enlarge continually; the axis of my
little life will coincide with the life of the infinite God,
His conscience and my own be one. Then my
character and my work will lie in the plane of His almighty action; no other will in me, His infinite wisdom, justice, holiness, and love, will flow into me, a
ceaseless tide, filling with life divine and new the little
creeklets of my humble soul. I shall be one with
God, feel His delight in me and mine in Him, and all
my mortal life run o'er with life divine and bless mankind. Let men abhor me, yea, scourge and crucify,
angels are at hand; yes, the Father is with me!

How we mistake. Men think if they can but get
wickedness dignified into a statute, enrolled in the
Capitol, signed by the magistrates, and popular with
the people, that all is secure. Then they rejoice and
at their "Thanksgiving dinner," say with the short-
lived tyrant in the play, after he had slain the rightful heirs of England's throne, and set his murderous
hoof on justice at every step to power,—

" Now is the winter of our discontent
Made glorious summer " . . .

and think that sin sits fast and rides secure.[5]   But no
statute of men is ever fixed on man till it be first the
absolute, the right, the law of God.   All else lasts
but its day, for ever this, for ever still the same.   By
" previous questions," men may stop debate, vote down
minorities with hideous grin, but the still small voice
of justice will whisper in the human heart, will be
trumpet-tongued in history to teach you that you cannot vote down God.

In your private character, if you would build securely, you must build on the natural law of God,
inherent in your nature and in His; if the nation would
build securely, it must build so.   Out of their caprice,
their selfishness, and their sin, may men make statutes,
to last for a day, built up with joyous huzzas, and the
chiming of a hundred guns, to come down with the
curses of the multitude, and smitten by the thunder of
God; but to build secure, you must build on the justice
of the Almighty.   The beatitudes of Jesus will outlast the codes of all the tyrants of the Old World and
the New.   So I have seen gamblers hurry and huddle
up their booths at a country muster, on the un-
smoothed surface of a stubble-field, foundation good
enough for such a structure, not a post plumb, to endure a single day of riot, drunkenness, and sin; but
to build a pyramid which shall outlast empires, men
lay bare the bosom of the primeval rock, and out
of primeval rock they build thereon their well-joined
work, outlasting Syria, Greece, Carthage, Rome,
venerable to time, and underneath its steadfast foot
the earthquakes pass all harmlessly away.

All things conspire to overturn a wrong.   Every

advance of man is hostile to it. Reason is hostile; religion is its deadly foe; the new-born generation will assail it, and it must fall. Of old it was written, "Though hand join in hand, the wicked shall not prosper," and the world's wide walls, from the remotest bounds of peopled space, laugh out their loud and long "Amen!" Let Iniquity be never so old and respectable, get all the most eminent votes, have the newspapers on her side, guns fired at her success, it all avails nothing; for this is God's world, not a devil's, and His eternal word has gone forth that right alone shall last for ever and for ever.

O young man, now in the period of the passions, reverence your conscience. Defer that to no appetite, to no passion, to no foolish compliance with other men's ways, to no ungodly custom, even if become a law. Ask always "Is it right for me?" Be brave and self-denying for conscience' sake. Fear not to differ from men; keeping your modesty, keep your integrity also. Let not even your discretion consume your valor. Fear not to be scrupulously upright and pure; be afraid neither of men's hate, nor even of their laugh and haughty scorn, but shudder at the thought of tampering with your sense of right, even in the smallest matters. The flesh will come up with deceitful counsels — the spirit teaching the commandments of God; give both their due. Be not the senses' slave, but the soul's freeman.

O brother man, who once wert young, in the period of ambition, or beyond it, if such a time there be, can you trust the selfishness, the caprice, the passions, and the sin of men, before your own conscience, renounce the law of God for the customs of men? When your volcanic mountain has been capped with snow, Interest, subtler than all the passions of the flesh, comes up to give her insidious counsel. " On our side," says she, " is the applause of men; feasting is with us; the wise and prudent are here also, yea, the ancient and honorable, men much older than thy father; and with gray hairs mottling thy once auburn head, wilt thou forsake official business, its solid praise and certain gain, for the phantom of natural duty, renounce allegiance to warm human lies for the cold truth of God remote and far!" Say, " Get thee behind me," to such counsellors; " I will not stain my age by listening to your subterranean talk."

O brother man, or old or young, how will you dare come up before your God and say: " O Lord, I heard, I heard Thy voice in my soul, at times still and small, at times a trumpet talking with me of the right, the eternal right, but I preferred the low counsels of the flesh; the commands of interest I kept; I feared the rich man's decorous rage; I trembled at the public roar, and I scorned alike my native duty and Thy natural law. Lo, here is the talent Thou gavest me, my sense of right. I have used each other sense, this only have I hid; it is eaten up with rust, but thus I bring it back to Thee. Take what is Thine!" Who would dare thus to sin against infinite justice? Who would wish to sin against it when it is also infinite love, and the law of right is but the highway on which the almightiness of the Father comes out to meet His prodigal, a great way off; penitent and returning home, or unrepentant still, refusing to be comforted, and famishing on chaff and husks, while there is bread of heavenly life enough and yet to spare, comes out to meet us, to take us home, and to bless us for ever and for ever?

XI

THE BOSTON KIDNAPPING

There are times of private, personal joy and delight, when some good deed has been done, or some extraordinary blessing welcomed to the arms. Then a man stops, and pours out the expression of his heightened consciousness; gives gladness words; or else, in manly quietness, exhales to heaven his joy, too deep for speech. Thus the lover rejoices in his young heart of hearts, when another breast beats in conscious unison with his own, and two souls are first made one; so a father rejoices, so a mother is filled with delight, her hour of anguish over, when their gladdened eyes behold the new-born daughter or the new-born son. Henceforth the day of newly welcomed love, the day of newly welcomed life, is an epoch of delight, marked for thanksgiving with a white stone in their calends of time,— their day of Annunciation or of Advent, a gladsome anniversary in their lives for many a year.

When these married mates are grown maturely wed, they rejoice to live over again their early loves, a second time removing the hindrances which once strewed all the way, dreaming anew the sweet prophetic dream of early hope, and bringing back the crimson mornings and the purple nights of golden days gone by, which still keep " trailing clouds of glory " as they pass. At their silver wedding, they are proud to see their children's manlifying face, and remember how, one by one, these olive-plants came up about their ever-widening hearth.

316

When old and full of memories of earth, their hopes chiefly of heaven now, they love to keep the golden wedding of their youthful joy, children and children's children round their venerable board.

Thus the individual man seeks to commemorate his private personal joy, and build up a monument of his domestic bliss.

So, in the life of a nation, there are proud days, when the people joined itself to some great idea of justice, truth, and love; took some step forward in its destiny, or welcomed to national baptism some institution born of its great idea. The anniversaries of such events become red-letter days in the almanac of the nation; days of rejoicing, till that people, old and gray with manifold experience, goes the way of all the nations, as of all its men.

Thus, on the twenty-second of December, all New England thanks God for those poor pilgrims whose wearied feet first found repose in this great wilderness of woods, not broken then. Each year, their children love to gather on the spot made famous now, and bring to mind the ancient deed; to honor it with speech and song, not without prayers to God. That day there is a springing of New England blood, a beating of New England hearts; not only here, but wherever two or three are gathered together in the name of New England, there is the memory of the pilgrims in the midst of them; and among the prairies of the West, along the rivers of the South, far off where the Pacific waits to bring gold to our shores of rock and sand,— even there the annual song of gladness bursts from New England lips.

So America honors the birth of the nation with a holiday for all the people. Then we look anew at the

national idea, reading for the six-and-seventieth time
the programme of our progress,— its first part a revolution; we study our history before and since, bringing back the day of small things, when our fathers
went from one kingdom to another people; we rejoice
at the wealthy harvest gathered from the unalienable
rights of men, sown in new soil. On that day the
American flag goes topmast high; and men in ships,
far off in the silent wilderness of the ocean, celebrate
the nation's joyous day. In all the great cities of
the Eastern world, American hearts beat quicker then,
and thank their God.

But a few days ago, the Hebrew nation commemorated its escape out of Egypt, celebrating its Passover. Though three and thirty hundred years have
since passed by, yet the Israelite remembers that his
fathers were slaves in the land of the stranger; that
the pyramids, even then a fact accomplished and
representing an obsolete idea, were witnesses to the
thraldom of his race; and the joy of Jacob triumphant
over the gods of Egypt lights up the Hebrew countenance in the melancholy Ghetto of Rome, as the recollection of the hundred-and-one pilgrims deepens the
joy of the Californian New Englanders delighting in
the glory of their nation, and their own abundant
gain. The pillar of fire still goes before the Hebrew,
in the long night of Israel's wandering; and still the
Passover is a day of joy and of proud remembrance.

Every ancient nation has thus its calendar filled with
joyful days. The worshipers of Jesus delight in
their Christmas and their Easter; the Mahometans, in
the Hegira of the Prophet. The year-book of mankind is thus marked all the way through with the red-
letter days of history. And most beautifully do those

days illuminate the human year, commemorating the
victories of the race, the days of triumph which have
marked the course of man in his long and varied, but
yet triumphant march of many a thousand years.
Thereby Hebrews, Buddhists, Christians, Mahometans,
men of every form of religion; English, French, Americans, men of all nations,— are reminded of the great
facts in their peculiar story; and mankind learns the
lesson they were meant to teach, writ in the great
events of the cosmic life of man.

These things should, indeed, be so. It were wrong
to miss a single bright day from the story of a man,
a nation, or mankind. Let us mark these days, and
be glad.

But there are periods of sorrow, not less than joy.
There comes a shipwreck to the man; and though he
tread the waters under him, and come alive to land,
yet his memory drips with sorrow for many a year
to come. The widow marks her time by dating from
the day which shore off the better portion of herself,
counting her life by years of widowhood. Marius,
exiled, hunted after, denied fire and water, a price set
on his head, just escaping the murderers and the sea,
" sitting a fugitive on the ruins of Carthage " which
he once destroyed, himself a sadder ruin now, folds his
arms and bows his head in manly grief.

These days also are remembered. It takes long to
efface what is written in tears. For ever the father
bears the annual wound that rent his child away: fifty
years do not fill up the tomb which let a mortal
through the earth to heaven. The anniversaries of
grief return. At St. Helena, on the eighteenth of
every June, how Napoleon remembered the morning
and the evening of the day at Waterloo, the beginning and the ending of his great despair!

So the nations mourn at some great defeat, and hate the day thereof. How the Frenchman detests the very name of Waterloo, and wishes to wipe off from that battle-field the monument of earth the allies piled thereon, commemorative of his nation's loss! Old mythologies are true to this feeling of mankind, when they relate that the spirit of some great man who died defeated comes and relates that he is sad: they tell that —

> "Great Pompey's shade complains that we are slow,
> And Scipio's ghost walks unrevenged amongst us."

An antique nation, with deep faith in God, looks on these defeats as correction from the hand of Heaven. In sorrow the Jew counts from the day of his exile, mourning that the city sitteth solitary that was full of people; that among all her lovers she hath none to comfort her; that she dwelleth among the heathen and hath no rest. But, he adds, the Lord afflicted her, because of the multitude of her transgressions; for Jerusalem had greatly sinned. How, in the day of her miseries, the Jew remembers her pleasant things that she had in the days of old; how her children have swooned from their wounds in the streets of their city, and have poured out their soul into their mother's bosom; Jerusalem is ruined, and Judah is forsaken, because their tongue and their doings were against the Lord, to provoke the eyes of His glory!

It is well that mother and Marius should mourn their loss; that Napoleon and the Hebrew should remember each his own defeat. Poets say that on the vigil of a fight, the old soldier's wounds smart afresh, bleeding anew. The poets' fancy should be a nation's fact.

But sometimes a man commits a wrong. He is false to himself, and stains the integrity of his soul. He comes to consciousness thereof, and the shame of the consequence is embittered by remorse for the cause. Thus Peter weeps at his own denial, and Judas hangs himself at the recollection of his treachery; so David bows his penitent forehead and lies prostrate in the dust. The anniversary of doing wrong is writ with fire on the dark tablets of memory. How a murderer convicted, yet spared in jail,— or, not convicted, still at large,— must remember the day when he first reddened his hand at his brother's heart! As the remorseless year brings back the day, the hour, the moment, and the memory of the deed, what recollections of ghastly visages come back to him!

I once knew a New England man who had dealt in slaves; I now know several such; but this man stole his brothers in Guinea to sell in America. He was a hard, cruel man, and had grown rich by the crime. But, hard and cruel as he was, at the mention of the slave-trade, the poor wretch felt a torture at his iron heart which it was piteous to behold. His soul wrought within him like the tossings of the tropic sea about his ship, deep fraught with human wretchedness. He illustrated the torments of that other "middle passage," not often named.

Benedict Arnold, successful in his treason, safe,— only André hanged, not he, the guilty man,— pensioned, feasted, rich, yet hated by all ingenuous souls not great enough to pity, hateful to himself; how this great public shame of New England must have remembered the twenty-fifth September, and have lived over again each year the annual treason of his heart!

It is well for men to pause on such days, the anni-
VIII—21

versary of their crime, and see the letters which sin has branded in their consciousness come out anew, and burn, even in the scars they left behind. In sadness, in penitence, in prayers of resolution, should a man mark these days in his own sad calendar. They are times for a man to retire within himself, to seek communion with his God, and cleanse him of the elephantine leprosy his sin has brought upon his soul.

There are such days in the life of a nation, when it stains its own integrity, commits treason against mankind, and sin against the most high God; when a proud king, or wicked minister,— his rare power consorting with a vulgar aim,— misled the people's heart, abused the nation's strength, organized iniquity as law, condensing a world of wicked will into a single wicked deed, and wrought some hideous Bartholomew massacre in the face of the sun. The anniversary of such events is a day of horror and of shivering to mankind; a day of sorrow to the guilty State which pricks with shame at the anniversary of the deed.

The twelfth of April is such a day for Boston and this State. It is the first anniversary of a great crime,— a crime against the majesty of Massachusetts law, and the dignity of the Constitution of the United States: of a great wrong,— a wrong against you and me, and all of us, against the babe not born, against the nature of mankind; of a great sin,— a sin against the law of God wrote in human nature, a sin against the Infinite God. It was a great crime, a great wrong, a great sin, on the side of American Government, which did the deed: on the people's part it was a great defeat; your defeat and mine.

Out of the iron house of bondage, a man, guilty of no crime but love of liberty, fled to the people of

Massachusetts. He came to us a wanderer, and Boston took him in to an unlawful jail; hungry, and she fed him with a felon's meat; thirsty, she gave him the gall and vinegar of a slave to drink; naked, she clothed him with chains; sick and in prison, he cried for a helper, and Boston sent him a marshal and a commissioner; she set him between kidnappers, among the most infamous of men, and they made him their slave. Poor and in chains, the government of the nation against him, he sent round to the churches his petition for their prayers;— the churches of commerce, they gave him their curse: he asked of us the sacrament of freedom, in the name of our God; and in the name of *their* trinity, the trinity of money, — Boston standing as godmother at the ceremony,— in the name of their God they baptized him a slave. The New England church of commerce said: " Thy name is Slave. I baptize thee in the name of the golden eagle, and of the silver dollar, and of the copper cent."

This is holy ground that we stand on: godly men laid here the foundation of a Christian church; laid it with prayers, laid it with tears, laid it in blood. Noble men laid here the foundation of a Christian state, with all the self-denial of New England men; laid that with prayers, with tears, laid that in blood. They sought a church without a bishop, a state without a king, a community without a lord, and a family without a slave. Yet even here in Massachusetts, which first of American colonies sent forth the idea of " inherent and unalienable rights," and first offered the conscious sacrament of her blood; here, in Boston, which was full of manly men who rocked the Cradle of Liberty,— even here the rights of man were of no

value and of no avail. Massachusetts took a man from
the horns of her altar — he had fled to her for protection,— and voluntarily gave him up to bondage
without end; did it with her eyes wide open; did it
on purpose; did it in notorious violation of her own
law, in consciousness of the sin; did it after " fasting
and prayer." [1]

It is well for us to come together, and consider the
defeat which you and I have suffered when the rights
of man were thus cloven down, and look at the crime
committed by those whom posterity will rank among
infidels to Christianity, among the enemies of man; it
is well to commemorate the event, the disgrace of
Boston, the perpetual shame and blot of Massachusetts. Yet it was not the people of Massachusetts
who did the deed: it was only their government. The
officers are one thing; and the people, thank God, are
something a little different.

If a deed which so outraged the people had been
done by the government of Massachusetts a hundred
years ago, there would have been a " day of fasting
and prayer," and next a muster of soldiers: one day
the people would have thought of their trust in God,
and the next looked to it that their powder was dry.
Now nobody fasts, save to the eye; he prays best who,
not asking God to do man's work, prays penitence,
prays resolutions, and then prays deeds, thus supplicating with heart and head and hands. This is a
day for such a prayer. The twelfth of last April
issued the proclamation which brings us here to-day.

We have historical precedent for this commemoration, if men need such an argument. After the Boston
Massacre of the fifth of March, 1770, the people had
annually a solemn commemoration of the event. They

had their great and honored men to the pulpit on
that occasion: Lovell, child of a Tory father,— the
son's patriotism brought him to a British jail; Tudor
and Dawes, honorable and honored names; Thacher,
" the young Elijah " of his times; Warren, twice called
to that post, but destined soon to perish by a British
hand; John Hancock,— his very name was once the
pride and glory of the town. They stood here, and,
mindful of their brothers slain in the street not long
to bear the name of " king," taught the lesson of
liberty to their fellow-men. The menace of British
officers, their presence in the aisles of the church, the
sight of their weapons on the pulpit-stairs, did not
frighten Joseph Warren,— not a hireling shepherd,
though he came in by the pulpit-window, while soldiers
crammed the porch. Did they threaten to stop his
mouth? It took bullet and bayonet both to silence
his lips. John Hancock was of eyes too pure to fear
the government of Britain. Once, when Boston was
in the hands of the enemy of freedom,— I mean the
foreign enemy,— the discourse could not be delivered
here; Boston adjourned to Watertown to hear " the
young Elijah " ask whether " the rising empire of
America shall be an empire of slaves or of freemen."
But on that day there was another commemoration held
hard by; " one George Washington " discoursed
from the " Heights of Dorchester;" and, soon after,
Israel Putnam marched over the Neck,— and there
was not a " Red-coat " south of the North End. The
March of '76 was not far from the July of '76, when
yet another discourse got spoken.

For twelve years did our fathers commemorate the
first blood shed here by soldiers " quartered among us
without our consent;" yes, until there was not a " Red-

coat " left in the land; and the gloom of the Boston Massacre was forgot in the blaze of American independence; the murder of five men, in the freedom of two millions.

The first slave Boston has officially sent back since 1770 was returned a year ago. Let us commemorate the act, till there is not a kidnapper left in all the North; not a kidnapper lurking in a lawyer's office in all Boston, or in a merchant's counting-room; not a priest who profanes his function by flouting at the higher law of God; till there is not a slave in America; and sorrow at the rendition of Thomas Sims shall be forgotten in the freedom of three million men. Let us remember the Boston Kidnapping, as our fathers kept the memory of the Boston Massacre.

It is a fitting time to come together. There was once a " dark day " in New England, when the visible heavens were hung with night, and men's faces gathered blackness less from the sky above than from the fears within. But New England never saw a day so black as the twelfth of April, 1851; a day whose Egyptian darkness will be felt for many a year to come.

New England has had days of misfortune before this, and of mourning at the sin of her magistrates. In 1761, a mean man in a high place in the British Island, thinking that " discussion must be suppressed," declared that citizens " are not to demand the reasons of measures; they must, and they easily may, be taught better manners." The British Ministry decided to tax the colonies without their consent. Massachusetts decided to be taxed only with her own consent. The Board of Trade determined to collect duties against the will of the people. The Government insisted; the

mercenaries of the custom-house in Boston applied
for "writs of assistance," authorizing them to
search for smuggled goods where and when they
pleased, and to call on the people to help in the matter. The mercenary who filled the governor's chair
favored the outrage. The court, obedient to power,
and usually on the side of prerogative and against the
right, seemed ready to pervert the law against justice.
Massachusetts felt her liberty in peril, and began the
war of ideas. James Otis, an irregular but brilliant
and powerful man from Barnstable, and an acute
lawyer, resigned his post of Advocate to the Admi-
ralty; threw up his chance of preferment, and was determined " to sacrifice estate, ease, health, applause,
and even life, to the sacred calls of my country," and
in opposition to that kind of power " which cost one
king of England his head, another his throne."

It was a dark day in Massachusetts when the " writs
of assistance " were called for; when the talents, the
fame, the riches, and the avarice of Chief-Justice
Hutchinson, the respectability of venerable men, the
power of the Crown and its officers, were all against
the right; but that brave lawyer stood up, his words
" a flame of fire," to demonstrate that all arbitrary
authority was unconstitutional and against the law.
His voice rang through the land like a war-psalm of
the Hebrew muse. Hutchinson, rich, false, and in
power, cowered before the " great incendiary " of New
England. John Adams, a young lawyer from
Quincy, who stood by, touched by the same inspiration,
declared that afterwards he could never read the Acts
of Trade without anger, nor " any portion of them
without a curse." If the court was not convinced, the
people were. It was a dark day when the " writs of

assistance " were called for; but the birthplace of
Franklin took the lightning out of that thundering
cloud, and the storm broke into rain which brought
forth the green glories of Liberty-tree, that soon blos-
somed all over in the radiance of the bow of promise
set on the departing cloud. The seed from that day
of bloom shall sow with blessings all the whole wide
world of men.

There was another dark time when the Stamp Act
passed, and the day came for the use of the stamps,
Nov. 1st, 1765: The people of Boston closed their
shops; they muffled and tolled the bells of the churches;
they hung on Liberty-tree the effigy of Mr. Huske,
a New Hampshire traitor of that time, who had removed to London, got a seat in Parliament, and was
said to have proposed the Stamp Act to the British
minister. Beside him they hung the image of Grenville, the ministerial author of the Act. In the after-
noon, the public cut down the images; carried them
in a cart, thousands following, to the town-house,
where the Governor and Council were in session; carried
the effigies solemnly through the building, and thence
to the gallows, where, after hanging a while, they were
cut down and torn to pieces. All was done quietly,
orderly, and with no violence. It was All-Saints Day:
two hundred and forty-eight years before, Martin
Luther had pilloried the papacy on a church-door at
Wittenberg, not knowing what would fall at the sound
of his hammer nailing up the Ninety-five Theses.

Nobody would touch the hated stamps. Mr. Oliver,
the secretary of the province, and " distributor of
stamps," had been hanged in effigy before. His
stamp-office had already given a name to the sea,
" Oliver's Dock " long commemorating the fate of the

building. Dismayed by the voice of the people, he
resigned his office. Not satisfied with that, the people
had him before an immense meeting at Liberty-tree;
and at noonday, under the very limb where he had been
hung in effigy, before a justice of the peace he took
an oath that he never would take any measures
. . . for enforcing the Stamp Act in America.
Then, with three cheers for liberty, Mr. Oliver was
allowed to return home. He ranked as the third
crown-officer in the colony. Where could you find
" one of his Majesty's justices of the peace " to administer such an oath before such a " town-meeting "?
A man was found to do that deed, and leave descendants to be proud of it; for, after three generations
have passed by, the name of Richard Dana is still on
the side of liberty.

No more of stamps in Boston at that time. In time
of danger, it is thought " a good thing to have a
man in the house." Boston had provided herself.
There were a good many who did not disgrace the
name. Amongst others, there was one of such " ob-
stinacy and inflexible disposition," said Hutchinson,
" that he could never be conciliated by any office or
gift whatever." Yet Samuel Adams was " not rich,
nor a bachelor." There was another, one John Adams,
son of a shoemaker at Quincy, not a whit less obstinate or hard to conciliate with gifts. When he heard
Otis in that great argument, he felt " ready to take
up arms against the ' writs of assistance.' " One day,
the twenty-second of December of that year, he writes
in his journal: " At home with my family, thinking."
In due time, something came of his thinking. He
wrote, " By inactivity we discover cowardice, and too
much respect for the Act."

The Stamp Act was dead in New England and in all America. Very soon the ministry were glad to bury their dead.

It was in such a spirit that Boston met the " writs of assistance " and the Stamp Act. What came of the resistance? When Parliament came together, the " great commoner " said,— every boy knew the passage by heart when I went to school,—" I rejoice that America has resisted. Three millions of people so dead to all the feelings of liberty as voluntarily to be slaves, would have been fit instruments to make slaves of all the rest." The ministry still proposed to put down America by armies. Mr. Pitt said: " America, if she fall, will fall like the strong man. She will embrace the pillars of the state, and pull down the Constitution along with her. But she will not fall." " I would advise," said he, " that the Stamp Act be repealed, absolutely, totally, and immediately;" " that the reason for the repeal be assigned; that it was founded on an erroneous principle." Repealed it was, " absolutely, totally, and immediately."

But the British Ministry still insisted on taxation without representation. Massachusetts continued her opposition. There was a merchants' meeting in Boston in favor of freedom. It assembled from time to time, and had a large influence. Men agreed not to import British goods: they would wear their old clothes till they could weave new ones in America, and kill no more lambs till they had abundance of wool. Boston made a non-importation agreement. Massachusetts wrote a " circular letter " to the other colonies asking them to make common cause with her,— a circular which the king thought " of the most dangerous and factious character." On the seventeenth of June, 1768, the town of Boston instructed its four representatives, Otis, Cushing, Adams, and Hancock: "It is our unalterable resolution at all times to assert and vindicate our dear and invaluable rights, at the utmost hazard of our lives and fortunes." [2] This seemed to promise another "seventeenth of June," if the Ministry persisted in their course.

On the fifteenth of May, 1770, she again issued similar instructions. "James I.," says the letter of instruction, "more than once laid down, that, as it was atheism and blasphemy in a creature to dispute what the Deity may do, so it is presumptuous and sedition in a subject to dispute what a king may do in the height of his powers." "Good Christians," said he, "will be content with God's will revealed in his word, and good subjects will rest in the king's will revealed in *his* law." That was the "No Higher Law Doctrine" of the time. See how it went down at Boston in 1770. "Surely," said the people of Boston, in town-meeting assembled, "nothing except the ineffable contempt of the reigning monarch diverted that indignant vengeance which would otherwise have made his illustrious throne to tremble and hurled the royal diadem from his forfeit head." [3] Such was the feeling of Boston towards a government which flouted at the eternal law of God.

The people claimed that law was on their side; even Sir Henry Finch having said, in the time of Charles I., "The king's prerogative stretcheth not to the doing of any wrong." But, Boston said, "Had the express letter of the law been less favorable, and were it possible to ransack up any absurd, obsolete

notions which might have seemed calculated to prop-
agate slavish doctrines, we should by no means have
been influenced to forego our birthright;" for " mankind will not be reasoned out of their feelings of
humanity." " We remind you, that the further nations recede and give way to the gigantic strides of
any powerful despot, the more rapidly will the fiend
advance to spread wide desolation." " It is now no
time to halt between two opinions." " We enjoin
you at all hazards to deport . . . like the faithful representatives of a free-born, awakened, and determined people, who, being impregnated with the
spirit of liberty in conception, and nurtured in the
principles of freedom from their infancy, are resolved
to breathe the same celestial ether, till summoned to
resign the heavenly flame by that omnipotent God
who gave it." That was the language of Boston in
1770.[4]

True there were men who took the other side; some
of them from high and honorable convictions; others
from sordid motives; some from native bigotry and
meanness they could not help. But the mass of the
people went for the rights of the people. It was
not a mere matter of dollars and cents that stirred the
men of Massachusetts then. True, the people had always been thrifty, and looked well to the " things of
this world." But threepence duty on a pound of tea,
six farthings on a gallon of molasses, was not very
burdensome to a people that had a school before there
was any four-footed beast above a swine in the colony
— a people that once taxed themselves thirteen shillings and eight pence in a pound of income! It was
the principle they looked at. They would not have
paid three barley-corns on a hogshead of sugar and

admit the right of Parliament to levy the tax. This same spirit extended to the other colonies: Virginia and Massachusetts stood side by side; New York with Boston.

It was a dark day for New England when the Stamp Act became a law; but it was a much darker day when the Fugitive Slave Bill passed the Congress of the United States. The Acts of Trade and the Stamp Act were the work of foreign hands, of the ministers of England, not America. A traitor of New Hampshire was thought to have originated the Stamp Act; but even he did not make a speech in its favor. The author of the Act was never within three thousand miles of Boston. But the Fugitive Slave Bill was the work of Americans; it had its great support from another native of New Hampshire; it got the vote of the member for Boston who faithfully represented the money which sent him there; though, God be thanked, not the men!

When the Stamp Act came to be executed in Boston, the ships hung their flags at half-mast; the shops were shut, the bells were tolled; ship, shop, and church all joining in a solidarity of affliction, in one unanimous lament. But, when the Fugitive Slave Bill came to Boston, the merchants and politicians of the city fired a hundred guns at noonday, in token of their joy! How times have changed! In 1765, when Huske of New Hampshire favored the Stamp Act, and Oliver of Boston accepted the office of distributor of stamps, the people hung their busts in effigy on Liberty-tree; Oliver must ignominiously forswear his office. After two of the Massachusetts delegation in Congress had voted for the Missouri Compromise in 1819, when they came back to Boston, they were hissed at on

'Change, and were both of them abhorred for the deed which spread slavery west of the great river. To this hour their names are hateful all the way from Boston to Lanesboro. But their children are guiltless: let us not repeat the fathers' name. But what was the Stamp Act or the Missouri Compromise to the Fugitive Slave Bill! One was looking at a hedge, the other stealing the sheep behind it. Yet when the representative of the money of Boston, who voted for the bill, returned, he was flattered and thanked by two classes of men; by those whom money makes "respectable" and prominent; by those whom love of money makes servile and contemptible. When he resigned his place, Boston sent another, with the command, "Go thou and do likewise;" and he has just voted again for the Fugitive Slave Bill,— he alone of all the delegation of Massachusetts.

The Stamp Act levied a tax on us in money, and Boston would not pay a cent, hauled down the flags, shut up the shops, tolled the church-bells, hung its authors in effigy, made the third officer of the Crown take oath not to keep the law, cast his stamp-shop into the sea. The Slave Act levied a tax in men, and Boston fired a hundred guns, and said, "We are ready; we will catch fugitive slaves for the South. It is a dirty work, too dirty for any but Northern hands; but it will bring us clean money." Ship, shop, and church seemed to feel a solidarity of interest in the measure; the leading newspapers of the town were full of glee.

The Fugitive Slave Bill became a law on the eighteenth of September, 1850. Eighty-five years before that date there was a town-meeting in Boston, at which the people instructed their representatives in the General Assembly of Massachusetts. It was just after the passage of the Stamp Act. Boston told her servants by no means to " join in any measures for countenancing and assisting in the execution of the same [the Stamp Act] ; but use your best endeavors in the General Assembly to have the inherent and un-alienable rights of the people of this province asserted, vindicated, and left upon the public record, that posterity may never have reason to charge the present times with the guilt of tamely giving them away." [5]

It was "voted unanimously that the same be accepted." This is the earliest use of the phrase " inherent and unalienable rights of the people " which I have yet found. It has the savor of James Otis, who had " a tongue of flame and the inspiration of a seer." It dates from Boston, and the eighteenth day of September, eighty-five years before the passage of the Fugitive Slave Bill. In 1850 where was the town-meeting of '65? James Otis died without a son; but a different man sought to " fence in " the Slave Act, and fence men from their rights.[6]

The passage of the Fugitive Slave Bill was a sad event to the colored citizens of the state. At that time there were 8975 persons of color in Massachusetts. In thirty-six hours after the passage of the bill was known here, five-and-thirty colored persons applied to a well-known philanthropist in this city for counsel.[7] Before sixty hours passed by, more than forty had fled. The laws of Massachusetts could not be trusted to shelter her own children: they must flee to Canada. " This arm, hostile to tyrants," says the motto of the State, " seeks rest in the enjoyment of liberty." Then it ought to have been changed, and read, " This arm, once hostile to tyrants, confederate with them now, drives off her citizens to foreign climes of liberty."

The word "commissioner" has had a traditional hatred ever since our visitation by Sir Edmund Andros; it lost none of its odious character when it became again incarnate in a kidnapper. With Slave Act commissioners to execute the bill, with such "ruling" as we have known on the Slave Act bench, such swearing by "witnesses" on the slave stand, any man's freedom is at the mercy of the kidnapper and his "commissioned" attorney. The one can manufacture "evidence" or "enlarge" it, the other manufacture "law;" and with such an administration and such creatures to serve its wish, what colored man was safe? Men in peril have a keen instinct of their danger; the dark-browed mothers in Boston, they wept like Rachel for her first-born, refusing to be comforted. There was no comfort for them save in flight: that must be not in the winter, but into the winter of Canada, which is to the African what our rude climate is to the goldfinch and the canary-bird.

Some of the colored people had acquired a little property, they got an honest living; had wives and children, and looked back upon the horrors of slavery, which it takes a woman's affectionate genius to paint, as you read her book; looked on them as things for the memory, for the imagination, not as things to be suffered again. But the Fugitive Slave Bill said to every black mother, "This may be your fate; the fate of your sons and your daughters." It was possible to all; probable to many; certain to some, unless they should flee.

It was a dark bill for them; but the blackness of the darkness fell on the white man. The colored men were only to bear the cross; the whites made it. I

would take the black man's share in suffering the
Slave Act, rather than the white man's sin in making
it: aye, as I would rather take Hancock's than Huske's
share of the history of the Stamp Act. This wicked
law has developed in the Africans some of the most
heroic virtues; in the Yankee it has brought out some
of the most disgraceful examples of meanness that
ever dishonored mankind.

The Boston Massacre,— you know what that was,
and how the people felt when a hireling soldiery, sent
here to oppress, shot down the citizens of Boston on
the fifth of March, 1770. Then the blood of America
flowed for the first time at the touch of British steel.
But that deed was done by foreigners; thank God,
they were not Americans born; done by hirelings, impressed into the army against their will, and sent here
without their consent. It was done in hot blood; done
partly in self-defense, after much insult and wrong.
The men who fired the shot were brought to trial.
The great soul of John Adams stood up to defend
them, Josiah Quincy aiding the unpopular work. A
Massachusetts jury set the soldiers free,— they only
obeyed orders, the soldier is a tool of his commander.
Such was the Boston Massacre. Yet hear how John
Hancock spoke on the fourth anniversary thereof,
when passion had had time to pass away: —

"Tell me, ye bloody butchers! ye villains high and
low! ye wretches who contrived, as well as you who
executed, the inhuman deed! do you not feel the goads
and stings of conscious guilt pierce through your
savage bosoms? Though some of you may think
yourselves exalted to a height that bids defiance to the
arms of human justice, and others shroud yourselves
beneath the mask of hypocrisy, and build your hopes
VIII—22

of safety on the low arts of cunning, chicanery, and falsehood; yet do you not sometimes feel the gnawings of that worm which never dies? Do not the injured shades of Maverick, Gray, Caldwell, Attucks, and Carr attend you in your solitary walks, arrest you even in the midst of your debaucheries, and fill even your dreams with terror?

"Ye dark, designing knaves! ye murderers! parricides! how dare you tread upon the earth which has drank in the blood of slaughtered innocents, shed by your wicked hands? How dare you breathe that air which wafted to the ear of Heaven the groans of those who fell a sacrifice to your accursed ambition? But if the laboring earth doth not expand her jaws; if the air you breathe is not commissioned to be the minister of death; yet hear it, and tremble! the eye of Heaven penetrates the darkest chambers of the soul; traces the leading clue through all the labyrinths which your industrious folly has devised; and you, however you may have screened yourselves from human eyes, must be arraigned, must lift your hands, red with the blood of those whose deaths you have procured, at the tremendous bar of God."

But the Boston kidnapping was done by Boston men. The worst of the kidnappers were natives of the spot. It was done by volunteers, not impressed to the work, but choosing their profession,— loving the wages of sin,— and conscious of the loathing and the scorn they are all sure to get, and bequeath to their issue. They did it deliberately; it was a cold-blooded atrocity: they did it aggressively, not in self-defense, but in self-degradation. They did it for their pay: let them have it; verily, they shall have their reward.

When the Fugitive Slave Bill became a law, it seems to me the Governor ought to have assembled the Legislature; that they should have taken adequate measures for protecting the eight thousand nine hundred and seventy-five persons thus left at the mercy of any kidnapper; that officers should have been appointed at the public cost, to defend these helpless men, and a law passed, punishing any one who should attempt to kidnap a man in this Commonwealth. Massachusetts should have done for justice what South Carolina has long ago done for injustice. But Massachusetts had often seen her citizens put into the jails of the North for no crime but their complexion and looked on with a drowsy yawn. Once, indeed, she did send two persons, one to Charleston and the other to New Orleans, to attend to this matter; both of them were turned out of the South with insult and contempt. After that, Massachusetts did nothing; the Commonwealth did nothing; the Commonwealth did not even scold: she sat mute as the symbolic fish in the State-house. The Bay State turned non-resistant; " passive obedience " should have been the motto then. So, when a bill was passed, putting the liberty of her citizens at the mercy of a crew of legalized kidnappers, the governor of Massachusetts did nothing. Boston fired her hundred guns under the very eyes of John Hancock's house; her servile and her rich men complimented their representative for voting away the liberty of nine thousand of her fellow-citizens. Was Boston Massachusetts? It is still the governor.

As the Government of Massachusetts did nothing, the next thing would have been for the people to come together in a great mass meeting, and decree, as their fathers had often done, that so unjust a law should

not be kept in the old Bay State, and appoint a
committee to see that no man was kidnapped and carried off; and, if the kidnappers still insisted on kidnapping our brothers here in Massachusetts, the
people could have found a way to abate that nuisance
as easily as to keep off the stamped paper in 1765.
The commissioners of the Slave Act might as easily
be dealt with as the commissioners of the Stamp Act.

I love law, and respect law, and should be slow to
violate it. I would suffer much, sooner than violate
a statute that was simply inexpedient. There is no
natural reason, perhaps, for limiting the interest of
money to six per cent. but as the law of Massachusetts
forbids more, I would not take more. I should hate to
interrupt the course of law, and put violence in its
place.

> "The way of ancient ordinance, though it winds,
> Is yet no devious way. Straightforward goes
> The lightning's path, and straight the fearful path
> Of the cannon-ball. Direct it flies, and rapid;
> Shattering that it may reach, and shattering what it
>   reaches.
> My son! the road the human being travels,—
> That on which blessing comes and goes,— doth follow
> The river's course, the valley's playful windings;
> Curves round the corn-field and the hill of vines,
> Honoring the holy bounds of property!
> And thus secure, though late, leads to its end."

But when the rulers have inverted their function,
and enacted wickedness into a law which treads down
the unalienable rights of man to such degree as this,
then I know no ruler but God, no law but natural
justice. I tear the hateful statute of kidnappers to
shivers; I trample it underneath my feet. I do it in
the name of all law; in the name of justice and of man;
in the name of the dear God.

But of all this nothing was done. The Governor did not assemble the Legislature, as he would if a part of the property in Massachusetts had thus been put at the mercy of legalized ruffians. There was no convention of the people of Massachusetts. True, there was a meeting at Faneuil Hall, a meeting chiefly of anti-slavery men; leading Free-soilers were a little afraid of it, though some of them came honorably forward. A venerable man put his name at the head of the signers of the call, and wrote a noble-spirited letter to the meeting; Josiah Quincy was a Faneuil Hall name in 1859, as well as in 1765. It was found a little difficult to get what in Boston is called a " respectable " man to preside. Yet one often true sat in the chair that night,— Charles F. Adams did not flinch, when you wanted a man to stand fire. A brave, good minister, whose large soul disdains to be confined to sect or party, came in from Cambridge, and lifted up his voice to the God who brought up Israel out of the iron house of bondage, and our fathers from thraldom in a strange land; thanking Him who created all men in His own image, and of one blood. Charles Lowell's prayer for all mankind will not soon be forgotten. The meeting was an honor to the men who composed it. The old spirit was there; philanthropy, which never fails; justice, that is not weary with continual defeat; and faith in God, which is sure to triumph at the last. But what a reproach was the meeting to Boston! " Respectability " was determined to kidnap.

At that meeting a Committee of Vigilance was appointed and a very vigilant committee it has proved itself, having saved the liberty of three or four hundred citizens of Boston. Besides, it has done many things not to be spoken of now. I know one of its

members who has helped ninety-five fugitives out of
the United States. It would not be well to mention
his name,— he has " levied war " too often,— the good
God knows it.

Other towns in the State did the same thing. Vigilance committees got on foot in most of the great
towns, in many of the small ones. In some places, all
the people rose up against the Fugitive Slave Bill; the
whole town a vigilance committee. The country was
right; off the pavement, Liberty was the watchword;
on the pavement, it was Money. But the government
of Massachusetts did nothing. Could the eight thousand nine hundred and seventy-five colored persons affect any election? Was their vote worth bidding for?

The controlling men of the Whig party and of the
Democratic party, they either did nothing at all, or
else went over in favor of kidnapping; some of them
had a natural proclivity that way, and went over
" with alacrity."

The leading newspapers in the great towns,— they,
of course, went on the side of inhumanity, with few
honorable exceptions. The political papers thought
kidnapping would " save the Union;" the commercial
papers thought it would " save trade," the great object for which the Union was established.

How differently had Massachusetts met the Acts of
Trade and the Stamp Act! How are the mighty
fallen! Yet, if you could have got their sacred ballot, I think fifteen out of every twenty voters, even in
Boston, would have opposed the law. But the leading politicians and the leading merchants were in
favor of the bill, and the execution of it.

There are two political parties in America: one of
them is very large and well organized; that is the

Slave-soil party. It has two great subdivisions; one is called Whig, the other Democratic: together they make up the great national Slave-soil party. It was the desire of that party to extend slavery; making a national sin out of a sectional curse. They wished to "re-annex" Massachusetts to the department of the slave soil, and succeeded. We know the history of that party: who shall tell the future of its opponent? There will be a to-morrow after to-day.

The practical result was what the leading men of Boston desired: soon we had kidnappers in Boston. Some ruffians came here from Georgia, to kidnap William and Ellen Craft. Among them came a jailer from Macon, a man of infamous reputation, and character as bad as its repute; notoriously a cruel man, and hateful on that account even in Georgia. In the handbills, his face was described as "uncommon bad." It was worthy of the description. I saw the face; it looked like total depravity incarnate in a born kidnapper. He was not quite welcome in Boston; Massachusetts had not then learned to "conquer her prejudices," yet he found friends, got "a sort of a lawyer" to help him kidnap a man and his wife: a fee will hire such men any day. He was a welcome guest at the United States Hotel, which, however, got a little tired of his company, and warned him off. The commissioner first applied to for aid in this business seemed to exhibit some signs of a conscience, and appeared a little averse to stealing a man. The Vigilance Committee put their eye on the kidnapper: he was glad to escape out of Boston with a whole skin. He sneaked off in a private way; went back to Georgia; published his story, partly true, false in part; got into a quarrel in the street at Macon,— I traced out his wriggling trail for some distance back,— it was not the first brawl he had been in; was stabbed to what is commonly called "the heart," and fell unmistakably dead. Some worthy persons had told him, if he went to Boston, he would "rot in a Massachusetts jail;" others, that they hoped it would turn out so, for such an errand deserved such an end. Poor men of Georgia! They knew the Boston of 1765, not of 1850;— the town of the Stamp Act, ruled by select men; not the city of the Slave Act ruled by a "Mayor." Hughes came to save the "Union!"

That time the kidnappers went off without their prey. Somebody took care of Ellen Craft, and William took care of himself. They were parishioners of mine. Mr. Craft was a tall, brave man; his countrymen, not nobler than he, were once bishops of Hippo and of Carthage. He armed himself, pretty well too. I inspected his weapons: it was rather new business for me; New England ministers have not done much in that line since the Revolution. His powder had a good kernel, and he kept it dry; his pistols were of excellent proof, the barrels true and clean; the trigger went easy; the caps would not hang fire at the snap. I tested his poniard; the blade had a good temper, stiff enough, yet springy withal; the point was sharp. There was no law for him but the law of nature; he was armed and equipped "as that law directs." He walked the streets boldly; but the kidnappers did not dare touch him. Some persons offered to help Mr. Craft to purchase himself. He said, "I will not give the man two cents for his 'right' to me. I will buy myself, not with gold, but iron!" That looked like "levying war," not like conquering his prejudices for liberty! William Craft did not obey with alacrity. He stood his ground till the kidnappers had fled; then he also must flee. Boston was no home for him. One of her most eminent ministers had said, if a fugitive came to him, " I would drive him away from my own door."

William and Ellen Craft were at the " World's Fair," specimens of American manufactures, the working-tools of the South; a proof of the democracy of the American State; part of the " outward evidences " of the Christianity of the American church. " It is a great country," whence a Boston clergyman would drive William from his door! America did not compete very well with the European States in articles sent to the Fair. A " reaping machine " was the most quotable thing; then a " Greek slave " in marble; next an American slave in flesh and blood. America was the only contributor of slaves; she had the monopoly of the article; it is the great export of Virginia, — it was right to exhibit a specimen at the World's Fair. Visitors went to Westminster Abbey, and saw the monument of marble which Massachusetts erected to Lord George Howe, and thence to the Crystal Palace to see the man and woman whom Massachusetts would not keep from being kidnapped in her capital.

In due time came the " Union meeting," on the twenty-sixth day of November, 1850, in Faneuil Hall, in front of the pictures of Samuel Adams and John Hancock,— in the hall which once rocked to the patriotism of James Otis, thundering against Acts of Trade and " writs of assistance," " more eloquent than Chatham or Burke." The Union meeting was held in the face and eyes of George Washington.

You remember the meeting. It was rather a remarkable platform; uniformly " hunker," but decidedly heterogeneous. Yet sin abolishes all historical and personal distinctions. Kidnapping, like misery, "makes strange bed-fellows." Three things all the speakers on that occasion developed in common: a hearty abhorrence of the right; a uniform contempt for the eternal law of God; a common desire to kidnap a man. After all, the platform did not exhibit so strange a medley as it seemed at first: the difference in the speakers was chiefly cutaneous, only skin-deep. The reading and the speaking, the whining and the thundering, were all to the same tune. Pirates, who have just quarreled about dividing the spoil, are of one heart when it comes to plundering and killing a man.

That was a meeting for the encouragement of kidnapping; not from the love of kidnapping in itself, but for the recompense of reward. I will not insult the common sense of respectable men with supposing that the talk about the " dissolution of the Union," and the cry, " The Union is in peril this hour," was anything more than a stage trick, which the managers doubtless thought was " well got up." So it was; but, I take it, the spectators who applauded, as well as the actors who grimaced, knew that the " lion " was no beast, but only " Simon Snug the joiner." Indeed, the lion himself often told us so. However, I did know two very " respectable " men of Boston, who actually believed the Union was in danger; only two, — but they are men of such incomprehensible exiguity of intellect, that their names would break to pieces if spoken loud.

Well, the meeting, in substance, told this truth: " Boston is willing; you may come here, and kidnap any black man you choose. We will lend you the marshal, the commissioner, the tools of perjury, supple

courts of law, clergymen to bless the transaction, and
editors to defend it!" That was the plain English
meaning of the meeting, of the resolutions and the
speeches. It was so understood North and South.

At the meeting itself it was declared that the Union
was at the last gasp; but the next morning the political doctors, the "medicine-men" of our mythology,
declared the old lady out of danger. She sat up that
day, and received her friends. The meeting was
"great medicine;" the crisis was passed. The Fugitive Slave Bill could be "executed in Boston," where
the "writs of assistance" and the Stamp Act had been
a dead letter: a man might be kidnapped in Boston
any day.

But the meeting was far from unanimous at the end.
At the beginning a manly speech would have turned
the majority in favor of the right. In November,
1850, half a dozen rich men might have turned Boston
against the wicked law. But their interest lay on the
other side; and "where the treasure is, there will the
heart be also." Boston is bad enough, but bad only
in spots; at that time the spots showed, and some men
thought all Boston was covered with the small-pox of
the Union meeting: the scars will mark the faces of
only a few. I wish I could heal those faces, which
will have an ugly look in the eyes of posterity.

The practical result of the meeting was what it was
designed to be: soon we had other kidnappers in Boston. This time they found better friends: like con-
sorteth with like. A certain lawyer's office in Boston
became a huckstery of kidnappers' warrants. Soon
the kidnappers had Shadrach in their fiery furnace,
heated seven times hotter than before for William and
Ellen Craft. But the Lord delivered him out of their

clutch; and he now sings " God save the Queen," in
token of his delivery out of the hands of the kidnappers
of " Republican " Babylon.　Nobody knows how he
was delivered; the rescue was officially declared " levying war," the rescuers guilty of " treason."　But,
wonderful to say, after all the violations of law by
the court, and all the browbeating by the attorneys,
and all the perjury and other " amendments and en-
largement of testimony " by witnesses, not a man
was found guilty of any crime.　Spite of " Union
meetings," there is some respect for Massachusetts
law; spite of judicial attempts to pack a jury, it is
still the great safeguard of the people; spite of
preaching, there is some virtue left; and, though a
minister would send back his mother into slavery, a
Massachusetts jury will not send a man to jail for
such an act as that.

The case of Shadrach was not the last.　Kidnappers came and kidnappers went: for a long time they
got no spoil.　I need not tell, must not tell, how they
were evaded, or what help came, always in season.
The Vigilance Committee did not sleep; it was in " permanent session " much of the whole winter; its eyes
were in every place, beholding the evil and the good.
The Government at Washington did not like this state
of things, and stimulated the proper persons, as the
keeper of a menagerie in private stirs up the hyenas
and the cougars and the wolves, from a safe distance.
There was a talk of " Sherman's flying-artillery "
alighting at Boston; but it flew over and settled at
Newport, I think.　Next there was to be a " garrison
of soldiers " to enforce the law; but the men in buck-
ram did not appear.　Then a " seventy-four gun ship "
was coming, to bombard Southack street, I suppose.

Still it was determined that the "Union" was not
quite safe; it was in danger of a "dissolution;" the
"medicine-men" of politics and commerce looked
grave. True, the Union had been "saved" again and
again, till her "salvation" was a weariness; she "was
nothing bettered, but rather grew worse." All winter
long the Union was reported as in a chronic spasm
of "dissolution." So the "medicine-men" prescribed:
a man kidnapped in Massachusetts, to be taken at
the South; with one scruple of lawyer, and two scruples
of clergyman. That would set the Union on her
legs. Boston was to furnish all this medicine.[8]

It was long before this city could furnish a kidnapped man. The Vigilance Committee parried the
blow aimed at the neck of the fugitive. The country
was on our side,— gave us money, help, men when
needed. The guardians of Boston could not bear the
taunt that she had not sent back a slave. New York
had been before her; the "City of Brotherly Love,"
the home of Penn and Franklin, had assisted in kidnapping; it went on vigorously under the arm of a
judge who appropriately bears the name of the great
first murderer. No judge could be better entitled;
Kane and kidnapping are names conjuring well.
Should Boston delay? What a reproach to the fair
fame of her merchants! The history of Boston was
against them; America has not yet forgotten the conduct of Boston in the matter of the Stamp Act and
Acts of Trade. She was deeply guilty of the Revolutionary War; she still kept its Cradle of Liberty, and
the bones of Adams and Hancock,— dangerous relics
in any soil; they ought to have been "sent back"
at the passage of the Fugitive Slave Bill, and Faneuil
Hall demolished. Bunker Hill Monument was within

sight. Boston was suspected of not liking to kidnap
a man. What a reproach it was to her! — 8975
colored persons in Massachusetts, and not a fugitive
returned from Boston. September passed by, October,
November, December, January, February, March; not
a slave sent back in seven months! What a disgrace
to the government of Boston, which longed to steal a
man; to the representative of Boston, who had voted
for the theft; to the Union meeting, which loved the
Slave Act; to Mr. Webster, who thought Massachusetts would obey " with alacrity,"— his Presidential stock looked down; to his kidnappers, who had
not yet fleshed their fangs on a fugitive. What a
reproach to the churches of commerce, and their
patron, Saint Hunker! One minister would drive a
fugitive from his door; another send back his own
mother: [9] what was their divinity worth, if in seven
months, they could not convert a single parishioner,
and celebrate the sacrament of kidnapping!

Yet, after all, not a slave went back from old Boston, though more than four hundred fled out of the
city from the stripes of America, and got safe to the
cross of England; not a slave went back from Boston,
spite of her representative, her government, her Union
meeting, and her clerical advice. She would comfort
herself against this sorrow, but her heart was faint in
her. Well might she say, " The harvest is passed,
the winter is ended, and we are not saved."

Yet the good men still left in Boston, their heart
not wholly corrupt with politics and lust of gain, rejoiced that Boston was innocent of the great trans-
gression of her sister-cities, and thought of the proud
days of old. But wily men came here: it was alleged
they came from the South. They went round to the

shops of jobbers, to the mills of manufactures, and looked at large quantities of goods, pretending a desire to purchase to a great amount; now it was a "large amount of domestics," then "a hundred thousand dollars' worth of locomotives." "But then," said the wily men, "we do not like to purchase here; you are in favor of the dissolution of the Union." "Oh, no," says the Northerner; "not at all." "But you hate the South," rejoins the feigned customer. "By no means," retorts the dealer. "But you have not sent back a slave," concludes the customer, "and I cannot trade with you."

The trick was tried in several places, and succeeded. The story got abroad; it was reported that large orders intended for Boston had been sent to New York, on account of the acquiescence of the latter city in the fugitive Slave Bill. Trade is timid; gold is a cowardly metal; how the tinsel trembles when there is thunder in the sky! Employers threatened their workmen: "You must not attend anti-slavery meetings, nor speak against the Fugitive Slave Bill. The Union is in imminent danger."

The country was much more hostile to man-stealing than the city: it mocked at the kidnappers. "Let them try their game in Essex county," said some of the newspapers in that quarter. Thereupon commercial and political journals prepared to "cut off the supplies of the country," and "reduce the farmers and mechanics to submission." It was publicly advised that Boston should not trade with the obnoxious towns; nobody must buy shoes at Lynn. In 1774, the Boston Port Bill shut up our harbor: it was a punishment for making tea against the law. But "penurious old Salem," whose enterprise is equaled by nothing but her " severe economy," opened her safe and commodious harbor to the merchants of Boston, with no cost of wharfage! But the Boston of 1850 was not equal to the " penurious old Salem " of 1774!

It was now indispensable that a slave should be sent back. Trade was clamorous; the administration were urgent; the administration of Mr. Fillmore was in peril; Mr. Webster's reputation for slave-hunting was at stake; the Union was in danger; even the marshal's commission was on the point of " dissolution," it is said. A descent was planned upon New Bedford, where the followers of Fox and Penn had long hid the outcast. That attempt came to nothing. The Vigilance Committee made a long arm, and " tolled the bell " of Liberty Hall in New Bedford. You remember the ghastly efforts at mirth made by some newspapers on the occasion. " The Vigilance Committee knows everything," said one of the kidnappers.

It now became apparent that Boston must furnish the victim. But some of the magistrates of Boston thought the marshal was too clumsy to succeed, and offered him the aid of the city. So, on the night of the third of April, Thomas Sims was kidnapped by two police-officers of Boston, pretending to the by-standers that he was making a disturbance, and to him that he was arrested for theft. He was had into the " court " of the kidnappers the next morning, charged with being a slave and a fugitive.

You will ask, How did it happen that Sims did not resist the ruffians who seized him? He did resist; but he was a rash, heedless young fellow, and had a most unlucky knife, which knocked at a kidnapper's bosom, but could not open the door. He was very imperfectly armed. He underwent what was called a " trial," a

trial without " due form of law;" without a jury, and
without a judge; before a Slave Act commissioner, who
was to receive twice as much for sacrificing a victim
as for acquitting a man! The Slave commissioner decided that Mr. Sims was a slave. I take it, nobody be-
forehand doubted that the decision would be against
the man. The commissioner was to receive five dollars
more for such a decision. The law was framed with
exquisite subtlety. Five dollars is a small sum, very
small; but things are great or little by comparison.

But, in doing justice to this remarkable provision of
the bill, let me do no injustice to the commissioner,
who decided that a man was not a man, but a thing.
I am told that he would not kidnap a man for five
dollars; I am told on good authority, that it would be
" no temptation to him." I believe it; for he also is
" a man and a brother." I have heard good deeds of
his doing, and believe that he did them. Total depravity does not get incarnated in any man. It is
said that he refused both of the fees in this case; the
one for the " examination," and the other for the
actual enslaving of Mr. Sims. I believe this also:
there is historical precedent on record for casting down
a larger fee, not only ten, but thirty pieces of silver,
likewise " the price of blood," money too base for a
Jew to put in the public chest eighteen hundred years
ago!

A noble defense was made for Mr. Sims by three
eminent lawyers, Messrs. Charles G. Loring, Robert
Rantoul, Jr., and Samuel E. Sewall, all honorable and
able men. Their arguments were productions of no
common merit. But of what use to plead law in such
a " court " of the Fugitive Slave Bill; to appeal to
the Constitution, when the statute is designed to thwart

VIII—23

justice, and to destroy "the blessings of liberty?"
Of what avail to appeal to the natural principles of
right before the tool of an administration which denies that there is any law of God higher than the
schemes of a politician? It all came to nothing. A
reasonable man would think that the human body and
soul were "free papers" from the Almighty sealed
with "the image and likeness of God;" but, of course,
in a kidnapper's "court," such a certificate is of no
value.

You all know the public account of the kidnapping
and "trial" of Mr. Sims. What is known to me in
private, it is not time to tell: I will tell that to your
children; no! perhaps your grandchildren.

You know that the arrest was illegal, the officers of
Massachusetts being forbidden by statute to help
arrest a fugitive slave. Besides, it appears that they
had no legal warrant to make the arrest; they lied, and
pretended to arrest him for another alleged offense.
He was on "trial" nine days,— arraigned before a
Slave Act commissioner,— and never saw the face of a
judge or any judicial officer but once. Before he
could be removed to slavery, it was necessary that the
spirit of the Constitution should be violated; that its
letter should be broken; that the laws of Massachusetts
should be cloven down; its officers, its courts, and its
people, treated with contempt. The Fugitive Slave
Bill could only be enforced by the bayonet.

You remember the aspect of Boston, from the
fourth of April till the twelfth. You saw the chains
about the court-house; you saw the police of Boston,
bludgeons in their hands, made journeymen kidnappers against their will. Poor fellows! I pitied
them. I knew their hearts. Once on a terrible time,

— it was just as they were taking Mr. Sims from the
court-house, a year ago this day,— somebody re-
proached them, calling them names fitting their conduct, and I begged him to desist; a poor fellow
clutched my arm, and said, "For God's sake don't
scold us: we feel worse than you do!" But with the
money of Boston against them, the leading clergy defending the crime against human nature, the city
government using its brief authority, squandering the
treasure of Boston and its intoxicating drink for the
same purpose, what could a police officer or a watch-
man do but obey orders? They did it most unwillingly
and against their conscience.

You remember the conduct of the courts of Massachusetts; the Supreme Court seemed to love the
chains around the court-house; for one by one the
judges bowed and stooped and bent and cringed and
curled and crouched down and crawled under the
chains. Who judges justly must himself be free.
What could you expect of a court sitting behind
chains; of judges crawling under them to go to their
own place? The same that you found. It was a
very appropriate spectacle,— the Southern chain on
the neck of the Massachusetts court. If the Bay
State were to send a man into bondage, it was proper
that the court-house should be in chains, and the
judges should go under.

You remember the "soldiers" called out, the celebrated "Sims Brigade," liquored at Court Square and
lodged at Faneuil Hall. Do you remember when
soldiers were quartered in that place before? It was
in 1768, when hireling "regulars" came, slaves
themselves, and sent by the British Ministry to "make
slaves of us all;" to sheathe their swords "in the

bowels of their countrymen!" That was a sight for the eyes of John Hancock— the " Sims Brigade," in Faneuil Hall called out to aid a Slave Act commissioner in his attempt to kidnap one of his fellow-citizens! A man by the name of Samuel Adams drilled the police in the street. Samuel Adams of the old time left no children. We have lost the true names of men; only Philadelphia keeps one.

You remember the looks of men in the streets, the crowds that filled up Court Square. Men came in from the country,— came a hundred miles to look on; some of them had fathers who fought at Lexington and Bunker Hill. They remembered the old times, when, the day after the battle of Lexington, a hundred and fifty volunteers, with the fire-lock at the shoulder, took the road from New Ipswich to Boston.

You have not forgotten the articles in the newspapers, Whig and Democratic both; the conduct of the " leading " churches you will never forget.

What an appropriate time that would have been for the Canadians to visit the " Athens of America," and see the conduct of the " freest and most enlightened people in the world!" If the great Hungarian could have come at that time, he would have understood the nature of " our peculiar institutions;" at least of our political men.

You remember the decision of the circuit judge,— himself soon to be summoned by death before the Judge who is no respecter of persons,— not allowing the destined victim his last hope, " the great writ of right." The decision left him entirely at the mercy of the other kidnappers. The court-room was crowded with " respectable people," " gentlemen of property and standing:" they received the decision

with " applause and the clapping of hands." Seize
a lamb out of a flock, a wolf from a pack of wolves,
the lambs bleat with sympathy, the wolves howl with
fellowship and fear; but when a competitor for the
Presidency sends back to eternal bondage a poor,
friendless negro, asking only his limbs, wealthy
gentlemen of Boston applaud the outrage.

> "O Judgment! thou art fled to brutish beasts,
> And men have lost their reason!"

You remember still the last act in this sad tragedy,
— the rendition of the victim. In the darkest hour
of the night of the eleventh and twelfth of April, the
kidnappers took him from his jail in Court Square,
weeping as he left the door. Two kindly men went
and procured the poor shivering boy a few warm
garments for his voyage: I will not tell their names;
perhaps their charity was " treason," and " levying
war." Both of the men were ministers, and had not
forgotten the great human word: " Inasmuch as ye
have done it unto one of the least of these my brethren,
ye have done it unto me." The chief kidnappers surrounded Mr. Sims with a troop of policemen, armed
with naked swords; that troop was attended by a
larger crew of some two hundred policemen, armed
with clubs. They conducted him, weeping as he went,
towards the waterside; they passed under the eaves of
the old State-house, which had rocked with the eloquence of James Otis, and shaken beneath the manly
tread of both the Adamses, whom the cannon at the
door could not terrify, and whose steps awakened the
nation. They took him over the spot where, eighty-
one years before, the ground had drunk in the African
blood of Crispus Attucks, shed by white men on the

fifth of March; brother's blood which did not cry in vain. They took him by the spot where the citizens of Massachusetts — some of their descendants were again at the place — scattered the taxed tea of Great Britain to the waters and the winds; they put him on board the " Acorn," owned by a merchant of Boston, who, once before, had kidnapped a man on his own account, and sent him off to the perdition of slavery, without even the help of a commissioner; a merchant to whom it is " immaterial what his children may say of him!"

" And this is Massachusetts liberty!" said the victim of the avarice of Boston. No, Thomas Sims, that was not " Massachusetts liberty;" it was all the liberty which the government of Massachusetts wished you to have; it was the liberty which the city government presented you; it was the liberty which Daniel Webster designed for you. The people of Massachusetts still believe that " all men are born free and equal," and " have natural, essential and unalienable rights " " of enjoying and defending their lives and liberties," " of seeking and obtaining their safety and happiness." Even the people of Boston believe that; but certain politicians and merchants, to whom it is " immaterial what their children say " of them,— they wished you to be a slave, and it was they who kidnapped you.

Some of you remember the religious meeting held on the spot, as this new " missionary " went abroad to a heathen land; the prayer put up to Him who made of one blood all nations of the earth; the hymns sung. They sang then, who never sang before, their " Missionary Hymn:"

"From many a Southern river
And field of sugar-cane,
They call us to deliver
Their land from slavery's chain."

On the spot where the British soldiers slew Crispus Attucks in 1770, other men of Boston resolved to hold a religious meeting that night. They were thrust out of the hall they had engaged. The next day was the Christian sabbath; and at night a meeting was held in a "large upper room," a meeting for mutual condolence and prayer. You will not soon forget the hymns, the Scriptures, the speeches, and the prayers of that night. This assembly is one of the results of that little gathering.

Well, all of that you knew before; this you do not know. Thomas Sims, at Savannah, had a fair and handsome woman, by the courtesy of the master called his "wife." Sims loved his wife; and, when he came to Boston, wrote, and told her of his hiding-place, the number in the street, and the name of the landlord. His wife had a paramour; that is a very common thing. The slave is "a chattel personal, to all intents, constructions, and purposes whatsoever." By the law of Georgia, no female slave owns her own virtue; single or married, it is all the same. This African Delilah told her paramour of her husband's hiding-place. Blame her not; perhaps she thought "the Union is in peril this hour," and wished to save it. Yet I doubt that she would send back her own mother; the African woman does not come to that; only a doctor of divinity and chaplain of the navy. I do not suppose she thought she was doing her husband any harm in telling of his escape; nay, it is likely that her joy was so full, she could not hold it in. The

Philistine had ploughed with Sims's heifer, and found out his riddle: the paramour told the master Sims's secret: the master sent the paramour of Mr. Sims's wife to Boston to bring back the husband! He was very welcome in this city, and got " the best of legal advice " at a celebrated office in Court street. Boston said, " God speed the paramour! " the Government of Massachusetts, " God speed the crime! " Money came to the pockets of the kidnappers; the paramour went home, his object accomplished, and the master was doubtless grateful to the city of Boston, which honored thus the piety of its founders!

He was taken back to Georgia in the " Acorn;" some of the better sort of kidnappers went with him to Savannah; there Sims was put in jail, and they received a public dinner. You know the reputation of the men: the workmen were worthy of their meat. In jail, Mr. Sims was treated with great severity; not allowed to see his relatives, not even his mother. It is said that he was tortured every day with a certain number of stripes on his naked back; that his master once offered to remit part of the cruelty, if he would ask pardon for running away. The man refused, and took the added blows. One day, the jail doctor told the master that Sims was too ill to bear more stripes. The master said, " Damn him! give him the lashes, if he dies;"— and the lashes fell. Be not troubled at that; a slave is only a " chattel personal." Those blows were laid on by the speakers of the Union meeting; it was only " to save the Union." I have seen a clerical certificate, setting forth that the " owner " of Mr. Sims was " an excellent Christian," and " uncommonly pious." When a clergyman would send back his own mother, such conduct is sacramental in a layman.

When Thomas Sims was unlawfully seized, and detained in custody against the law, the Governor of Massachusetts was in Boston; the Legislature was in session. It seems to me it was their duty to protect the man, and enforce the laws of the State; but they did no such thing.

As that failed, it seems to me that the next thing was for the public to come together in a vast multitude, and take their brother out of the hands of his kidnappers, and set him at liberty. On the morning of the sixth of March, 1770, the day after the Boston Massacre, Faneuil Hall could not hold the town-meeting. They adjourned to the Old South and demanded " the immediate removal of the troops;" at sundown there was " not a red-coat in Boston." But the people in this case did no such thing.

The next thing was for the Vigilance Committee to deliver the man: the country has never forgiven the committee for not doing it. I am chairman of the executive committee of the Vigilance Committee; I cannot now relate all that was done, all that was attempted. I will tell that when the time comes. Yet I think you will believe me when I say the Vigilance Committee did all they could. But see some of the difficulties in their way.

There was in Boston a large number of crafty, rich, designing, and " respectable " men, who wanted a man kidnapped in Boston, and sent into slavery; they wanted that for the basest of purposes,— for the sake of money; they wanted the name of it, the reputation of kidnapping a man. They protected the kidnappers,— foreign and domestic; egged them on, feasted them. It has been said that fifteen hundred men volunteered to escort their victim out of the State;

that some of them are rich men. I think the majority of the middle class of men were in favor of freedom; but, in Boston, what is a man without money? and, if he has money, who cares how base his character may be? You demand moral character only of a clergyman. Some of the richest men were strongly in favor of freedom; but, alas! not many, and for the most part they were silent.

The city government of that period I do not like to speak of. It offers to a man, as cool as I am, a temptation to use language which a gentleman does not wish to apply to any descendant of the human race. But that government, encouraging its thousand and five hundred illegal groggeries, and pretending a zeal for law, was for kidnapping a man; so the police force of the city was unlawfully put to that work; soldiers were called out; the money of the city flowed freely, and its rum. I do not suppose that the kidnapping was at all disagreeable to the "conscience" of the city government; they seemed to like it, and the consequences thereof.

The prominent clergy of Boston were on the same side. The dollar demanded that; and whither it went, thither went they. "Like people, like priest," was a proverb two thousand five hundred years ago, and is likely to hold its edge for a long time to come. Still there were some very noble men among the ministers of Boston: we found them in all denominations.

Then the courts of Massachusetts refused to issue the writ of habeas corpus. They did not afford the smallest protection to the poor victim of Southern tyranny.

Not a sheriff could be got to serve a writ; the high sheriff refused, all his deputies held back. Who could expect them to do their duty when all else failed?

The Legislature was then in session. They sat from January till May. They knew that eight thousand nine hundred and seventy-five citizens of Massachusetts had no protection but public opinion, and in Boston that opinion was against them. They saw four hundred citizens of Boston flee off for safety; they saw Shadrach captured in Boston; they saw him kidnapped, and put in jail against their own law; they saw the streets filled with soldiers to break the laws of Massachusetts, the police of Boston employed in the same cause; they saw the sheriffs refuse to serve a writ; they saw Thomas Sims kidnapped and carried from Boston; and, in all the five months of the session, they did not pass a law to protect their fellow-citizens; they did not even pass a " resolution " against the extension of slavery! The Senate had a committee to investigate the affair in Boston. They sat in the Senate-hall, and were continually insulted by the vulgarest of men; insulted not only with impudence, but impunity, by men who confessed that they were violating the laws of Massachusetts.

Massachusetts had then a Governor who said he would not harbor a fugitive slave. What did he do? He sat as idle as a feather in the chair of state; he left the sheriffs as idle as he. While the laws of Massachusetts were broken nine days running, the successor of John Hancock sat as idle as a feather in the chair of state, and let kidnapping go on! I hate to say these things. The Governor is a young man, not without virtues; but think of such things in Massachusetts!

This is my public defense of the Vigilance Committee. The private defense shall come, if I live long enough.

It was on the ninteenth day of April that Thomas Sims was landed at Savannah, and put in the public jail of the city. Do you know what that day stands for in your calendar? Some of your fathers knew very well. Ten miles from here is a little monument at Lexington, "sacred to liberty and the rights of mankind," telling that on the 19th of April, 1775, some noble men stood up against the army of England, "fired the shot heard round the world," and laid down their lives "in the sacred cause of God and their country." Six miles further off is another little monument at Concord; two miles further back, a third, all dating from the same day. The War of the Revolution began at Lexington, to end at Yorktown. Its first battle was on the nineteenth of April. Hancock and Adams lodged at Lexington with the minister. One raw morning, a little after daybreak, a tall man, with a large forehead under a three-cornered hat, drew up his company of seventy men on the green, farmers and mechanics like himself; only one is left now, the boy who "played" the men to the spot. They wheeled into line to wait for the regulars. The captain ordered every man to load his piece "with powder and ball." "Don't fire," were his words, "unless fired upon; but, if they want a war, let it begin here."

The regulars came on. Some Americans offered to run away from their post. The captain said, "I will order the first man shot dead that leaves his place." The English commander cried out, "Disperse, you rebels; lay down your arms and disperse." Not a man stirred. "Disperse, you damned rebels!" shouted he again. Not a man stirred. He ordered the vanguard to fire; they did so, but over the heads of

our fathers. Then the whole main body leveled their
pieces, and there was need of ten new graves in Lexington. A few Americans returned the shot. British
blood stained the early grass, which " waved with the
wind." " Disperse and take care of yourselves," was
the captain's last command! And, after the British
fired their third round, there lay the dead, and there
stood the soldiers; there was a battle-field between
England and America, never to be forgot, never to be
covered over. The " mother-country " of the morning was the " enemy " at sunrise. " Oh, what a glorious morning is this!" said Samuel Adams.

The nineteenth of April was a good day for Boston
to land a fugitive slave at Savannah, and put him in
jail, because he claimed his liberty. Some of you
had fathers in the battle of Lexington, many of you
relations; some of you, I think, keep trophies from
that day, won at Concord or at Lexington. I have
seen such things,— powder-horns, shoe-buckles, a
firelock, and other things, from the nineteenth of
April, 1775. Here is a Boston trophy from April
nineteenth, 1851. This is the coat of Thomas
Sims.[10] He wore it on the third of April last. Look
at it. You see he did not give up with alacrity, nor
easily " conquer " his " prejudices " for liberty. See
how they rent the sleeve away! His coat was torn
to tatters. " And this is Massachusetts liberty!"

Let the kidnappers come up and say, " Massachusetts! knowest thou whether this be thy son's coat
or not?"

Let Massachusetts answer: " It is my son's coat!
An evil beast hath devoured him. Thomas is without
doubt rent in pieces!"

Yes, Massachusetts, that is right! It was an evil

beast that devoured him, worse than the lion which comes up from the swelling of Jordan: it was a kidnapper. Thomas was rent with whips! Go, Massachusetts! keep thy trophies from Lexi ton. I will keep this to remind me of Boston, and her dark places, which are full of cruelty.

After the formation of the Union, a monument was erected at Beacon Hill, to commemorate the chief events which led to the American Revolution, and helped secure liberty and independence. Some of you remember the inscriptions thereon. If a monument were built to commemorate the events which are connected with the recent " Salvation of the Union," the inscriptions might be: —

Union saved by Daniel Webster's Speech at Washington, March 7, 1850.

Union saved by Daniel Webster's Speech at Boston, April 30, 1850.

Union saved by the Passage of the Fugitive Slave Bill, Sept. 18, 1850.

Union saved by the Arrival of Kidnapper Hughes at Boston, Oct. 19, 1850.

Union saved by the " Union Meeting" at Faneuil Hall, Nov. 26, 1850.

Union saved by Kidnapping Thomas Sims at Boston, April 3, 1851.

Union saved by the Rendition of Thomas Sims at Savannah, April 19, 1851.—

" Oh, what a glorious morning is this!"

Sicut Patribus sit Deus Nobis.

The great deeds of the American Revolution were also commemorated by medals. The Boston kidnapping is worthy of such commemoration, and would be an appropriate subject for a medal, which might bear on one side a bas-relief of the last scene of that act: the court-house in chains; the victim in the hollow square of Boston police, their swords and bludgeons in their hands. The motto might be —" The Great Object of Government is the Protection of Property at Home." [11] The other side might bear a Boston church, surrounded by shops and taverns taller than itself, with the twofold inscription: "No Higher Law"; and, " I would send back my own Mother."

What a change from the Boston of John Hancock to the Boston of the Fugitive Slave Bill; from the town which hung Grenville and Huske in effigy, to the city which approved Mr. Webster's speech in defense of slave-catching! Boston tolled her bells for the Stamp Act, and fired a hundred holiday cannons for the Slave Act! Massachusetts, all New England, has been deeply guilty of slavery and the slave-trade. An exile from Germany finds the chief street of Newport paved by a tax of ten dollars a head on all the slaves landed there; the little town sent out Christian New England rum and brought home heathen men — for sale. Slavery came to Boston with the first settlers. In 1639, Josselyn found here a negro woman in bondage refusing to become the mother of slaves. There was much to palliate the offense: all northern Europe was stained with the crime.[12] It did not end in Westphalia till 1789. But the consciences of New England never slept easy under that sin. Before 1641, Massachusetts ordered that a slave should be set free after seven years' service, reviving a merciful ordinance of the half-barbarous Hebrews a thousand years before Christ. In 1645, the General Court of Massachusetts sent back to Guinea two black men illegally enslaved, and made a law forbidding the sale of slaves, except captives in war, or men sentenced to sale for crime. Even they were set free after seven

years' service. Still slavery always existed here, spite
of the law; the newspapers once contained advertisements of " negro-babies to be given away " in Boston!
Yet New England never loved slavery; hard and cruel
as the Puritans were, they had some respect for the
letter of the New Testament. In 1700, Samuel Sewall
protested against " the selling of Joseph;" as another
Sewall, in 1851, protested against the selling of
Thomas. There was a great controversy about slavery
in Massachusetts in 1766; even Harvard College took
an interest in freedom, setting its young men to look at
the rights of man! In 1767, a bill was introduced to
the General Assembly to prevent " the unnatural and
unwarrantable custom of enslaving mankind." It was
killed by the Hunkers of that time. In 1774, a bill of
a similar character passed the Assembly, but was
crushed by the veto of Governor Hutchinson.

In 1788, three men were illegally kidnapped at Boston by " one Avery, a native of Connecticut," and
carried off to Martinico. Then we had John Hancock for governor, and he wrote to all the governors
of the West India Islands in favor of the poor creatures. The Boston Association of Congregational
Ministers petitioned the Legislature to prohibit Massachusetts ships from engaging in the foreign or domestic slave-trade. Dr. Belknap was a member of the
Association,— a man worthy to have Channing for a
successor to his humanity. The Legislature passed a
bill for the purpose. In July the three men were
brought back from the West Indies: Dr. Belknap
says, " It was a day of jubilee for all the friends of
justice and humanity." [13]

What a change from the Legislature, clergy, and
governor of 1788 to that of 1851! Alas! men do not

gather figs of thistles.   The imitators of this Avery
save the Union now: he saved it before it was formed.
How is the faithful city become a harlot!   It was full
of judgment: righteousness lodged in it, but now
murderers.

What is the cause of this disastrous change!   It is
the excessive love of money which has taken possession
of the leading men.   In 1776, General Washington
said of Massachusetts: "Notwithstanding all the
public spirit that is ascribed to this people, there is no
nation under the sun that I ever came across, which
pays greater adoration to money than they do."
What would he say now?   Selfishness and covetousness have flowed into the commercial capital of New
England, seeking their fortune.   Boston is now a
shop, with the aim of a shop, and the morals of a shop,
and the politics of a shop.

Thomas Jefferson said: Governments are instituted amongst men to secure the natural and unalienable right to life, liberty, and the pursuit of
happiness.   All America said so on the fourth of
July, 1776.   But we have changed all that.   Daniel
Webster said, at New York, 1850: "The great object of government is the protection of property at
home, and respect and renown abroad."   John Hancock had some property to protect; but he said the
design of government is "security to the persons and
the properties of the governed."   He put the persons
first, and the property afterwards; the substance of
man before his accidents.   Hancock said again: "It
is the indispensable duty of every member of society
to promote, as far as in him lies, the prosperity of
every individual."   The Governor of Massachusetts
says, "I would not harbor a fugitive."   A clergyman
VIII—24

says, "I would send back my own mother!" If the great object of government is the protection of property, why should a governor personally harbor a fugitive, or officially protect nine thousand colored men? Why should not a clergyman send to slavery his mother, to save the Union, or to save a bank, or to gain a chaplaincy in the navy? But, if this be so, then what a mistake it was in Jesus of Nazareth to say, "A man's life consisteth not in the abundance of things that he possesseth!" Verily the meat is more than the life; the body less than raiment! Christ was mistaken in his "beware of covetousness:" he should have said, "Beware of philanthropy; drive off a fugitive; send back your mother to bondage. Blessed are the kidnappers, for they shall be called the children of God."

Even Thomas Paine had a Christianity which would choke at the infidelity and practical atheism taught in the blessed name of Jesus in the Boston churches of commerce to-day. The gospel relates that Jesus laid his hands on men to bless them — on the deaf, and they heard; on the dumb, and they spoke; on the blind, and they saw; on the lame, and they walked; on the maimed and the sick, and they were whole. But Christian Boston lays its hands on a whole and free man, and straightway he owns no eyes, no ears, no tongue, no hands, no foot: he is a slave!

In 1761, the Massachusetts of John Hancock would not pay threepence duty on a pound of tea, to have all the protection of the British Crown; ninety years later, the Boston of Daniel Webster, to secure the trade of the South, and a dim, delusive hope of a protective tariff, will pay any tax in men. It is no new thing for her citizens to be imprisoned at Charleston

and New Orleans, because they are black. What
merchant cares? It does not interrupt trade. Five
citizens of Massachusetts have just been sent into
bondage by a Southern State. Of what consequence
is that to the politicians of the Commonwealth? Our
property is worth six hundred million dollars. But
how much is a man worth less than a dollar! The
penny wisdom of " Poor Richard " is the great gospel
to the city which cradled the benevolence of Franklin.

Boston capitalists do not hesitate to own Southern
plantations and buy and sell men; Boston merchants
do not scruple to let their ships for the domestic slave-
trade, and carry the child from his mother in Baltimore, to sell him to a planter in Louisiana or Alabama;
some of them glory in kidnapping their fellow-citizens
in Boston. Most of the slave-ships in the Atlantic
are commanded by New England men. A few years
ago, one was seized by the British government at
Africa, " full of slaves;" it was owned in Boston, had
a " clearance " from our harbor, and left its name on
the books of the insurance offices here. The controlling men of Boston have done much to promote, to
extend, and to perpetuate slavery. Why not, if the
protection of property be the great object of government? Why not, if interest is before justice? Why
not, if the higher law of God is to be sneered at in
State and Church?

When the Fugitive Slave Bill passed, the six New
England States lay fast asleep: Massachusetts slept
soundly, her head pillowed on her unsold bales of
cotton and of woolen goods, dreaming of " orders
from the South." Justice came to waken her, and
whisper of the peril of nine thousand citizens; and
she started in her sleep, and, being frighted, swore a

prayer or two, then slept again.   But Boston woke,—
sleeping, in her shop, with ears open, and her eye on
the market, her hand on her purse, dreaming of goods
for sale,— Boston woke broadly up, and fired a hundred guns for joy.   O Boston, Boston! if thou couldst
have known, in that thine hour, the things which belong
unto thy peace!   But no: they were hidden from her
eyes.   She had prayed to her god, to Money; he
granted her the request, but sent leanness into her
soul.

Yet at first I did not believe that the Fugitive Slave
Bill could be executed in Boston; even the firing of
the cannons did not convince me; I did not think men
bad enough for that.   I knew something of wickedness; I knew what love of money could do, I had seen
it blind most venerable eyes.   I knew Boston was a
Tory town; the character of upstart Tories — I
thought I knew that: the man just risen from the
gutter knocks down him that is rising.   But I knew
also the ancient history of Boston.   I remembered the
first commissioner we ever had in New England, Sir
Edmund Andros, sent here by the worst of the Stuarts
"to rob us of our charters in North America."   He
was a terrible tyrant.   The liberty of Connecticut fled
into the great oak at Hartford: —

> "The Charter Oak it was the tree
> That saved our blesséd liberty."

"All Connecticut was in the oak."   But Massachusetts laid her hands on the commissioner,—he was
her governor also,— put him in jail, and sent him
home for trial in 1689.   William of Orange thought
we "served him right."   The name of "commissioner" has always had an odious meaning to my mind.

I did not think a commissioner at kidnapping men would fare better than Sir Edmund kidnapping charters. I remembered the " writs of assistance," and thought of James Otis; the Stamp Act, " Adams and Liberty " came to my mind. I did not forget the way our fathers made tea with salt water. I looked up at that tall obelisk; I took courage, and have since reverenced that " monument of piled stones." I could not think Mr. Webster wanted the law enforced, spite of his speeches and letters. It was too bad to be true of him. I knew he was a bankrupt politician, in desperate political circumstances, gaming for the Presidency, with the probability of getting the vote of the county of Suffolk, and no more. I knew he was not rich: his past history showed that he would do almost anything for money, which he seems as covetous to get as prodigal to spend. I knew that " a man in falling will catch at a red-hot iron hook." I saw why Mr. Webster caught at the Fugitive Slave Bill: it was a great fall from the coveted and imaginary Presidency down to actual private life at Marshfield. It was a great fall. The Slave Act was the red-hot iron hook to a man " falling like Lucifer, never to hope again." The temptation was immense. I could not think he meant to hold on there; he did often relax his grasp, yet only to clutch it the tighter. I did not like to think he had a bad heart. I hoped he would shrink from blasting the head of a single fugitive from that dreadful " thunder " of his speech; that he would not like to execute his own law. Men in Boston said it could not be executed. Even cruel men that I knew shuddered at the thought of kidnapping a man who fills their glasses with wine. The law was not fit to be executed: that was the general opinion in Boston at

first. So, when kidnapper Hughes came here for
William Craft, even the commissioner applied to was
a little shy of the business. Yet that commissioner
is not a very scrupulous man. I mean in the various
parties he has wriggled through, he has not left the
reputation of any excessive and maidenly coyness in
moral matters, and a genius for excessive scrupulous-
ness as to means or ends. Even a hunker minister
informed me that he " would certainly aid a fugitive."
But, after the Union Meeting, the clouds of darkness
gathered together, and it set in for a storm; the kidnappers went and rough-ground their sword on the
grindstone of the church, a navy chaplain turning the
crank; and all our hopes fell to the ground.

> " Vice is a monster of such frightful mien,
>   As, to be hated, needs but to be seen;
>   But seen too oft, familiar with her face,
>   We first endure, then pity, then embrace."

The relentless administration of Mr. Fillmore has
been as cruel as the law they framed.[14] Mr. Webster
has thrust the red-hot iron hook into the flesh of thousands of his fellow-citizens. He and his kidnappers
came to a nation scattered and peeled, meted out and
trodden down; they have ground the poor creatures
to powder under their hoof. I wish I could find an
honorable motive for such deeds, but hitherto, no
analysis can detect it, no solar microscope of charity
can bring such motive to light. The end is base, the
means base, the motive base.

Yet one charge has been made against the government, which seems to me a little harsh and unjust. It
has been said the administration preferred low and
contemptible men as their tools; judges who blink at
law, advocates of infamy, and men cast off from

society for perjury, for nameless crimes, and sins not
mentionable in English speech; creatures " not so good
as the dogs that licked Lazarus's sores; but, like flies,
still buzzing upon anything that is raw." There is
a semblance of justice in the charge: witness Philadelphia, Buffalo, Boston; witness New York. It is true
for kidnappers the government did take men that
looked " like a bull-dog just come to man's estate;"
men whose face declared them, " if not the devil, at
least his twin-brother." There are kennels of the
courts wherein there settles down all that the law breeds
most foul, loathsome, and hideous and abhorrent to the
eye of day; there this contaminating puddle gathers
its noisome ooze, slowly, stealthily, continually,
agglomerating its fetid mass by spontaneous cohesion,
and sinking by the irresistible gravity of rottenness into
that abhorred deep, the lowest, ghastliest pit in all
the subterranean vaults of human sin. It is true the
Government has skimmed the top and dredged the bottom of these kennels of the courts, taking for its purpose the scum and sediment thereof, the Squeers, the
Fagins, and the Quilps of the law, the monsters of
the court. Blame not the Government; it took the
best it could get. It was necessity, not will, which
made the selection. Such is the stuff that kidnappers
must be made of. If you wish to kill a man, it is not
bread you buy: it is poison. Some of the instruments
of Government were such as one does not often look
upon. But, of old time, an inquisitor was always " a
horrid-looking fellow, as beseemed his trade." It is
only justice that a kidnapper should bear " his great
commission in his look."

In a town full of British soldiers in 1774, on the
anniversary of the Boston Massacre, John Hancock
said: —

" Surely you never will tamely suffer this country to be a den of thieves. Remember, my friends, from whom you sprang. Let not a meanness of spirit, unknown to those whom you boast of as your fathers, excite a thought to the dishonor of your mothers. I conjure you by all that is dear, by all that is honorable, by all that is sacred, not only that ye pray, but that you act; that, if necessary, ye fight, and even die, for the prosperity of our Jerusalem. Break in sunder, with noble disdain, the bonds with which the Philistines have bound you. Suffer not yourselves to be betrayed by the soft arts of luxury and effeminacy into the pit digged for your destruction. Despise the glare of wealth. That people who pay greater respect to a wealthy villain than to an honest, upright man in poverty, almost deserve to be enslaved: they plainly show that wealth, however it may be acquired, is, in their esteem, to be preferred to virtue.

" But I thank God that America abounds in men who are superior to all temptation, whom nothing can divert from a steady pursuit of the interest of their country, who are at once its ornament and safeguard. And sure I am I should not incur your displeasure, if I paid a respect so justly due to their much-honored characters, in this place; but, when I name an Adams, such a numerous host of fellow-patriots rush upon my mind, that I fear it would take up too much of your time, should I attempt to call over the illustrious roll: but your greatful hearts will point you to the men; and their revered names, in all succeeding times, shall grace the annals of America. From them let us, my friends, take example; from them let us catch the divine enthusiasm; and feel, each for himself, the godlike pleasure of diffusing happiness on all around us; of

delivering the oppressed from the iron grasp of
tyranny; of changing the hoarse complaint and bitter
moans of wretched slaves into those cheerful songs
which freedom and contentment must inspire. There
is a heartfelt satisfaction in reflecting on our exertions
for the public weal, which all the sufferings an en-
raged tyrant can inflict will never take away, which the
ingratitude and reproaches of those whom we have saved
from ruin cannot rob us of. The virtuous assertor of
the rights of mankind merits a reward, which even a
want of success in his endeavors to save his country,
the heaviest misfortune which can befall a genuine
patriot, cannot entirely prevent him from receiving."

But, in 1850, Mr. Webster bade Massachusetts
" conquer her prejudices." He meant the " prejudices " in favor of justice, in favor of the unalienable
rights of man, in favor of Christianity. Did Massachusetts obey? The answer was given a year ago.
" Despise the glare of wealth," said the richest man in
New England in 1774: " the great object of government is the protection of property," said " the great intellect " of America in 1850! John Hancock, seventy-
eight years ago, said, " We dread nothing but slavery:"
Daniel Webster, two years ago, said Massachusetts will
obey the Fugitive Slave Bill " with alacrity." Boston
has forgotten John Hancock.

In 1775, Joseph Warren said, " Scourges and death
with tortures are far less terrible than slavery." Now
it is " a great blessing to the African." [15] Said the
same Warren, " The man who meanly submits to wear
a shackle contemns the noblest gift of Heaven, and im-
piously affronts the God that made him free." Now
clergymen tell us that kidnappers are ordained of God,
and passive obedience is every man's duty! The town

of Boston in 1770 declared, " Mankind will not be reasoned out of the feelings of humanity." In 1850 the pulpit of Boston says, Send back your brother.

The talk of dissolution is no new trick. Hear General Warren, in the spirit of 1775 : " Even anarchy itself, that bugbear held up by the tools of power, is infinitely less dangerous to mankind than arbitrary government. Anarchy can be but of short duration ; for, when men are at liberty to pursue that course which is most conducive to their own happiness, they will soon come into it, and from the rudest state of nature, order and good government must soon arise. But tyranny, when once established, entails its curses on a nation to the latest period of time, unless some daring genius, inspired by Heaven, shall, unappalled by danger, bravely form and execute the design of restoring liberty and life to his enslaved and murdered country." Now a man would send his mother into slavery to save the Union !

Will Boston be called on again to return a fugitive? Not long since, some noble ladies in a neighboring town, whose religious hand often reaches through the darkness to save men ready to perish, related to me a fresh tale of woe. Here is their letter of the first of March : —

" Only ten days ago, we assisted a poor, deluded sufferer in effecting his escape to Canada, after having been cheated into the belief by the profligate captain who brought him from the South, that he would be in safety as soon as he reached Boston. . . . He had accumulated two hundred dollars which he put into the captain's hands, upon his agreeing to secrete him, and bring him to Boston. The moment the vessel touched the wharf, the scoundrel bade the poor fellow be off in a moment; and he then discovered his liability to be pursued and taken. It was then midnight and the cold was intense. He wandered about the streets, and in the morning strolled into the —— Depot, and came out to —— in the earliest cars. On reaching this town, he had the sense to find out the only man of color who lives here, ——, a very respectable barber. Mr. —— sheltered him that day and the following night; and early the next morning a sufficient sum had been collected for him to pay his passage to Canada, and supply his first wants after arriving there; but, in the meanwhile, the villainous captain bears off his hard earnings in triumph."

I must not give the names of the ladies: they are liable to a fine of a thousand dollars each, and imprisonment for six months. It was atrocious in the captain to steal the two hundred dollars from the poor captive; but the Government of the United States would gladly steal his body, his limbs, his life, his children, to the end of time. The captain was honorable in comparison with the kidnappers. Perhaps he also wished to " Save the Union."— *Sicut Patribus sit Deus Nobis!*

What a change from the Boston of our fathers! Where are the children of the patriots of old? Tories spawned their brood in the streets: Adams and Hancock died without a child. Has nature grown sterile of men? Is there no male and manly virtue left? Are we content to be kidnappers of men? No! Here still are noble men, men of the good old stock; men of the same brave, holy soul. No time of trial ever brought out nobler heroism than last year. Did we want money, little Methodist churches in the country, the humanest churches in New England, dropped their widow's mite into the chest. From ministers of all modes of faith but the popular one in money, from all churches but that of commerce, there came gifts, offers of welcome, and words of lofty cheer. Here in Boston, there were men thoroughly devoted to the defense of their poor, afflicted brethren; even some clergymen faithful among the faithless. But they were few. It was only a handful who ventured to be faithful to the true and right. The great tide of humanity, which once filled up this place, had ebbed off: only a few perennial springs poured out their sweet and unfailing wealth to these weary wanderers.

Yet Boston is rich in generous men, in deeds of charity, in far-famed institutions for the good of man. In this she is still the noblest of the great cities of the land. I honor the self-sacrificing, noble men; the women whose loving-kindness never failed before. Why did it fail at this time? Men fancied that their trade was in peril. It was an idle fear; even the dollar obeys the " higher law," which its worshipers deny. Had it been true, Boston had better lose every farthing of her gold, and start anew with nothing but the wilderness, than let her riches stand between us and our fellow-man. Thy money perish, if it brutalize thy heart!

I wish I could believe the motives of men were good in this; that they really thought the nation was in peril. But no; it cannot be. It was not the love of country which kept the " compromises of the Constitution " and made the Fugitive Slave Bill. I pity the politicians who made this wicked law, made it in the madness of their pride. I pity that son of New England, who, against his nature, against his early history, drew his sword to sheathe it in the bowels of his brother-man.[16] The melancholiest spectacle in all this land, self-de-

spoiled of the luster which would have cast a glory on
his tomb, and sent his name a watchword to many an
age,— now he is the companion of kidnappers, and a
proverb amongst honorable men, with a certainty of
leaving a name to be hissed at by mankind.

I pity the kidnappers, the poor tools of men almost
as base.   I would not hurt a hair of their heads; but I
would take the thunder of the moral world, and dash
its bolted lightning on this crime of stealing men, till
the name of kidnapping should be like Sodom and
Gomorrah.   It is piracy to steal a man in Guinea; what
is it to do this in Boston?

I pity the merchants who, for their trade, were glad
to steal their countrymen; I wish them only good.   Debate in yonder hall has shown how little of humanity
there is in the trade of Boston.   She looks on all the
horrors which intemperance has wrought, and daily
deals in every street; she scrutinizes the jails,— they
are filled by rum; she looks into the alms-houses,
crowded full by rum; she walks her streets and sees the
perishing classes fall, mowed down by rum; she enters
the parlors of wealthy men, looks into the bridal
chamber, and meets death: the ghosts of the slain
are there,— men slain by rum.   She knows it all, yet
says, " There is an interest at stake! "— the interest
of rum; let man give way!   Boston does this to-day.
Last year she stole a man; her merchants stole a man!
The sacrifice of man to money when shall it have an
end?   I pity those merchants who honor money more
than man.   Their gold is cankered, and their soul is
brass,— is rusted brass.   They must come up before
the posterity which they affect to scorn.   What voice
can plead for them before their own children?   The
eye that mocketh at the justice of its son, and scorneth

to obey the mercy of its daughter, the ravens of posterity shall pick it out, and the young eagles eat it up!

But there is yet another tribunal: "After the death the judgment!" When he maketh inquisition for the blood of the innocent, what shall the stealers of men reply? Boston merchants, where is your brother, Thomas Sims? Let Cain reply to Christ.

Come, Massachusetts! take thy historic mantle, wrought all over with storied memories of two hundred years, adorned with deeds in liberty's defense, and rough with broidered radiance from the hands of sainted men; walk backwards, and cover up and hide the naked public shame of Boston, drunk with gain, and lewdly lying in the street. It will not hide the shame. Who can annul a fact? Boston has chronicled her infamy, and on the iron leaf of time,— ages shall read it there!

Then let us swear by the glory of our fathers and the infamy of this deed, that we will hate slavery, hate its cause, hate its continuance, and will exterminate it from the land; come up hither as the years go by, and here renew the annual oath, till not a kidnapper is left lurking in the land; yes, till from the Joseph that is sold into Egypt, there comes forth a man to guide his people to the promised land. Out of this " Acorn " a tall oak may grow.

Old mythologies relate, that, when a deed of sin is done, the souls of men who bore a kindred to the deed çome forth and aid the work. What a company must have assisted at this sacrament a year ago! What a crowd of ruffians, from the first New England commissioner to the latest dead of Boston murders! Robert Kidd might have come back from his felon-grave at " Execution Dock," to resume his appropriate place,

and take command of the " Acorn," and guide her on
her pirate-course. Arnold might sing again his glad
Te Deum, as on that fatal day in March. What an
assembly there would be,— " shapes hot from Tar-
tarus."

But the same mythologies go fabling on, and say
that at such a time the blameless, holy souls who made
the virtues blossom while they lived, and are themselves
the starriest flowers of heaven now, that they return to
bless the old familiar spot, and witness every modern
deed ; and, most of all, that godly ministers, who lived
and labored for their flocks, return to see the deed they
cannot help, and aid the good they bless. What a
gathering might there have been of the just men made
perfect ! The patriots who loved this land, mothers
whose holy hearts had blessed the babes they bore ; pure
men of lofty soul who labored for mankind,— what a
fair company this State could gather of the immortal
dead ! Of those great ministers of every faith, who
dearly loved the Lord, what venerable heads I see : John
Cotton and the other " famous Johns ; " Eliot, bearing
his Indian Bible, which there is not an Indian left to
read ; Edwards, a mighty name in East and West, even
yet more marvelous for piety than the depth of thought ;
the Mathers, venerable men ; Chauncy and Mayhew, both
noble men of wealthy soul ; Belknap, who saw a brother
in an African ; Buckminster, the fairest, sweetest bud
brought from another field, too early nipped in this ;
Channing and Ware, both ministers of Christ, who,
loving God, loved too their fellow-men ! How must
those souls look down upon the scene ! Boston delivering up — for lust of gold delivering up — a poor,
forsaken boy to slavery ; Belknap and Channing mourning for the church !

I turn me off from the living men, the living courts, the living churches,— no the churches dead; from the swarm of men all bustling in the streets; turn to the sainted dead. Dear fathers of the State; ye blessed mothers of New England's sons;— O holy saints who laid with prayer the deep foundations of New England's church is then the seed of heroes gone? New England's bosom, is it sterile, cold, and dead? "No!" say the fathers, mothers, all,—"New England only sleeps; even Boston is not dead! Appeal from Boston drunk with gold, and briefly mad with hate, to sober Boston in her hour to come. Wait but a little time; have patience with her waywardness; she yet shall weep with penitence that bitter day, and rise with ancient energy to do just deeds of lasting fame. Even yet there's justice in her heart, and Boston mothers shall give birth to men!"

Tell me, ye blessed, holy souls, angels of New England's church, shall man succeed, and gain his freedom at the last? Answer, ye holy men; speak by the last great angel of the church who went to heaven. Repeat some noble word you spoke on earth!

Hear their reply:—

"Oppression shall not always reign:
   There comes a brighter day,
When Freedom, burst from every chain,
   Shall have triumphant way.
Then Right shall over Might prevail,
And Truth, like hero armed in mail,
The hosts of tyrant Wrong assail,
   And hold eternal sway.

What voice shall bid the progress stay
   Of Truth's victorious car?—
What arm arrest the growing day,
   Or quench the solar star?
What reckless soul, though stout and strong,

Shall dare bring back the ancient wrong,—
Oppression's guilty night prolong,
  And Freedom's morning bar?

The hour of triumph comes apace,—
  The fated, promised hour,
When earth upon a ransomed race
  Her bounteous gifts shall shower.
Ring, Liberty, thy glorious bell!
Bid high thy sacred banners swell!
Let trump on trump the triumph tell
  Of Heaven's redeeming power!" [17]

NOTES

NOTES

I

A SERMON OF SLAVERY

This sermon was preached on January 31, 1841, and repeated June 4, 1843. It is included in Frances Power Cobbe's edition of Parker's Collected Works: Vol. V., pp. 1–16.

Page 4, note 1. The view here expressed of the effect of slavery is questionable. Since the beginning of the world a multitude of nations have endured the condition of bondage, and sociologists declare that in the past slavery has been a school in which the barbarian has been raised from warfare and idleness to habits of industry, absorbing also from his masters some traits of culture. Theodore Parker and his fellows have no patience with the notion that African slavery has exercised anything but a harmful influence.

Page 5, note 2. In bringing the African to America, the North, as Parker elsewhere admits, was no less involved than the South, New England ships and men being largely concerned in the slave-trade. This Abraham Lincoln had clearly in view, deeming it just that the North should share in the cost of emancipation.

Page 14, note 3. The admission that the non-existence of slavery in the North is due rather to its material unprofitableness than to any acute moral sense of its iniquity, deserves to be noted. Men of Parker's school too seldom recognize this fact, too often expressing themselves as if the South were involved in iniquity which the North did not share. Parker's admission here is candid.

II

THE MEXICAN WAR

This speech was delivered at the anti-war meeting in Faneuil Hall, Boston, February 4, 1847. It is included in Miss Cobbe's edition of Parker's Collected Works, Vol. IV., pp. 41–76.

Probably Theodore Parker never showed more courage than upon this occasion. Though New England sentiment did not sustain the Mexican War, yet the sentiment and country-at-large pushed it, and it was manly to defy with such intrepidity the bayonets of the administration assembled before him. Few now defend the war with Mexico. Texas having been acquired by methods not to be approved, weak Mexico was browbeaten and humiliated into a hostile attitude, where she could not at all sustain herself, the result being further losses of her territory to the United States, thus greatly strengthening and enriching her unscrupulous rival.

Page 23, note 1. This reference is to John Quincy Adams.

III

A LETTER ON SLAVERY

This " Letter to the People of the United States Touching the Matter of Slavery " bears date of December 22, 1847. It is reprinted from the Boston edition of 1848. It is included in Miss Cobbe's edition of Parker's Collected Works, Vol. V., pp. 17–84.

Page 36, note 1. The odium in which slavery was held in the North at an early day is exaggerated here. Probably as much compunction with relation to slavery was at this time felt at the South as at the North, which Parker elsewhere seems to admit: had conditions at the North changed as they did at the South, making slavery profitable, it is not likely that the New England conscience would have found it hard to become reconciled to it.

Page 37, note 2. The South played an important part in initiating and passing the Ordinance of 1787, though the claim cannot be sustained that it was drafted by Jefferson, the author of the Declaration of Independence.

Page 53, note 3. The sense here is not obvious. The Swiss at one time served in many countries of Europe as mercenary bailiffs and guards to such an extent that the word " Swiss " became almost a term of opprobrium. This may have been in Parker's mind.

Page 75, note 4. This requires some abatement. However neglected the slaves may have been in general, instances abound where humane and religious masters were zealously careful of the spiritual welfare of those in bonds. The negro Sunday-schools of Stonewall Jackson in Virginia, the religious classes of Bishop Leonidas Polk of Louisiana, and the paternal care of Joseph Le Conte in Georgia, are instances in point. See the lives of these men.

Page 102, note 5. The course of the Civil War was soon to show that the existence of slavery was to the South an element of military strength. To the surprise of the North, and perhaps to the equally great surprise of the South, there was between 1861 and 1865, no attempt at an uprising of the slaves against their masters. While accepting freedom as the northern armies gradually advanced southward, the mass of negroes remained quiet on the plantations, making no effort to break their bonds. They faithfully tilled the land; and with the army, were teamsters and servants, built the fortifications, indeed rendered all the service of which soldiers are capable except standing on the firing line. This docility of the negroes was quite unlooked for. The white soldiers of the South were substantially relieved of all labors except marching and fighting, which greatly enhanced their efficiency.

Page 110, note 6. Here is suggested a picture of the ruthlessness with which barbarians treat each other. In the case of the North American Indians, however great may have been the cruelties inflicted upon them by the whites, it is certain that those practised among the tribes themselves were far greater. The Iroquois, just before the coming of the whites, exterminated the Eries. The Jesuit missionaries witnessed and recorded the extermination of the Hurons. La Salle and his companions witnessed that of the Illinois. At the other end of the confederacy of the Six Nations the Mohawks treated as mercilessly the western tribes of New England. It is not probable that any sufferings inflicted upon the Africans by the whites, surpassed or even equaled their suffering while in barbarism, exposed only to the whips and spears of their fellow-savages.

Page 112, note 7. Certainly this language is extravagant. In past times the nations of the world in general have practised slaveholding whenever they had the power so to do, with motives as sordid, inhumanities as marked as those of the slaveholders of America. Until within a century of Theodore Parker's time, man's moral sense, refining only slowly, had scarcely begun to recognize slavery as an ill. An evil so inveterate and all-permeating could only disappear by gradual stages.

Page 113, note 8. The divine sentence against slavery, Theodore Parker might have said, appears in the way it ought to appear,— upon the whites, the sinners; — not upon the blacks, the victims. While through anguish and bloody sweat, these latter, innocent as they are, have been in a measure lifted up, the whites have undergone degradation and sorrow.

IV

THE DESTINATION OF AMERICA

This address on " The Political Destination of America and the Signs of the Times " was delivered before several literary societies in 1848. It is included in Miss Cobbe's edition of Parker's Collected Works, Vol. IV., pp. 77–110.

Page 129, note 1. Agreeing fully that in Athens, Corinth and Rome the master-class was cursed by slavery, the philosophical historian will at the same time point out that vast multitudes of barbarians from the orient, from Africa, and northern Europe came through enforced servitude under the influence of Greek refinement and Roman order, thereby undergoing discipline that helped them toward civilization.

Page 147, note 2. To-day this passage reads oddly. In great part through the immense foreign infusion of the last sixty years, it can no longer be said that we do not know how to play. Each great city has its Coney Island or its equivalent. Forty thousand will gather into a stadium to witness an athletic contest. In schools and colleges the passion for sport threatens seriously to overwhelm the passion for study. No work of philanthropy is more widely approved than the establishment of play-grounds. The country now well understands how to make holiday.

Page 153, note 3. When this passage was written, Emerson, whom Parker praises, was famous, but Hawthorne, Whittier, Lowell, Longfellow, Holmes, Howells, were just beginning their work. It would be wide of the mark to say to-day that America has no literature that smacks of the soil. Within the decade in which the critic thus discoursed, the Scarlet Letter, the House of Seven Gables, Uncle Tom's Cabin, Evangeline and Hiawatha, Biglow Papers, the Autocrat of the Breakfast Table, brought this criticism to naught.

V

THE ABOLITION OF SLAVERY BY THE FRENCH REPUBLIC

This speech was delivered at a meeting of the American Anti-Slavery Society called to celebrate this event on April 6, 1848. It is included in Miss Cobbe's edition of Parker's Collected Works, Vol. V., pp. 85–92.

In this beautiful speech no passage occurs which requires explanation or stricture.

Page 165, note 1. This reference is to Mr. Wendell Phillips.

Page 171, note 2. See the *Courier des Etats Unis,* for November, 1847, which contains passages from M. Lamartine's programme, which set forth all the schemes that the provincial government had afterwards tried to carry out.

Page 174, note 3. John Quincy Adams is here referred to, the dramatic incidents of whose death were at the moment fresh in the minds of men.

VI

THE ANTI-SLAVERY CONVENTION

This speech was delivered at Faneuil Hall, Boston, on May 31, 1848, before the New England Anti-Slavery Convention. It is included in Miss Cobbe's edition of Parker's Collected Works, Vol. V., pp. 93–102.

Page 180, note 1. South Carolina had passed laws requiring that negroes coming as sailors into her ports, though freemen, should be taken from their ships and kept in prison during their stay in the State. In 1844, Hon. Samuel Hoar was sent from Massachusetts to South Carolina as a commissioner to test the law, but was not allowed to do so, or to remain in the State. See Hart, Slavery in the American Nation, p. 277.

Page 180, note 2. This was a sentiment offered at a public dinner given by the citizens of Charleston, S. C., to Hon. Daniel Webster.

Page 183, note 3. This reference is to Rev. Cyrus Pierce, teacher of the Normal School at Newton.

Page 183, note 4. This reference is to Hon. Horace Mann.

Page 185, note 5. The men here referred to are Messrs. Garrison, Phillips, and Quincy.

Page 186, note 6. A true forecast, though it did not at all enter the mind of the prophet, touching in light, almost humorous terms upon the coming struggle, what terrible experiences for his country were close at hand.

VII

THE FREE SOIL MOVEMENT

This address, " Some Thoughts on the Free-soil Party and the Election of General Taylor," was delivered in December, 1848. It is included in Miss Cobbe's edition of Parker's Collected Works, Vol. IV., pp. 111–134.

Page 197, note 1. The Free-soil party, organized on the principle stated in the text, held its Convention in 1848, at Buffalo, N. Y., where Martin Van Buren and Charles Francis Adams were nominated for President and Vice-President.

Page 197, note 2. It is a strange reading of history to make John Quincy Adams a favorer at any time of the slave power.

Page 201, note 3. This reference is to William Lloyd Garrison.

Page 206, note 4. Mr. Parker here made a footnote. " The following table shows the facts of the case:

Cost of post-office in slave states for the year ending July 1st, 1847, $1,318,541.	Cost of post-office in free states for the year ending July 1st, 1847, $1,038,219.
Receipts from post-office, $642,380.	Receipts from post-office, $1,459,631.

So the Southern post-office cost the nation $694,161 and the Northern post-office paid the nation $421,412, making a difference of $1,115,573 against the South."

Page 208, note 5. This reference is to Mr. John P. Hale.

Page 212, note 6. This reference is to Hon. Daniel Webster.

Page 213, note 7. Cavaignac was a figure much in the foreground in the French Revolution of 1848, at one time wielding much authority.

Page 215, note 8. There are better authorities for Van Buren's record than Theodore Parker.

Page 217, note 9. Here Parker has noted:

" The following extract, from the Charleston Mercury, shows the feeling of the South: ' Pursuant to a call, a meeting of the citizens of Orangeburg District was held to-day, 6th November, in the court-house, which was well filled on the occasion. . . . Gen. D. F. Jamison then rose, and moved the appointment of a committee of twenty-five, to take into consideration the continued agitation by Congress of the question of slavery; . . . the committee, through their chairman, Gen. Jamison, made the following report: —

" ' The time has arrived when the slaveholding States of the confederacy must take decided action upon the continued attacks of the North against their domestic institutions, or submit in silence to that humiliating position in the opinions of mankind, that longer acquiescence must inevitably reduce them to. . . . The agitation of the subject of slavery commenced in the fanatical murmurings of a few scattered abolitionists, to whom it was a long time confined; but now it has swelled into a torrent of popular opinion at the North; it has invaded the fireside and the church, the press and the halls of legislation; it has seized upon the deliberations of Congress, and at this moment is sapping the foundations, and about to overthrow the fairest political structure that the ingenuity of man has ever devised.

" ' The overt efforts of abolitionism were confined for a long period to annoying applications to Congress, under color of the pretended right of petition; it has since directed the whole weight of its malign influence against the annexation of Texas, and had well-nigh cost to the country the loss of that important province; but emboldened by success and the inaction of the South, in an unjust and selfish spirit of national agrarianism it would now appropriate the whole public domain. It might well have been supposed that the undisturbed possession of the whole of Oregon Territory would have satisfied the non-slaveholding States. This they now hold, by the incorporation of the Ordinance of 1787 into the bill of the last session for establishing a territorial government for Oregon. That provision, however, was not sustained by them from any apprehension that the territory could ever be settled from the States of the South, but it was intended as a gratuitous insult to the Southern people, and a malignant and unjustifiable attack upon the institution of slavery.

" ' We are called upon to give up the whole public domain to the fanatical cravings of abolitionism, and the unholy lust of political power. A territory, acquired by the whole country for the use of all, where treasure has been squandered like chaff, and Southern blood poured out like water, is sought to be appropriated by one section, because the other chooses to adhere to an institution held not only under the guaranties that brought this confederacy into existence, but under the highest sanction of Heaven. Should we quietly fold our hands under this assumption on the part of the non-slaveholding States, the fate of the South is sealed, the institution of slavery is gone, and its existence is but a question of time. . . . Your committee are unwilling to anticipate what will be the result of the combined wisdom and joint action of the southern portion of the confederacy on this question; but as an initiatory step to a concert of action on the part of the people of South Carolina, they respectfully recommend, for the adoption of this meeting, the following resolutions: —

" ' Resolved, That the continued agitation of the question of slavery, by the people of the non-slaveholding States, by their legislatures, and by their representatives in Congress, exhibits not only a want of national courtesy, which should always exist between kindred States, but is a palpable violation of good faith towards the slaveholding States, who adopted the present Constitution " in order to form a more perfect union."

" ' Resolved, That while we acquiesce in adopting the boundary between the slaveholding and non-slaveholding States, known as the Missouri Compromise line, we will not submit to any further restriction upon the rights of any Southern man to carry his property and his institutions into territory acquired by Southern treasure and by Southern blood.

" ' Resolved, That should the Wilmot Proviso, or any other restriction, be applied by Congress to the territories of the United States, south of 36° 30' north latitude, we recommend to our representative in Congress, as the decided opinion of this portion of his district, to leave his seat in that body, and return home.

" ' Resolved, That we respectfully suggest to both houses of the Legislature of South Carolina, to adopt a similar recommendation as to our senators in Congress from this State.

" ' Resolved, That upon the return home of our senators and representatives in Congress, the Legislature of South Carolina should be forthwith assembled to adopt such measures as the exigency may demand.'

" The resolutions were then submitted, seriatim, and, together with the report, were unanimously adopted."

VIII

REPLY TO WEBSTER

This speech was delivered in Faneuil Hall, March 25, 1853, at a meeting of the citizens of Boston, called to consider the speech of Mr. Webster. It is included in Miss Cobbe's edition of Parker's Collected Works, Vol. IV., pp. 212–234.

Page 219, note 1. The four great men were Webster, Clay, Calhoun and Cass.

Page 220, note 2. The most succinct statement of the difference between Parker and those whom he criticized would be that while he put first American emancipation and second the preservation of the Union, the party over against him put first the Union, and second emancipation. By the Wilmot Proviso the territory acquired from Mexico was to remain free.

Page 221, note 3. This reference is to Mr. John Quincy Adams.

Page 222, note 4. The Ordinance of 1787, which shut slavery out of the Northwest, was favored by statesmen both from the North and South, Jefferson being a leading spirit; though strict accuracy would require a different statement than that it was the proviso of Jefferson. See Bassett, The Federalist System. American Nation, vol. XV., p. 185.

Page 238, note 5. This picture is very moving, a picture of the sufferings of an escaping slave not at all exaggerated. Ellen Craft, according to another writer, came North in men's clothes, her light skin enabling her to pass for a white planter, her husband accompanying her as an attendant. At Baltimore where it was necessary for her to give her signature, she being unable to write, tied up her right hand as if injured. The pair for that time escaped. Hart, Slavery in the American Nation, vol. XVI., p. 227.

Page 239, note 6. What to Parker seemed impossible, we, at this distance can accept and understand. Undoubtedly Webster genuinely feared the disruption of the Union as a consequence of the passage of the Wilmot Proviso, with most excellent reason. Parker was short-sighted, Webster foresaw truly.

IX

THE SLAVE POWER

This speech was delivered at the New England Anti-Slavery Convention in Boston, May 29, 1850. It is included in Miss Cobbe's edition of Parker's Collected Works, Vol. V., pp. 103–133.

Page 249, note 1. This reference is to Mr. Silgeström.

Page 249, note 2. W. Gilmore Simms, the Southern novelist and man of letters, claimed that he was one of the pioneers in asserting that slavery in the South was a blessing, about 1837. See Rhodes, Hist. of U. S. from Compromise of 1850, vol. I., p. 68.

Page 252, note 3. Annal. Lib. XIV., cap. 42 et seq.

Page 263, note 4. Executive Documents, House of Representatives, No. 17, p. 3.

Page 267, note 5. Mr. Parker added here in the printed pamphlet the following note:

" Since the delivery of the above, Mr. Webster has introduced his bill, providing a trial by jury for fugitive

slaves.   If I understand it, Mr. Webster does not offer
it as a substitute for the Judiciary Bill on the subject,
does not introduce it as an amendment to that or to
anything else.   Nay, he does not formally introduce it
— only lays it before the Senate, with the desire that
it may be printed!   The effect it is designed to produce, it is very easy to see.   The retainers can now say
— See! Mr. Webster himself wishes to provide a trial
by jury for fugitives!   Some of the provisions of the
bill are remarkable, but they need not be dwelt on here."

Page 275, note 6.   Robert C. Winthrop, Speaker of
the House, and successor of Webster in the Senate,
when the latter became Secretary of State, was like
Webster, Everett, Fillmore and Abraham Lincoln, an
old-line Whig who put the saving of the Union first,
emancipation second.   He parted from Lincoln when
the latter became the candidate of what Winthrop
thought a " sectional party ": there must be in his view
" no North and no South."   Winthrop opposed Lincoln's second election also, and always looked askance
at him until after the assassination.   At that time no
eulogy was more cordial than Winthrop's, and it was
evident from his language, that as he looked back, he
approved what Lincoln had done.   See R. C. Winthrop, Letters and Speeches, vol. II., p. 661.

X

THE FUNCTION OF CONSCIENCE

This " Sermon for the Times " on " The Function
and Place of Conscience in Relation to the Laws of
Men " was preached at the Melodeon on Sunday, September 22, 1850.   It is included in Miss Cobbe's edition of Parker's Collected Works, Vol. V., pp. 134–
163.

The ethical system of Theodore Parker receives

treatment at length elsewhere in this volume, and may perhaps be studied to best advantage in the Intuitive Morals of Miss Frances Power Cobbe, his English disciple and editress.

Page 289, note 1. Mr. Parker here noted: " The terms *laws of the human spirit, spiritual laws,* etc., are sometimes used to denote, exclusively those laws which man *must* keep, not merely what he *ought* to keep, laws in relation to which man has no more freedom than a mass of marble. The records are used above in a different sense."

Page 299, note 2. The hymn here alluded to is as follows:

Why dost thou, Tyrant, boast abroad
    thy wicked works to praise?
Dost thou not know there is a God,
    whose mercies last alwaies?

On mischiefe why sett'st thou thy minde,
    and wilt not walke upright?
Thou hast more lust false tales to find,
    than bring the truth to light.
Thou dost delight in fraud and guile,
    in mischiefs, bloud and wrong.
Thy lips have learned the flattering stile,
    oh false deceitful tongue.

Therefore shall God for aye confound,
    and pluck thee from thy place;
Thy seed root out from off the ground,
    and so shall thee deface.
The just, when they behold thy fall,
    with feare shall praise the Lord;
And in reproach of thee withall,
    crie out with one accord: —

" Behold the man that woulde not take
    the Lord for his defense;
But of his goods his God did make,
    and trust his corrupt sense.
But I, as olive, fresh and green,
    shall spring and spread abroad;
For why? my trust all times has been,
    upon the living God!

" For this therefore will I give praise
    to Thee with heart and voyce;
I will set forth Thy name alwayes,
    wherein Thy saints rejoyce."

Psalm lii. in Sternhold and Hopkins.

Page 309, note 3. Mr. Parker here noted that " so
it appeared in September, 1851; but since then the
Whig party has vindicated its claim to the same bad
eminence as the Democratic party."

Page 311, note 4. Mr. Parker here made a footnote: " The person referred to fled away from Boston,
and in one of the British provinces found the protection
for his undeniable rights which could not be allowed him
in New England."

Page 313, note 5. This refers to a speech of Mr.
Webster, occasioned by the passage of the Fugitive
Slave Law.

XI

THE BOSTON KIDNAPPING

This discourse was delivered before the Committee
of Vigilance, at the Melodeon in Boston, on the first
anniversary of the rendition of Thomas Sims, April
12, 1852. The printing of this discourse was occasioned by the following letter.

Rev. Theodore Parker:

DEAR SIR,— We know that we express the earnest and unanimous wish of all who listened to your appropriate and eloquent address last Monday, in asking a copy of it for the press.

Yours respectfully,

Wendell Phillips
Henry I. Bowditch
Timothy Gilbert ⎫ Committee
John P. Jewett ⎬ of
M. P. Hanson ⎭ Arrangements.
John M. Spear

Boston, April 15, 1852.

Page 324, note 1. Mr. Parker here noted that " the annual day of ' fasting and prayer ' came between the seizure of Mr. Sims and his rendition."

Page 331, note 2. See Town Records of that date.

Page 331, note 3. See Town Records.

Page 332, note 4. See Town Records.

Page 335, note 5. See Town Records.

Page 335, note 6. This reference is to Hon. Harrison Gray Otis.

Page 335, note 7. This reference is to Mr. Francis Jackson.

Page 349, note 8. A more stringent law for the return of fugitive slaves was an important feature of the Compromise of 1850. Parker's statement, though impassioned, is accurate as to the facts. The horrors of the situation are not exaggerated, but passages like this show that Parker was quite blind to what threatened. He mocks at the cry that the Union was in danger; no doubt esteeming the safety of the Union a thing of small importance. Not far off was a Civil War in which more than a million of men perished and perhaps, in the North alone, five billion in treasure wasted. Webster saw the danger and relaxed in his early anti-slavery energy, hoping that by forbearance in the North the danger might be averted. Parker, short-sighted, had no patience with the temporizing of Webster and his kind, and poured out upon them vials of unmeasured wrath. Abraham Lincoln, quite unknown, was until 1848, like Webster a Whig, and afterward differed not much from Webster in his views. At any rate, the policy of Lincoln, which saved the country, and in the end put a period to slavery, would have been probably approved by Webster. Had Parker lived, his denunciation of Lincoln would have been as severe no doubt as his denunciation of Webster. For a more detailed account, see Introduction.

Page 350, note 9. The reference is to a remark made in heat by Rev. Dr. Orville Dewey. For a defense of Dr. Dewey see Chadwick, Theodore Parker, p. 256. Parker often refers to the outburst of Dr. Dewey, which was the venial lapse of a well-meaning man.

Page 365, note 10. At this point in the delivery of his discourse the coat was exhibited.

Page 367, note 11. This is a remark of Mr. Webster's.

Page 367, note 12. This complicity of early New England with slavetrading and slaveholding is voluminously attested in documents of the period, and was not always remembered by the abolitionists.

Page 368, note 13. A comparison not fair as regards the Boston of 1852.

Page 374, note 14. Millard Fillmore was a Unitarian whose religious views differed little from those of Theodore Parker. He was a man thoroughly amiable and of much moral earnestness. James Ford Rhodes, the most authoritative historian of the period, justifies his signature of the Fugitive Slave Law in his History of United States, I, 188, and in general declares that as President he acquitted himself with " ability and honor." He was much under the influence of Webster, his intellectual superior, and conscientiously felt that as between the two terrible evils which lay before him, the sufferance of slavery for a time and the destruction of the Union, in choosing the former he chose the lesser evil. It may be plausibly maintained that Fillmore's policy postponed the Civil War ten years,— thereby deferring the crisis to a time when the North was able to cope with it.

Page 377, note 15. To the abolition heart no proposition seemed more outrageous than that slavery could benefit the slave, and yet sociologists of high authority declare that in past ages the condition of bondage has been a great school in which the nations have been slowly trained into something better than barbarism. See Introduction.

Page 380, note 16. This reference is to Mr. Webster.

Page 385, note 17. These are the words of Henry Ware, Jr., a minister eminent for religion, who had lately died in Boston.